GATEKEEPERS OF GROWTH

GATEKEEPERS OF GROWTH

THE INTERNATIONAL POLITICAL ECONOMY OF CENTRAL BANKING IN DEVELOPING COUNTRIES

Sylvia Maxfield

PRINCETON UNIVERSITY PRESS PRINCETON, NEW JERSEY

Published by Princeton University Press, 41 William Street,
Princeton, New Jersey 08540
In the United Kingdom: Princeton University Press, Chichester, West Sussex

Library of Congress Cataloging-in-Publication Data

Maxfield, Sylvia.
Gatekeepers of Growth : the international political economy of central banking in developing countries / Sylvia Maxfield.
p. cm.
Includes bibliographical references and index.
ISBN 0-691-02687-4 (cloth : alk. paper)
1. Banks and banking, Central—Developing countries. I. Title.
HG3550.M39 1997
332.1'1'091724—dc20 96-27217 CIP

This book has been composed in Palatino

Princeton University Press books are printed
on acid-free paper and meet the guidelines
for permanence and durability of the Committee
on Production Guidelines for Book Longevity
of the Council on Library Resources

Printed in the United States of America by Princeton Academic Press

10 9 8 7 6 5 4 3 2 1

THE CENTRAL BANK CAN BE SEEN AS THE REPOSITORY OF REASON AGAINST THE SHORT-TERM CLAIM OF PASSION...

—Jon Elster, *Ulysses and the Sirens: Studies in Rationality and Irrationality*

Contents

Acknowledgments

I DAYDREAMED many times during the evolution of this project about writing the acknowledgments. This book, which began as a simple attempt to draw out the comparative implications of my monograph on Mexico, became much more than that, and it is complete thanks to the support of my friends and colleagues. First and foremost, I am grateful to Alex Cukierman, Robert Franzese, Robert Kaufman, and Steven Webb for their exceptionally close readings and astute commentary on the penultimate version. For comments, suggestions, invitations to present draft chapters, and logistical assistance, thanks go to Susan Rose Ackerman, Leslie Armijo, Bob Bates, Dwight Brothers, Gail Buyske, David Cameron, Scott Christiansen, Bill Clark, Gerald Corrigan, Andrew Crockett, Rick Doner, Denise Dresser, Sebastian Edwards, Jeff Frieden, Stephan Haggard, Randy Henning, Miles Kahler, Bob Keohane, Rosa Lastra, Susanne Lohmann, Jim Mahon, Harry Makler, Seong Park, Lou Pauly, Jesus Reyes Heroles, Ron Rogowski, Ben Schneider, Pierre Siklos, Tom Skidmore, Pam Starr, Steven Topik, John Waterbury, Eliza Willis, Jeff Winters, Carol Wise, and anonymous reviewers. I especially thank Manuel Pastor, for permitting me to report results from our joint research in Chapter 9, and Patcharee Siroros, whose work on the Bank of Thailand contributed substantially to mine.

This book includes four very labor intensive case studies of central bank history. Two of these draw on primary source material written in languages I do not read or speak. I am indebted to the research assistants who worked with me in locating and interpreting Korean and Thai language materials: Jung-Kwan Cho, Helen Kim, Seok-Jin Lew, and Don Nakornthob. For excellent research assistance I am also grateful to Ingrid Cerwinka, Kent Eaton, Eric Feldman, Josh Hoffman, Nancy Neiman, Mitsue Sakamoto, and Bill Summerhill. I could never have completed the book without substantial financial assistance from the North-South Center of the University of Miami and several smaller grants from the Yale Center for International and Area Studies.

My final debts are to my family. When I wasn't absent physically on long trips to Asia or Latin America, I was often absent mentally. I am grateful to Max for trying to be patient with far less motherly attention than most children demand and receive. Kate and Zoë, the twins, were born in the middle of this project. They had the (unwitting) good grace to pretend that nothing could be better than a mother inseparable from her computer. For strong drinks proffered at crucial moments, and other help of which they are only too aware, I thank Maria Maxfield, Virginia Herndon, John Cunningham, and Isabelle and Arthur Bulger. Chris suffered my vagaries of mood, often *too* silently. I hardly need to say that this book is for him.

GATEKEEPERS OF GROWTH

One

Central Bank Independence: Why the Interest?

COUNTRIES ranging from Eritrea to Malta, France, Kazahkstan, New Zealand, England, and Chile have recently approved, or contemplated, new central bank legislation. Between 1990 and 1995 at least thirty countries, spanning five continents, legislated increases in the statutory independence of their central banks. This represents a rate of increase in central bank independence many times greater than in any other decade since World War II (see Table 1.1).

Central banks shape monetary policy, affect exchange rates, and guard financial stability. They condition economic variables crucial to national development and growth. Central banks also play a role in determining the nature of international financial and monetary cooperation. The independent authority of central banks can enhance or circumscribe democratic governance. Central banks are clearly important economic and political institutions. The adage among international observers is "New nations acquire a flag, write a national anthem, and constitute a central bank." Why, then, has concern with central banks, central banking, and independence reached new heights in the 1990s?

The answer lies in several different real world events: the end of the fixed exchange rate system devised at Bretton Woods, the seeming ineffectiveness of monetary policy in regulating the trade-off between inflation and unemployment, the globalization of financial markets, and European economic transformation, including integration and post-Communist transition. The rationalist revolution in some of the social sciences has also contributed theoretical reasons to study central banking. Growing interest in central banking has fueled normative debate about independence that has, in turn, sparked further interest.

Early research on the political economy of central banking focused on the consequences of central bank independence, particularly for inflation and growth. But recent trends have spurred research on why and when government politicians delegate authority to central banks. Central banks have great potential to influence national economies. Why would government politicians give up control over the economy, especially when economic performance influences political popularity? Most answers to this question assume a political economy isolated

TABLE 1.1
Change in Legal Central Bank Independence by Decade

Decade	*No. of +*	*Average Magnitude*	*Overall Increase*	*No. of –*	*Average Magnitude*	*Overall Decrease*
1960s	6	.10	0.60	5	.07	0.35
1970s	8	.06	0.48	7	.08	0.56
1980s	3	.12	0.36	3	.06	0.18
1990s	30	.26	2.86	*N.A.*	*N.A.*	*N.A.*

Source: Calculated from data in Alex Cukierman, Steven B. Webb, and Bilin Neyapti, "Measuring the Independence of Central Banks," *World Bank Economic Review*, 6, 3 (September 1992), and coding of post-1989 charters.

Note: "No. of +" refers to the number of central banks with positive changes in their legal independence; "no. of –" refers to negative changes. *N.A.* = Not available.

from its international context. In a world of global financial markets, however, this assumption is false. In most developing countries national and international financial circumstances are inseparable. The following chapters argue that financial events are an important part of the story of politicians' decisions to cede authority to central banks or to honor and protect previous decisions regarding central bank discretion. In short, of the events spurring interest and debate over central banking, this book suggests that one, the globalization of financial markets, is of central importance.

The argument, elaborated in Chapter 3, is that politicians use central bank independence to try to signal their nation's creditworthiness to potential investors. The more global financial markets become, the more politicians must concern themselves with signaling investors. Specifically, this book argues that the likelihood politicians will use central bank independence to try to signal creditworthiness is greater (1) the larger their country's need for balance of payments support, (2) the greater the expected effectiveness of signaling, (3) the more secure their tenure as politicians, and (4) the fewer their country's restrictions on international financial transactions.

This chapter outlines what central banks typically do and then summarizes the events and debates that have led both policymakers and academics to a heightened concern with central banking. In addition to the events noted above, two debates, one meta-theoretical and one normative, have also played a role: the debate over rational expectations models in the social sciences and concern over the economic and political beneficence of central bank independence. Chapter 2 surveys research on central bank politics and lays out the domain of possible explanations for variations in central bank independence, and Chapter

3, as noted, outlines the argument of the book. Chapters 4 through 9 present results from three different empirical exercises designed to probe the investor-signaling argument by "triangulating" (attacking the problem from different angles).[1] Chapter 4 summarizes cross-regional variation in central bank politics in the 1990s and suggests that it is consistent with an argument emphasizing politicians' perceptions of international financial pressures. Chapters 5–8 examine the investor-signaling argument in the context of central bank history in Thailand, Mexico, South Korea, and Brazil. The final chapter presents the results of an indirect econometric "test" of the investor-signaling explanation for central bank independence.

What Does a Central Bank Do?

Much of the politics of central banking arises from the central banks' role in making monetary policy. Monetary policy, efforts to control the supply and price (interest rate) of money, can limit or aggravate economic fluctuations, inflation, unemployment, and growth. Each of these affects different groups in society differently. Political concerns arise because politicians often delegate considerable discretion over monetary policy to experts, typically in the central bank. In their decisions about central bank discretion, government leaders have to think about how monetary policy can be both guided by experts and responsive to its varying impact throughout society.

Central banks not only seek to control the money supply but also perform other functions; they aim to protect financial stability, guarantee the domestic and international payments system, and provide some range of financial services to the government. Compared with monetary policy, financial stability is easier to portray as equally important to all groups in society, at least in countries where most individuals have bank accounts. In the extreme, financial instability involves a public rush to withdraw assets from deposit institutions (banks) because individuals fear these institutions do not have sufficient assets to cover potential withdrawals. (Bank deposits are among a bank's "liabilities," because the bank is liable to produce cash on demand for the depositor.) To guard against financial instability, a situation in which banks cannot produce cash to back deposits, central banks regulate commercial bank licensing, set standards for minimum bank capital, and supervise at least a portion of the financial system through the use of inhouse examiners or auditors hired from an outside firm. Supervision usually involves periodic inspections of commercial banks. When supervision has failed to detect early warnings of commercial bank failure, the central bank can serve as lender of last resort. One of the trickiest decisions central bankers face concerns whether to lend to a troubled bank in the hope that a small loan can speed recovery, or to refuse to lend and thus oversee liquidation of the bank. In other words, central bankers have to decide if a financial institution's problems are short-term cash-flow or "liquidity" problems, or more fundamental "solvency" problems. To make this decision they must also consider the impact of one bank's troubles on the entire banking system.

The task of preserving financial stability overlaps partially with the task of guaranteeing an effective payments system. An effective payments system is one in which individuals willingly accept money and money substitutes in exchange for goods and services. In addition to actions designed to protect financial stability, the central bank bolsters the payments system by establishing reserve accounts for commercial banks, aiding in the check clearing process, and replacing worn-out currency. The central bank may also play a role in the international payments system. The central bank often manages foreign exchange reserves and, in some cases, has some degree of responsibility for the regulation of foreign exchange rates and procedures.

As fiscal agent for the government, the central bank typically receives deposits and issues checks for government agencies, issues and redeems government securities, and contributes to international exchange rate management, at least to the extent of conducting official reserve transactions with other countries. The central bank's role as fiscal agent for the government is also politically charged. As banker to the government, the central bank is in a position to cover the government's overdrafts. A central bank can finance the government in several ways: it can buy government securities, it can make unsecured loans from its reserves, it can print money. Theoretically, the central bank can impose fiscal discipline on the government.

Central bank independence can have varied meaning and importance depending on the category of central bank functions. The extent of independence from the government has the greatest direct impact on the central bank's ability to control the money supply. It is difficult, for example, to control the money supply if the government makes excessive demands for financing that the central bank feels it cannot deny. Independence from commercial banks is more important than independence from the executive for effective regulation and supervision of financial institutions.

The primary concern in this book is with the relationship between central bank authority vis-à-vis government, on the one hand, and price stability, on the other. The key components of authority are the ability to freely choose instruments to pursue the primary objective of price stability and to command government respect for central bank advice on government finance and fiscal policy. When central bank independence is high, fiscal policy should be partly influenced by monetary policy.[2] Chapter 2 says more about conceptualizing and measuring central bank independence. This chapter turns next to the events and debates that have given rise to heightened interest in central bank independence in the 1990s.

Exchange Rate Rules and the Importance of Central Bank Independence

To control inflation policymakers seek an anchor for prices. The exchange rate system devised in Bretton Woods, New Hampshire, at a global economic summit after World War II provided an exchange rate anchor. The rules of the Bretton Woods agreement set a fixed rate for exchanging nondollar currencies to dollars and dollars to gold. Prices were anchored to a fixed dollar exchange rate. When President Richard Nixon devalued the U.S. dollar relative to gold in 1971, the global fixed exchange rate regime fell apart. As the price of the dollar floated, policymakers searched for new price anchors. Policymakers viewed central bank independence as one of several possible ways to limit price instability in a floating exchange rate world. Yet change in the international exchange rate regime in the 1970s, though an important part of the context of growing interest in central bank independence, is not an adequate explanation for the dramatic rise in central bank independence in the 1990s. We must also review other considerations.

Central Banking and the End of the Long-Run Inflation-Unemployment Trade-Off

For many government politicians the value of directly controlling monetary policy themselves shapes the decision to increase or protect existing central bank discretion over monetary policy. That value has declined since the 1970s, in part because monetary policy is no longer an effective tool for determining national employment levels. If controlling monetary policy does not buy politicians the ability to generate desired levels of employment, why not cede more discretion over monetary policy to the central bank?

At the same time, there is another twist to the connection between monetary policy effectiveness and central bank discretion. Policymakers may hope that by creating a world of independent central banks, they may return to the world in which monetary policy *is* effective in fine-tuning employment levels. Both factors, a decline in monetary policy effectiveness that therefore lowers the value of government discretion over monetary policy, and a desire to reconstitute monetary policy effectiveness, may be behind the current wave of interest in central banking. There is a difference between them, however. The former suggests that the current trend of increased central bank independence may continue over the long term; the latter indicates the potential for a reversal of current trends as the value politicians assign to controlling monetary policy themselves rises again.

Although this is not the place to recount the history of macroeconomic theory, some discussion is necessary to clarify the connection between the unemployment-inflation trade-off, monetary policy effectiveness, and current interest in central banking.[3] In 1958 the economist A. William Phillips showed that there had been a consistent relationship between unemployment and inflation in the United Kingdom for more than a century.[4] Over the long run, an increase or decrease in employment yielded a predictable change in inflation. Other economists studied the long-run trade-off between inflation and unemployment in other countries and generated similar results. Once this relationship was hypothesized, policymakers believed monetary policy could be used to reach a desired level of inflation and unemployment. Control over monetary policy was therefore quite valuable to government politicians, who could thereby respond to constituents' demands or tolerance for unemployment and inflation.

In the 1970s belief in the effectiveness of monetary policy to fine-tune long-run inflation and unemployment levels began to unravel, both because academic economists changed their theories and because policymakers found that monetary policy was not working as expected. The introduction of rational expectations into economic theory led academic economists to question the underlying micro-level logic of the models associating monetary policy tools with inflation and unemployment. The logic of the Phillips curve works, went the economists' thinking, only if inflation is unexpected. But rational individuals anticipate government manipulation of monetary policy and its impact on inflation and unemployment.

Perhaps more important than theoretical developments was the practical experience of policymakers. By the 1970s it seemed that to buy lower inflation policymakers would have to pursue very tight monetary policy and suffer the political consequences of very large increases in unemployment. Economists coined the term "stagflation" to refer to this new world in which inflation stayed the same no matter how great unemployment. By the 1980s this persistent inflation lowered the value of government discretion over monetary policy.[5] But this was not the only change in economic reality that contributed to the wave of interest in central banking.

Central Banking and the Globalization of Financial Markets

A further reason for growing interest in central banks lies in the consequences of financial globalization. Financial globalization raises the cost of poor monetary policy and increases the value of central bank independence. As barriers to the international movement of currency and other financial assets decline and as national governments increasingly permit free international operation of financial institutions, national financial markets are becoming more and more integrated into one large international market. In this context, currency sales creating pressures for devaluation and/or sale of equity or bond holdings that can negatively affect the price of these assets and often the financial health of the issuers (companies or governments) quickly penalize national governments that follow economic policies distasteful to financial market actors.

Currency traders and investors in emerging market securities tend to observe central bank actions closely and take them as signals of future national economic policy and asset performance. *Forbes* magazine, for example, exhorts investors to "watch the central banks . . . [as a] rough rule of thumb for avoiding the carnage . . . [that can] prove treacherous to emerging stock markets."[6] Interest in central banking has risen with the internationalization of finance, and particularly with the growth of global securities markets.

From the point of view of government politicians, the internationalization of securities markets is influential in a very specific way. When domestic financial regulation and controls on international capital flows limit the investment options of a country's national residents, governments can sell debt at relatively low interest rates. Internationally isolated and "repressed" financial markets can create artificially high demand for government securities. Especially when other sources of government revenue are low relative to government expenditures, as is typically the case in developing countries, the cost of raising funds through the sale of government bonds is very important. When financial markets are deregulated and become increasingly internationally integrated, government politicians no longer enjoy a captive market for government securities. When the government has to compete with myriad other investment vehicles to sell its securities, the value of central bank independence rises because it can serve as a signal to investors. In this way, if no other, the internationalization of securities markets has increased investor and issuer interest in central bank independence.

This particular source of interest in central bank independence, specific to the internationalization of securities markets in the 1990s, is the basis for the more general argument derived in this book. Yet it is instructive to explore other reasons for the rising interest in central bank politics in the 1990s as well.

European Integration and Transition

Another reason for the explosion of interest in central banks stems from the stipulation of central bank independence criteria for joining the European Union under the terms of the Maastricht Treaty. The Maastricht Treaty makes central bank independence a requirement for accession. This stipulation has engendered considerable national debate as European countries try to bring their central bank laws into line with Maastricht requirements. In this regard we see the connection between central banking and nationhood quite clearly. British concern about the central bank provisions of the Maastricht Treaty does not center on fear that Bundesbank leadership of union monetary policy will be inflationary. It is rather, in Paul Volcker's terms, "about Queen and sovereignty and parliament and . . . [being] in control of things."[7]

The association of central banking with national sovereignty is also part of the reason for the flurry of central bank legislation in the transitional economies of Central and Eastern Europe. Nonetheless, nations trying to make the transition from centrally guided to market economies also have a variety of more mundane reasons to be concerned with central banking. One is inflation, which is among the primary problems confronting transitional economies. Policymakers perceive independent central banks with a strong mandate to achieve price stability as bulwarks against inflation. This is part of the reasoning, correct or not, that has given rise to a wave of new central bank legislation across Central and Eastern Europe (and in countries of other regions with transitional economies).[8]

Other reasons for interest in central banking in transitional economies relate to the central bank functions already discussed. Eastern and

Central European countries, in particular, face the challenge of creating efficient payments systems and effective, competitive, sound, private banking sectors. As governments privatize state-owned banks and as new commercial banks arise to meet ballooning credit demands associated with the growth of the market economy, the importance of the central bank's role as commercial bank supervisor, regulator, and lender of last resort grows. The traditional central bank role in establishing and maintaining an effective payments system also focuses special attention on the importance of central banking in the transitional economy nations of Eastern and Central Europe.

Individual Rationality and Equilibrium in the Social Sciences

Debate over the Phillips curve was part of a rationalist revolution in the social sciences. The social world consists of equilibrium, according the rational expectations view, best explained by modeling the behavior of interest-maximizing, that is, rational, individuals. For example, the Phillips curve suggestion of a predictable long-run trade-off between inflation and employment falls apart if we assume that workers are rational and adjust their wage demands to expectations about government policy.

The rationalist revolution spurred interest in central banks among economists in the following way. The original Phillips curve story ignored the possibility of rational expectations and the related problem that the best strategy for a rational actor to achieve his or her goals may vary over time in response to the actions of others. In the rational expectations story about inflation and output, policymakers have goals for the state of the economy. Policymakers choose the best policies for achieving their goals. Public actions in response to government policy affect the optimality of the chosen policies. Public reactions are based on expectations about future government policy actions. The public expects the government to change its policy course. Citizens know that rational government leaders will have every incentive to try to espouse a commitment to low inflation in the long run, while violating it in the short term when electoral needs demand.

Economists refer to this as the "time inconsistency" problem.[9] The best government policy choice prior to policy implementation is not necessarily consistent with the best policy choice after implementation, because the public responds anticipating a change in government policy. Concretely, there is inconsistency between the politician's optimal long-run interest-maximizing strategy of commitment to low inflation and the optimal short-run strategy once citizens have taken actions (like wage bargaining) on the basis of the announced long-run policy.

Economists began to focus on central banks because they viewed turning policy discretion over to an autonomous institution as a way to minimize the policy problems resulting from public expectations of inconsistent government policy. Rational expectations models focused attention on how central bank independence could increase the credibility of government commitment to a particular policy path by making it more costly for the government to cede to short-run temptations for cheating.[10]

Political scientists as well as economists model a multitude of political outcomes as equilibrium resulting from the aggregation of interest-maximizing behavior. From this viewpoint central bank independence is a puzzle. Why would interest-maximizing politicians cede discretion over monetary policy, which has widespread economic—and therefore political—effects, to a central bank? Credibility and improved policy effectiveness is an answer easily borrowed from the economists. But scholars have gone beyond this answer, searching for explanations that make central bank independence consistent with a rationality-based equilibrium view of politics. One argument is that politicians want to be able to deny responsibility for unpopular monetary policy.[11] Another is that legislators want a highly informed third party (the central bank) to help them monitor the monetary policy of a government they mistrust.[12] Still another story, told in the context of the founding of the Bank of England, is that government leaders seek creditworthiness.[13] Finally, political scientists also argue that central bank independence results when leaders of a party losing office want to make it difficult for the incoming party to change monetary policy.[14] The next chapter discusses these arguments in more detail. The point here is that the introduction of rational expectations to social science spurred academic interest in institutions, particularly central banks.

Normative Arguments for and against Central Bank Independence

The interest of academics and policymakers in central banking both reinforces and is reinforced by a broader normative debate about the social value of central bank independence. Some arguments demonstrate the beneficence of central bank independence; others proclaim its malevolence. The main argument for central bank independence is improved economic performance. The two arguments frequently invoked against central bank independence are that it hinders policy coordination, which has a negative impact on the economy, and that it contravenes democratic governance.

Improved Economic Performance

Many central bankers propagate the idea that central bank independence is a key to a healthy economy. Alan Greenspan, chair of the Federal Reserve Bank in the mid-1990s, argued before Congress that "the independence of central banks is an element in keeping inflation down, and just as importantly, the lower rates of inflation, the higher the growth rate in productivity."[15] Nonetheless the empirical evidence supporting this claim is mixed.

Early research on central banks focused predominantly on the relationship between their independence and economic performance. While evidence suggests that central bank independence is associated with low inflation, at least in highly industrialized economies, there is less corroboration of a hypothesized connection between central bank independence and *overall* economic health. And in non-OECD countries, empirical support is also mixed for the argument that central bank independence improves economic performance.

Quantitative studies of inflation in OECD (Organization for Economic Cooperation and Development) countries find that countries with more nearly independent central banks, as defined legally, have lower and less variable inflation than countries with less legally autonomous central banks.[16] Clark and his colleagues find that OECD countries with more independent central banks are less prone to political business cycles.[17] But other studies find that although legal central bank independence is associated with lower inflation, it does not produce faster or less volatile growth or greater employment.[18] And one study of political business cycles in OECD countries partially contradicts the Clark et al. findings. Alesina and Summers find no evidence of political manipulation of economic policy leading to electoral cycles in growth or unemployment.[19]

These mixed results are difficult to interpret. For example, one approach to uncovering the impact of central bank independence on output and employment focuses on "sacrifice" ratios. The argument is that legal central bank independence should help return us to a world where individuals expect steady, low inflation. This should be a short-run Phillips curve world where changes in inflation rates are unusual and surprising and have an inverse relationship to change in employment and output. Inflation reduction is inevitably associated, to a moderate degree, with recession. If central bank independence increases faith in government policy commitments, we would expect greater central bank independence to have an impact on the amount of output the central bank must sacrifice in order to achieve the desired level of inflation. A country with a dependent central bank might have to give up two units of employment and output to gain one unit of price stability, whereas a country with an independent central bank might only suffer a one-unit output penalty for each unit of price stability. Empirical evidence suggests that legally independent central banks in OECD countries suffer a greater "sacrifice ratio" than dependent central banks.[20] But this result is questionable on several grounds.[21] It may be possible that while the average sacrifice level is higher, lower variance in inflation suggests that the sacrifice is borne less frequently. Another possibility is that the impact of monetary contraction and monetary expansion is different; research failing to distinguish between the two cases is not an adequate test of the "improved performance" argument.

The strength of empirical support for the case that central bank independence improves economic performance becomes more complex once we turn away from studies based on OECD countries. Legal independence in non-OECD countries is not significantly correlated with low inflation or high growth. Yet regressions run using the central banks' governor turnover as a measure of their independence do find an association with improved economic performance, both lower inflation and higher growth.[22]

In sum, the evidence does not clearly support an argument for central bank independence in OECD countries based on protecting growth and employment performance. But proponents of central bank independence for OECD countries are on firm ground in arguing that it protects against price inflation. In non-OECD countries there is no growth-enhancing *or* inflation-controlling rationale for *legal* central bank independence. But the empirical evidence does support a central bank autonomy argument, whether legally enshrined or not, on the grounds that behavioral independence in developing countries protects against inflation.[23] Researchers have not demonstrated a clear negative link between growth and central bank independence in developing countries.[24]

Policy Coordination

Opponents of central bank independence sometimes argue that efficient fiscal and monetary policy formulation and implementation require coordination. Central bank independence, the argument goes, undermines fiscal and monetary policy coordination. In his popular critique of the U.S. Federal Reserve Bank, Greider used the analogy of a "car with two drivers."[25] Central bank independence, he argued, leads to "over-steering" because the fiscal policy driver compensates for anticipated monetary policy and vice versa. The result is an outcome that is suboptimal from the standpoint of social welfare maximization in neoclassical economics. Analysts describe the coordination dilemma as a strategic game over economic policy between two equally powerful players. If the central bank is independent and has a preferred macroeconomic outcome different from that of the fiscal authority, the strategic game that ensues might take the form of "chicken" or Stackelberg warfare.[26] For example, if the central bank anticipates a more expansionary fiscal policy than it believes desirable, it might implement tighter monetary policy than otherwise called for, in turn leading the fiscal authority to hold fast to its expansionary path.

During the Reagan administration, opponents of central bank independence have argued, lack of coordination led to unnecessarily tight monetary policy and loose fiscal policy. One of several socially suboptimal outcomes was that, fearing expansionary fiscal policy, the central bank instituted policies that pushed interest rates up, arguably inhibiting capital formation. Another negative consequence of lack of policy coordination in the Reagan years was currency overvaluation, which in turn contributed to the United States' growing trade deficit in those years. Some have argued that overvaluation induced firm behaviors that were largely irreversible and left the United States with a permanent tendency toward trade deficit.[27]

A final problem with lack of coordination, and the game of policy "chicken" that can result, is a decline in the credibility of both monetary and fiscal policies. If each party in this strategic, noncooperative game holds fast to a relatively extreme policy position, the public may cease to believe in the policy commitments made by either.

There is relatively little empirical research on this topic. But the logic of the argument itself raises some concerns. Most important, policy coordination is necessary to maximize social welfare because of the small number of policy instruments, such as monetary, fiscal, or exchange rate policy, available to policymakers trying to achieve many different economic targets: inflation, savings, investment, growth, and so on. Yet lack of policy coordination can stem from a variety of factors other than central bank independence. Furthermore, depending on how analysts structure the payoffs in a strategic game model of an uncoordinated macroeconomic policy process, they can construe the net social cost as relatively small, especially compared with the potential social costs associated with political control of the central bank.[28]

Democratic Accountability

Typically, central banks are accountable to voters only indirectly, through their accountability to the executive. Giving central banks greater independence from the executive and greater policy jurisdiction, opponents of independence argue, weakens voters' ability to influence the economic policymaking process. U.S. Representative Henry B. Gonzalez, for example, has proposed legislation to require greater popular access to Federal Reserve Board decision making through virtually immediate public release of videotapes of Fed deliberations.[29] Even Republicans on the House Banking Committee appear to feel some change is necessary in U.S. central banking procedures in order to increase democratic control of the Fed.[30] Complaints about the Fed's lack of democratic ability have been voiced periodically in both the House and Senate since the Fed's founding in 1917. The possibility that a European central bank might be created before the creation of a "symmetrical political authority" has also raised concern about a potential "democracy deficit" in Europe.[31]

Concretely, the dilemma arises from the supposition that central bankers will always prefer more monetary restraint than the median voter. "Shielded as they are from public opinion, cocooned within an anti-inflationary temple," warns one well-known economist, "central bankers can all too easily deny . . . that there is a short-run tradeoff between inflation and unemployment."[32] What is to prevent an independent central bank from pursuing an excessively anti-inflationary policy that is either suboptimal from a social welfare standpoint or simply far from the preferences of the electorate?

One response to this concern starts from the contention that central bank independence is not legally determined; rather, politics, through the strength of a hard-money group or a coalition, or the form of political institutions, or the process of wage bargaining or party competition, determines both independence and monetary policy.[33] Central bank independence is not usually enshrined constitutionally; this heightens the likelihood that politics overrides law.[34] Another point relevant to this argument is that some have modeled the situation so that the median voter actually *wants* the central bank to choose a policy more conservative than her own "ideal point."[35]

Those arguing that central bank independence and the globalization of financial markets go hand in hand, and effectively contribute to a shift in central bank accountability from domestic political actors to international market actors, construe central bank independence as the rise of potentially undemocratic technocracy.[36] The current trend toward central bank independence, Freeman contends, "is antithetical to popular sovereignty" because independent central banks and the owners of mobile capital they essentially "represent" are usurping national power to "decide the distribution of power and wealth."[37] Epstein argues that the growth of international financial integration has increased central banks' power and independence and that independent central banks can "thwart a Keynesian coalition of labor and industry that supports expansionary policy; . . . it can veto expansionary power that a labor-led government might support."[38] Central bankers often add fuel to this fire with their rhetoric. For example, Carlos Ciampi of the Bank of Italy justified central bank independence on the grounds that "a sound currency is a cornerstone of just democracy."[39] The Bundesbank, the central bank of Germany, has also made this claim.

These are important concerns and later chapters address them more fully. At least for OECD countries, however, the weak empirical relationship between independence, on the one hand, and employment and growth, on the other, suggests that fears that central bank independence will strangle social democracy may be misplaced for the present. For developing countries the evidence is less clear. In these countries concern that central bank independence may heighten the tensions national politicians face between the demands of internationally mobile capital and the exigencies of domestic politics, especially where national, expansion-oriented political coalitions are strong, may be more valid.

Conclusion

To varying degrees, central banks control monetary policy. They also protect financial stability and facilitate domestic and international financial payments. Central banks serve as fiscal agents to the government. Independence is important in different ways and extents depending on the central bank task in question. This book focuses primarily on central bank independence from executive branch pressure that would interfere with the bank's monetary policy and inflation performance goals. While it is important to recognize that independence has different meanings and varying importance depending on the task under consideration, to some extent conditions for effective performance of all central bank tasks are intertwined. Erosion of monetary control can jeopardize financial stability and the payments system. Conversely, central banks carry out monetary policy through the financial system. Central banks control the money supply either directly or indirectly. Central bankers exercise direct control through interest rates, reserve requirements, or credit controls. They can indirectly control the money supply through the sale and purchase of government securities, known as open market operations, or regulation of credit provision for use in stock purchases (margin requirements). The most efficient method of money supply control is through the open market for government securities. The more robust and stable the national financial markets, other things equal, the more likely the central bank can maintain price stability. And of course financial stability is more likely if price stability can be achieved.[40] This circularity aside, distinctions among central bank tasks are important to keep in mind when debating and analyzing central bank independence.

Three "world-historical" events contributed to heightened interest in central banking in the 1990s: the rise of stagflation, the globalization of financial markets, and European transition. The preceding pages discuss these events in roughly chronological order, but as the next two chapters outline, this book's argument places great causal weight on the globalization of finance. The rational expectations revolution helped put central banking on the agenda within the ivory tower, while global trends raised normative issues for debate outside the ramparts. The normative debate centers on two issues. The first is whether central bank independence improves economic performance or whether it precludes policy coordination and negatively affects the economy. The second concern is that central bank independence is less than democratic. These are important issues for our times; they are revisited in the conclusion. The intervening chapters return to the central question of this book, which is positive, rather than normative. That is, why and when do politicians give discretion to, and respect the authority of, their country's central bank? The next chapter surveys the literature attempting to answer this question, pointing out an important lacuna. Where most existing explanations assume a closed economy, this book argues that international financial pressures are an important part of the cost-benefit calculations leading politicians to grant and/or protect central bank discretion and authority.

Two

The Political Sources of Central Bank Independence

THE INITIAL FOCUS in literature on central banks was on the economic consequences of central bank independence. More recently the literature has begun to explore the political sources of central bank independence. We know that central bank independence affects economic performance to some extent, but when and why do government politicians give discretion to central banks? Under what circumstances do they honor and protect previous decisions to cede authority to central banks? Answers to these questions focus on (1) the political strength of different sectoral groups with varying preferences for employment and price stability, (2) the nature of political institutions and party systems, and (3) the financial needs of government. The relative weight of these factors and the nature of their interaction is still unclear. Comparison of empirical results is challenging because authors use different definitions of independence and different methodologies. What *is* clear from recent scholarship is that first, central bank independence does not come from the legislators' pen alone. Laws stipulating independence may be necessary, but they are certainly not a sufficient condition for central bank independence. Second, the sources of central bank independence vary with levels of economic development. Results that hold for OECD countries are typically not robust for non-OECD countries. A third point stems from the closed-economy assumptions characteristic of most existing models and arguments about the sources of central bank independence. The literature on central banks makes the increasingly false assumption that national and international financial considerations are separable. This book builds on these conclusions and tries to move beyond them by exploring the interaction between domestic political and financial conditions for de facto central bank independence in developing countries.

Definitions and Measures of Central Bank Independence

Most typically, central bank independence refers to independence from the executive branch of government. But it can also refer to independence from the legislature or protection from "capture" by the commercial banks it must regulate.[1] Even if we accept the most common conceptual usage of central bank independence vis-à-vis the executive branch, definitions and indicators still vary considerably. An important distinction is between independence *from* and freedom *to*. Analysts separate freedom from the executive branch from the freedom to choose policy instruments. At its extreme, freedom from the executive implies that the central bank need not comply with stipulations for monetary policy designed to keep economic outcomes in line with voter preferences. This might more accurately be termed central bank discretion following Calvert and his colleagues' definition of discretion as "the departure of agency decisions from the positions agreed upon by the executive and the legislature at the time of delegation and appointment."[2] Yet an important distinction in the conceptual understanding of central bank independence is between discretion over the goals of monetary policy and discretion over the tools with which to reach goals set by others. The latter captures the more widely accepted definition of central bank independence: freedom to choose policy instruments with which to conduct policy that accords with directly or indirectly determined electoral mandates for economic policy.

Another issue concerns whether the term "independence" captures the situation of mutual consultation between the monetary and fiscal authority. In particular, fiscal authorities consult closely with many of the central banks thought of as most independent. For example, during much of its history the Bank of Thailand has enjoyed a virtual veto over government fiscal policy.[3] The conceptual distinction here is whether or not the central bank has the authority to shape decisions tangential to, but nonetheless affecting, its discretion over the goals or tools of monetary policy. In this book central bank independence refers to discretion over both goals and tools of monetary policy and authority, as just defined (see Table 2.1).

Quantitative indicators used to measure central bank independence also vary widely. Japan's ranking places it anywhere from the bottom to the third quartile, depending on which set of legal independence measures one follows.[4] The standard components of legal independence include some or all of the following, equally or differentially weighted, categories of statutory stipulations: personnel appointment (most important, the proportion of central bank policy board members appointed by the government and the length of term), government finance (nature of limits), policy process (specifically, relations with government), policy objectives and instruments, mechanisms for resolving bank–executive branch conflict, and extent of constitutional guarantee. Inconsistency in quantitative measures of legal central bank independence stems in part from emphasis on different aspects of central bank

TABLE 2.1
Conceptual Definitions of Central Bank Independence

Discretion over Tools of Monetary Policy	Central bank has discretion to choose tools with which to try to meet monetary policy goals set by the government.
Discretion over Goals and Tools of Monetary Policy	Central bank has discretion to set goals of monetary policy and choose tools.
Authority	Central bank is consulted, and its views are seriously considered regarding policy tangential to, but potentially effecting, monetary policy.

legislation, leading scholars to code the same legal texts differently. In reality, it may not be possible to identify the most important legal specifications for independence without understanding the political context. For example, the Dutch cite their legislation's provision for the resolution of disputes between the central bank and government, requiring the government to report to parliament any decision to override the central bank, as an important source of central bank independence. However, the protection this provides the central bank is a function of the Dutch political context. In a parliamentary system with no clear majority party, the cost of politicizing monetary policy is severe: a likely vote of no confidence, bringing down the government.

Quantitative measures of central bank independence can also be based on calculations of the extent of central bank action beyond that predicted by economic fundamentals (called a "reaction function"), or the coding of qualitative responses by economic policymakers, including central bankers themselves. Incidence of change in the central bank governorship, particularly relative to change in government leadership, is another measure. This measure is known as "governor turnover," and it suffers from the obvious shortcoming that central bank governors can last a long time in their positions precisely because they are highly subservient to politicians.

De jure independence is a questionable proxy for behavioral independence. History is replete with cases of formally independent central banks, like Weimar Germany's Reichsbank, that presided over galloping inflation because politicians demanded it. Johnson and Siklos use the deviation of interest rates from underlying market forces (the reaction function) as a measure of central bank independence in OECD countries.[5] The rankings they derive are not consistent with those based on the coding of legal statutes, leading the authors to comment that "statutorily independent central banks behave as dependent entities while statutorily dependent central banks seem to act independently within government."[6] Many central bankers themselves emphasize the disjuncture between formal and informal independence. Governor Eddie George, for example, protested during the debate over increasing Bank of England independence in 1993 that increasing the formal independence of the bank would be a "poisoned chalice" unless accompanied by strong political support for an independent central bank.[7]

Important theoretical findings are implicit in the different results obtained by scholars using different concepts and indicators of central bank independence. Although never complete, law, for example, appears to be a better explanation of behavioral central bank independence in OECD countries than in non-OECD countries. Cukierman and his colleagues find that the correlation between legal independence and central bankers' subjective evaluations of the central banks for which they worked was only .06 for developing countries, while it was .33 for developed countries.[8]

The assumption that law is an important determinant of central bank independence suggests that we should see change in central bank authority only after the law changes; yet the country histories in this book suggest that this is not the case. The non-OECD country central bank histories delineated in Chapters 5–8 show more variation in central bank independence than in central bank law. The role of law is one of several differences between developed and developing countries apparent in the literature on the political economy of central banking. These differences become even more evident in the survey of literature on the political sources of central bank authority that follows.

Sectoral Groups as Political Constituencies

The first constellation of arguments about sources of central bank independence focuses on the organization and political strength of different sectoral groups with different relative preferences for employment and price stability. The assumption is that these groups' preferences for macroeconomic policy translate into preferences for central bank independence. Groups favoring price stability will also favor central bank independence. Groups preferring full employment will argue for political control of the central bank. The financial sector is most likely to support central bank independence, and labor-intensive industry and labor are most likely to oppose central bank independence. Goodman shows that in 1981 government actors and private financiers pushed for an increase in Italian central bank independence. They succeeded in part thanks to labor's quiescence.[9] Posen recently extended this argument.[10] His regression analysis, for example, purports to show that financial sector strength predicts inflation and legal central bank independence in OECD countries. Although methodological problems leave Posen's findings open to question, others have tried to improve on his research.

Clark tests the sectoral argument for a country sample including both OECD and developing countries and uses both behavioral and legal measures of central bank independence.[11] He explores the inverse argument implied by Posen's association of financial sector strength and central bank independence. Clark postulates that where labor and heavy industry are strong, central bank independence will be low. When he conducts separate analyses of developing and advanced industrial countries, Clark finds that the sectoral argument explains central bank independence in developing countries, but not in advanced industrial countries.

Of course these researchers recognize that there are multiple causal influences on central bank independence. Those making the case for the strength of different sectors as determinants of central bank independence typically focus on the way political institutions shape the varying policy influence of different sectoral groups. Viewed this way, these arguments shade into the arguments discussed in the next section, which focus on political institutions and party competition. What distinguishes those here is the relative weight attached to sectoral preferences and partisanship versus how party institutions and political competition shape the time horizons and strategic choices of government leaders. One could say that the former is more "society-oriented" and latter more "statist" or that the former corresponds more closely to partisan versions of political business cycle theory and the latter to opportunistic versions of political business cycle theory.

In any case, Posen rightly suggests that the size of the financial sector, the extent of its intra-sector coherence and its links to industry, are insufficient indication of a sector's ability to influence policy and institutional design. Sectoral influence is a function of the extent to which political authority is vulnerable to interest group pressure. Posen finds that the influence of the financial sector, and therefore central bank independence, is greater when there are few political parties of relatively equal strength (low party fractionalization) in a federalist system. Why? Because, argues Posen, this combination of political institutions and party characteristics yields high national government decisiveness about and commitment to issues, such as central bank independence, deemed important enough to be put above the interregional fray.

Clark hypothesizes slightly differently about how political institutions and party characteristics mediate between sectoral preferences and central bank independence. Like Posen, Clark finds the centralization and insulation of government decision making a significant mediating variable in both developing and advanced industrial countries. But its impact on central bank independence is negative, rather than positive as Posen claims. According to Clark's results, the more political competition, measured by the frequency of democratic regimes and the rarity of large electoral mandates, the more independent the central bank.[12] The seemingly contradictory findings could be reconciled in several ways. Regime type could be a significant intervening variable determining the sign of the impact of political competition on central bank independence. The relationship between political competition and central bank independence could also be non-linear. Both too little or too much political competition could be threatening to independence. For both Posen and Clark the characteristics of political competition are mediating variables.

Franzese's perspective about the political economy of inflation implies a different sectoral argument about sources of central bank independence.[13] He argues that the employment and output costs associated with central bank independence will be lower the larger the traded goods sector and the more centralized the wage bargaining. The exchange rate appreciation that monetary contraction can induce hurts producers of traded goods. The more independent the central bank, the less likely it is that it will have to induce sharp monetary contraction. Extrapolating from Franzese's model we should expect more support for central bank independence in countries where large traded goods sectors coexist with coordinated wage bargaining systems. Franzese derives his results from a study of OECD countries. Notice that his ideal conditions for central bank independence rarely exist among non-OECD countries.

While these sectoral arguments rely on a causal logic extending sectoral preferences for macroeconomic policy to preferences for central bank independence, there is another, arguably more plausible, causal link between strong financial sectors and central bank independence. Most students of central bank independence would agree with central bankers when they point to technical expertise and credibility as the most important determinants of central bank authority. This, in turn, is arguably a function of the depth of domestic financial markets. Central banks most efficiently achieve money supply control through open market operations. Open market operations are in turn most efficient when there are primary and secondary markets for government bonds. The more sophisticated the markets, the more necessary technical expertise and information are to predict market behavior. The quality of the central bank's personnel and information become more valuable the more difficult it is for the layperson, average politician, or even the Treasury Department to understand how financial and money markets move. Bank of Japan staff, for example, note that the higher quality of their staff and information is an important resource in policy debates with the Ministry of Finance. Central bank authority grows as the central bank gains a reputation for understanding and being able to lead financial markets efficiently and effectively.[14]

Institutions and the Nature of Political Competition

In a direct challenge to sectoral arguments, Hall argues that even where labor and industry are strong, central bank independence and low inflation are possible if corporatist political institutions exist.[15] A focus on political institutions typifies the second set of perspectives on central bank independence. Like Franzese, Hall focuses on one corporatist political institution in particular: coordinated wage bargaining. Coordinated wage bargaining lowers the costs of inflation control; it allows central banks to control inflation with lower rates of unemployment than in countries without coordinated wage bargaining. Coordinated wage bargaining essentially alters the political environment in which central banks operate, making tight monetary policy less unpopular.

Hall's is the exception to the rule among the "institutionalist" arguments about sources of central bank independence. Most depart from the notion that central bank independence is somehow related to the costs associated with institutional change. Sectoral arguments essentially posit that central banks are an epiphenomenon of sectoral forces and assume that politicians bear no cost in changing central bank discretion or authority. Most so-called institutionalist studies focus on how the extent of political competition shapes the cost of change. The conclusion that more, rather than less, political competition is good for central banks' legal independence is rapidly becoming the accepted wisdom for institutionalist scholars studying OECD countries. Nonetheless, political competition has a variety of components, and some confusion exists about which are most important. There is also discord over whether political competition is important regardless of different parties' substantive economic objectives. These controversies reinforce the importance of distinguishing between legal versus de facto independence and OECD versus non-OECD country contexts.

Studies concluding that the extent of political competition is a primary determinant of central bank independence in OECD countries focus to varying degrees on government politicians' time horizons or perspective on their tenure in office, the size of electoral mandates, the number of political parties and their positions in policy space, and the number of "veto gates" or procedural hurdles in the process of legislative change. There is agreement that the more veto gates, the weaker the threat of legally undermining central bank independence. The weaker the legal threat, the less need for the central bank to comply with informal political pressure from the government. If the independent central bank is willing to risk a public appeal to preserve its autonomy in the face of executive pressure, then the smaller the government's electoral mandate, the less likely it is that the government will succeed in undermining central bank independence. This combination of factors leads Lohmann to argue that Bundesbank independence is rarely threatened because divided party control of a federalist system yields a large number of veto gates and weak party control of government.[16] The regression results of Banaian and his colleagues showing correlation between federalism and central bank independence support this conclusion.[17]

Others note that the more equal political parties' strengths, the more likely it is that any given party's electoral mandate will be low. Goodman makes the parsimonious, and related, argument that central bank independence in advanced industrial countries is simply a function of government politicians' time horizons.[18] The longer their time horizon, the more government politicians will desire the greatest possible economic policy flexibility, which implies low central bank independence.

There is less agreement about the implication of distance between parties' economic policy preferences and about the substance of the governing party's preferences for the argument that political competition is a necessary condition of central bank independence in industrialized democracies. Bernhard, for example, argues that in a two-party system central bank independence will only occur if the two parties are "catch-all" parties and share similar policy preferences (that is, lie close together in policy space).[19] This is because the executive is able to pursue policies that might harm its party's legislative supporters. (A catch-all party that lies close in general policy space to its competitor has incoherent preferences about monetary policy and can appeal to the second party to support whichever monetary policy it decides to pursue.) When the executive has this option, legislators will seek a legally independent central bank to help them prevent the government from pursuing monetary policy contrary to their interests. The independent central bank does this by monitoring and providing legislators information about government actions.

Bernhard argues that the United States and Austria fit this model. In the United States the Democratic and Republican parties share relatively similar ideologies, compared with the differences between Britain's Labor and Conservative parties, for example. The Federal Reserve Bank governor regularly testifies to Congress about economic policy, thereby providing information Congress can use in policy debates with the executive. Bernhard stresses appointment procedures in his definition of central bank independence. Independent central banks have appointment procedures guaranteeing that appointees reflect the distribution of economic policy preferences in the legislature. In the United States the Federal Reserve Bank's decision-making body includes a balance of regional interests similar to those in Congress. This leads Congress to trust the information provided regularly to it by the Federal Reserve governor.

Bernhard argues that central bank independence is more likely the less party polarization there is. Alesina, Clark, and Cukierman argue the opposite.[20] Alesina and Cukierman claim that in constitutional democracies central bank legal independence is more likely the *greater* the party polarization, in other words, the greater the difference in the parties' macroeconomic policy preferences. The potential for large fluctuations in economic policy, and therefore for poor economic performance, is high in this situation. The two parties have an incentive to agree on a legally independent central bank that will pursue a consistent policy roughly halfway between the two parties' preferred policies. Although hardly an institutionalized democracy, Chile in 1989 illustrates this argument. The outgoing right-wing government of General Pinochet and the more social democratic coalition expecting to succeed him agreed to central bank independence. Pinochet wanted to prevent a complete policy change after he left office.[21] The incentive for the party in power to cheat on the agreement is high, however, meaning that behavioral independence will be low unless other aspects of the political situation raise the penalty for cheating. For example, in a parliamentary system where the governing party has a narrow electoral mandate, cheating could lead to a vote of no confidence.

Notice that this literature usually abstracts from the monetary policy preferences of the party in power. Goodman's statement is typical. The longer politicians' time horizons, the greater their tenure security; "*regardless of their economic objectives*, they will be unlikely to favor an increase in central bank [legal] independence."[22] Others disagree. Clark not only emphasizes the importance of distance between parties, but also suggests that the impact of longer time horizons on composite measures of actual and legal central bank independence is indeterminate without specification of the governing party's preferences regarding expected central bank policy.[23] The higher the governing politician's subjective evaluation of his or her reelection probability, the more likely is political interference with the central bank *if* he or she dislikes expected central bank policy. Zielinski adopts this line of argument.[24] In his view, an increase in central bank independence is most probable if a right-wing (fiscally conservative) party is in power facing poor reelection prospects in a contest with a left-wing party whose macroeconomic policy ideal is very distant from that of the governing party.

In countries without institutionalized democracy, conclusions regarding the contribution of political competition to central bank independence are less clear. In contrast to Boylan's conclusions, which are based on two observations, Cukierman and Webb's "large-*n*" study suggests that the impact of short time horizons on central bank independence is negative in developing countries, especially when short time horizons reflect a history of frequent changes in the type of regime (authoritarian versus democratic).[25] This finding is consistent with work showing that political instability has a negative impact on economic performance, particularly inflation, in developing countries.[26] Cukierman and Webb find that central bank independence is at greatest risk in non-OECD countries experiencing frequent regime changes. Short of regime change, the probability of politicians' rescinding authority delegated to the central bank after a change in the head of government or party in government is twice as great in non-OECD countries as in OECD countries.[27]

Clark finds that tenure security or insecurity, measured as the size of the governing party's majority or plurality in the legislature, bears no statistically significant relationship to central bank independence in developing countries.[28] But Clark's results are not necessarily inconsistent with those of Cukierman and Webb for at least two reasons. First, it is possible that tenure security measured through party dominance in the legislature may be significant for the subset of developing countries with stable democracies. Second is the possibility that tenure security is positively related to central bank independence as Cukierman and Webb suggest, but that it is not adequately captured through party dominance of the legislature in a set of countries where party systems and legislative power are only recently becoming consistent, stable, influential features of domestic politics.

While popular sentiment in the United States often sees central bank independence as threatening democracy, democracy can create incentives for politicians to delegate authority to the central bank. Shifting monetary policy authority to a separate institution allows politicians to avoid at least some of the responsibility and blame for economic performance. But this is an untested hypothesis. Explaining differences in central bank independence among well-functioning democracies will remain difficult until we have conclusive empirical results that pinpoint the precise causal story linking political competition to central bank independence. Scholarship to date also suggests that political competition in the absence of well-established democratic rules is not healthy for central bank independence. Cukierman and Webb find that central bank independence measured through governor turnover relative to change in government leadership was highest among those non-OECD countries under firmly established authoritarian regimes.[29] Until democratic governance becomes fully institutionalized in non-OECD countries, these results suggest that we should continue to expect reversals of central bank independence.

Government Financial Needs and Central Bank Independence

The third main set of arguments about central bank independence focuses on the incentives created by government needs for finance.[30] North and Weingast argue that the English government founded the Bank of England because it sought new loans to continue its war with France. This is consistent with Cukierman's more ahistorical formalization, concluding that "the delegation of authority to the central bank is used as a device to reduce interest charges on new government debt."[31] I find a version of this argument illustrative in the histories of central bank independence in newly industrializing countries.[32]

The logic of this financial incentives argument is clear in the history of the Bank of England. In the early 1690s the government of William III found itself out of money and uncreditworthy "due to previous repudiations of debts and confiscations of wealth."[33] Government credibility was so low that creditors were hesitant to lend at any interest rate. To raise funds in these circumstances governments and their potential creditors devised a novel exchange that involved creating a central bank or, as it was called at the time, a state bank. Creditors would subscribe to a large new government loan in exchange for the government's granting monopoly privileges to a new bank incorporated by the creditors. By statute this new bank would handle government accounts and issue notes. This provided the creditors a guarantee of repayment and monopoly rents. The Bank of England statute also prohibited lending money to the Crown or buying Crown land without parliamentary approval (creditors dominated Parliament).

A central bank was founded, but its independence by contemporary standards is questionable. The bank made repeated loans to the government throughout the eighteenth century, usually in return for reiteration of its monopoly privileges. The onset of the Napoleonic Wars coincided with an end to specie convertibility, and the government prevailed "on the Bank to help finance the wars through inflation.[34] The fixed but freely convertible exchange rates of the gold standard years bolstered the central bank's inflation-fighting capacity, perhaps more than its legal charter. The role played by the gold standard in this history suggests the need to integrate domestic and international forces in the political economy of central bank independence.

Similar stories could be told about the origins of many state banks in other advanced industrial countries and in developing countries.[35] In most cases the state bank's lack of independence is clear. The need for government finance calls forth a quasi-central bank through an exchange of monopoly privilege for bank loans to the government. Typically, under government pressure, bank loans far exceed statutory limits, if these exist. These state banks become fonts of inflationary government finance, as did the Bank of England during and after the Napoleonic Wars.

Brazil illustrates this logic. The Portuguese colonial government founded the first Banco do Brasil to finance the costs of the Portuguese court, which had been transplanted in the 1820s from Lisbon to Rio de Janiero because of war in Europe. Legal stipulations aside, the bank extended credit to the government virtually on demand. Not surprisingly, the Banco do Brasil failed and was reincarnated several times throughout the nineteenth and twentieth centuries. In the twentieth century it became an important source of finance for the government subsidy of coffee exporters. An alternate institution, with more potential for independence, was not founded until the 1960s. Debate over central bank independence and the inflationary role of the Banco do Brasil still rages today.

If we try to extend this argument to explain variation over time in the authority of contemporary central banks, ambiguity arises in the logic connecting government revenue imperatives to central bank independence. The creation of a central bank or greater independence accorded an existing central bank can reduce the cost of government borrowing by raising government credibility, lowering expectations of inflation, and lowering risk premia charged the government. This is the logic of the Bank of England story and that of Cukierman, who argues that central bank independence is higher the larger the amount of funds that the government plans to borrow on the capital market.[36] Alternatively, the creation of a central bank that lacks independence or a decrease in the authority of an existing central bank permits government to inflate away its existing debt burden and raise the portion of revenue earned through the seignorage that is earned by having a monopoly to print money.

The impact of government need for finance on central bank authority is clearly significant. But as with politicians' time horizons, its positive or negative relation to central bank independence depends on government interest in inflationary versus noninflationary finance. Such interest is a function of the relative economic and political costs political leaders associate with different financing options. To date the revenue imperative argument for central bank independence has been explored largely in a closed-economy context. In protected domestic financial systems with considerable government regulation, governments can "force" investment in government bonds. When investors have few options other than buying government debt, the cost of inflationary policy and the commensurate need for central bank independence is low. Presumably the internationalization of capital markets heightens the costs of inflationary finance and should increase the probability of central bank independence. This causal mechanism is one of several in the open-economy argument about central bank independence outlined in the next chapter. Before turning to a detailed discussion of this book's argument, however, there are two other explanations of central bank independence to address.

Leadership and Ideology

One further argument seeking to explain central bank independence rests on the quality of the leadership exercised by the governor of the central bank.[37] A second is that economic ideology explains the creation and re-creation of independent central banks.

To the reader familiar only with central banking in the United States, the issue of central bank independence may bring to mind the supposed collaboration of Federal Reserve Board governor Arthur Burns with President Richard Nixon's electorally motivated interest in expansionary monetary policy in 1972. This cooperation contrasted sharply with the tight monetary policy central bank governor Paul Volcker pursued to the detriment of Jimmy Carter's reelection efforts in 1979. Observers often attribute this difference in Fed behavior to the particular personalities of the two Fed governors. But there are several problems with the "great man or woman" theory of central bank power.[38] First is the problem of "endogeneity" in governor appointment. In many cases governors are appointed by the president or prime minister. Those presidents or prime ministers who want an authoritative central bank may appoint a governor with leadership potential. The source of leadership skill poses a different problem. Leadership skills may be hard to identify a priori; in many cases they are honed through praxis. In the case of central bank governors it may be the protection that is or is not afforded them by government politicians that shapes the opportunity for strong leadership to emerge. Leadership arguments are weak because they neglect the underlying importance of the motives of government politicians.

Another argument often employed to explain choice of economic policy could easily be extended to politicians' choice of central bank independence: the weight of economic ideology. The problem is that this type of explanation does not identify why and when policymakers adopt particular ideologies. For example, in a book ostensibly about the force of ideas in shaping economic policy patterns, Hall argues that ultimately the likelihood of political leaders' adoption of Keynesian economic ideas and policies was shaped by "the kind of financial instruments that each state developed to fund its debt, the regulatory regime imposed on the banking sector and the general character of the capital markets."[39] Of course prevailing economic ideologies will shape politicians' estimates of the costs and benefits of central bank independence. In this sense they contribute to temporal trends in the independence of that institution. The challenge is to specify the relative weight of economic ideology compared with market forces as explanations of overall trends in central bank authority.

Toward an International Political Economy of Central Bank Independence

International conditions will increasingly influence macroeconomic policy choices in both OECD and non-OECD countries, yet most of the models of central banking just reviewed are closed-economy models. These assume we can understand the dynamics of authority delegation to central banks without consideration of a country's international situation. Yet the link between international conditions and central bank authority seems evident in the history of the founding of central banks in many developing countries. In many instances in developing countries, official central banks, as opposed to the quasi-central banks often referred to as state banks, were founded when international financial pressures tipped the political scale in favor of those national actors arguing for a central bank. In the 1920s, for example, the League of Nations, the Federal Reserve Bank of New York, and the Bank of England actively promoted the founding of central banks throughout Eastern Europe and Latin America.[40] These actors, writes Simmons, "along with prominent members of the American and British financial sectors, often conditioned their stabilization assistance on improvements in the institutional independence of national central banks."[41] A similar pattern is evident in the 1950s and 1990s. The founding and bolstering of central banks appears to come in waves associated with periods when foreign capital inflows are highly prized and the leverage of international creditors and their domestic allies rises commensurably.

Adding an international component to the story of central bank authority helps clarify some of the puzzles that emerge from the existing research. Take the sectoral argument, for example. A potential explanation for the contradictory findings reported above is that financiers' abilities to exploit a nation's international economic vulnerabilities shape the effectiveness of financial sector demands on government to protect central bank independence. When government leaders prize foreign capital inflows highly, domestic proponents of central bank independence, usually in the financial sector, can use the exclusivity of their links to international financiers to bolster the proposition that international capital inflows will follow from the creation of, or improvement in, central bank independence.

The economic history of Latin America since World War II provides many examples. In Mexico the relative influence of private domestic bankers and their allies has varied with the nation's international financial situation. In the 1920s Mexico was in default on its international debts but needed to renegotiate and receive fresh funds. In this period the bankers were relatively successful in imposing their preferences for tight monetary and fiscal policy on the government. The bankers were less successful in the following two decades, when Mexico once again fell into default but could not hope to gain much by restructuring its debt when international markets were in chaos. As multilateral lending rose in the 1950s and access to these funds took on corresponding importance, the fortunes of the bankers improved. Excess global liquidity in the 1970s once again eroded the bankers' influence over government economic policy, while the debt crisis restored it.[42]

Similarly, the extent of international integration of domestic financial markets (partly a function of capital account openness) and the mix of outstanding financial obligations can explain whether a government's need for finance translates into more or less central bank independence. On the assumption that the behavior of domestic creditors follows that of international ones, the more internationally financially integrated the economy, the more likely it is that government need for finance will yield central bank independence, because it is taken as both a sign of government commitment to desirable economic policies and an opportunity for increased creditor influence over government policy via a more independent central bank. The argument is simple. Creditors and politicians are rational and have long understood what academic research has seemingly discovered only recently: "That which buttresses the credibility of the central bank, then, will dampen the inflationary monetary bias . . . and *encourage capital inflows*."[43] Such an argument would lead us to expect identifiable temporal trends in central bank authority across the globe. Johnson and Siklos, for example, find that "central bank behavior is significantly different in the post–Bretton Woods period relative to the Bretton Woods era."[44] As the authors note, the OECD-oriented studies that aim almost exclusively to explain cross-national variations in (assumed to be constant) levels of legal independence "mask subtle changes in central bank behavior over time" that are related to changing objective and subjective international financial conditions. This book takes up the challenge left by the existing literature on central banking to try to illuminate the interaction and relative weight of increasingly inseparable national and international financial factors, along with domestic political considerations, in government politicians' calculations about central bank independence, particularly in non-OECD countries.

Three

International Capital Flows and the Politics of Central Bank Independence

> We have to learn about these capital flows and how they might actually matter to governments and national interests.
>
> —John Woolley

> The only way to ensure . . . [central bank] independence is to create laws and institutions which act to tie the hands of both the government and the central bank. . . . The adoption of IMF standby agreements is an important traditional way to achieve this result.
>
> —Mart Laar, Prime Minister of Estonia

THE WAVE of central bank reform during the 1990s in countries all over the globe lends credibility to the argument that global financial forces are at work.[1] This chapter sketches an argument suggesting that the financial pressures on politicians in middle-income developing countries shape their decisions regarding central bank independence in several specific ways. The 1990s witnessed a wave of increase in legal central bank independence because government leaders were trying to attract and retain capital. Put telescopically, the likelihood that politicians in middle-income developing countries will attempt to signal creditworthiness by increasing central bank independence is an increasing function of their nation's objective need for balance of payments support, the expected effectiveness of signaling, and politicians' tenure security. It is a decreasing function of the extent of financial regulation in the politician's country.[2] Chapter 4 suggests that the pattern of cross-regional variation in central bank reform in the 1990s is consistent with this argument.

This book argues that actual central bank independence in middle-income developing countries varies with a country's need for credit and investment, as perceived by government politicians. Politicians try to signal their country's creditworthiness by ceding central bank discretion and recognizing central bank authority.[3] International financial asset holders should be more willing, ceteris paribus, to invest in countries with independent central banks for two reasons. First, investors expect central banks with discretion and authority to help keep national economic policy on a stable, consistent course. Therefore central bank independence increases the extent to which international investors can predict their relative returns. International investors view the costs politicians pay to reverse central bank independence as a partial guarantee of stable, consistent economic policy.

Central bank independence may also increase the confidence of some international investors in a second way. Concerned about host-country policies that threaten anticipated returns, international investors may believe that their ability to influence policy is greater the more independent the central bank is from the executive branch. Foreign investors read central bank independence as a signal of the strength of domestic proponents of sound monetary policy, both within the government and among domestic social groups, with whom the investors might implicitly or explicitly ally in an effort to influence policy.

Obviously politicians' use' of central bank independence to signal creditworthiness in middle-income developing countries will rise with the objective need for international financial resources measured through the balance of payments. This objective need is discussed briefly at the end of the chapter. Objective balance of payments conditions equal, three other factors increase the likelihood that the need for international financial resources will lead politicians to increase central bank discretion and government recognition of central bank authority. The expected responsiveness of investors partially guides politicians' use of central bank independence to increase creditworthiness. If the global supply of financial resources vastly exceeds demand, as in the 1970s, costly efforts to signal creditworthiness will be foolish. Furthermore, not all international investors will be equally responsive to central bank independence. One of the main objectives of this chapter is to delineate how and why investor responsiveness varies by asset type (foreign direct investment, international bank loans, foreign bonds, foreign equity shares). The following section explains how and why investor responsiveness varies with four characteristics: asset-specificity, risk structure, access to local information, and number of investors. Politicians' use of central bank independence to increase creditworthiness also rises with more extensive financial liberalization for the host country and longer effective time horizons and tenure security for its leaders. Subsequent sections explain these mechanisms in turn.

The Effectiveness of Signaling Creditworthiness

Politicians seek creditworthiness in the eyes of international investors to improve the quantity and price of financial resources offered to their country. The effectiveness of efforts to increase creditworthiness will vary with the characteristics of international financial markets. Two characteristics are important: the relationship between supply and demand for international financial resources and the predominant form of international financial intermediation. This section evaluates the latter and explores how the nature of the assets through which international funds flow to middle-income developing countries affects how and to what extent political leaders will try to build creditworthiness.[4]

Asset-specificity, mobility, or liquidity, all references to the same asset characteristic, are crucial to understanding the international financial pressures government politicians face.[5] If an investment such as foreign direct investment in a factory is "stuck" in a recipient country there is little the investor can do if host-country policy changes threaten to lower anticipated returns. The recipient country has considerable leeway to deviate from policies expected by the investor initially; it is difficult to liquidate a factory. Of course, new foreign investors may become wary of investing in the country. But the point is that, other things equal, pressure on recipient countries to stick to the policy path "promised" at the time an investment is made rises with the liquidity of the investment stock.[6] International investors in government bonds or equities, for example, can normally sell them immediately on news of an unfavorable change in the policy environment. This liquidity increases pressure on political leaders who desire international investment to maintain a favorable policy environment. The predominant form of capital flow from "north" to "south" will shape the marginal benefit from efforts to signal improved creditworthiness.

Another way to say this is that the greater the elasticity of supply and price of international funds, the more valuable are politicians' marginal efforts to increase creditworthiness. Other things equal, the elasticities are low for foreign direct investment, moderate for commercial bank loans, and great for bond and equity investments.

In the world of more liquid investments, the distribution and nature of risk on returns should also shape investor responsiveness to signals about the future investment environment. The more risk borne by the investor, the more responsive the investor should be to market signals.[7] The greater the default risk, the more responsive the investor should be.[8] This helps us distinguish between government bonds and equities.[9] The return on government securities is fixed, which is why government bonds are called "fixed-income" securities. The return on an equity investment is variable, and risk is shared between investor and borrower. But because government bonds mature on a specific date, the investor runs a risk that the government will not have funds to liquidate the security. (A security in this case is literally a piece of paper, or "note.") Default risk is thus lower for equity shares than for fixed-income securities because an equity borrower facing liquidity problems can lower the dividend paid, while a government facing a liquidity problem may have to default. Cross-border investment complicates the analysis. Unless they insure themselves, investors in foreign securities expose themselves to exchange risk. If a government issues bonds denominated in a foreign currency (like dollars), investors should be very responsive to changes in the policy environment affecting the supply of foreign exchange. If a government issues bonds denominated in the local currency, investors should be very responsive to policies threatening exchange rate stability. A corporate equity issued on a foreign market denominated in a foreign currency is usually backed by a commitment from a sponsoring bank to provide the foreign currency. (This is how American Depository Receipt issues work on the New York Stock Exchange.)[10] The investor is exposed to a decline in the exchange-adjusted price of the stock but faces less risk of outright default than the investor in foreign government bonds.

The risks and policy sensitivities of commercial banks making loans to governments, "sovereign" loans, are similar to those of investors in government securities. Both should be more sensitive to changes in the macroeconomic policy environment than equity investors, who will be more sensitive than investors in debt instruments to sectorally oriented policies. But international bank lenders tend to be fewer in number than holders of government securities. The comfort in numbers and large exposure lower international bank sensitivity to the policy environment. The small community of international bankers, in its efforts to directly pressure the borrowing country government for policy changes or to appeal to home country governments or multilateral institutions such as the IMF to intervene on the investors' behalf, can hold out greater hope of success than the typically larger community of bondholders.[11]

Asset-specificity, risk structure, access to local information, and numbers all may shape the responsiveness of international investors to particular kinds of signals of creditworthiness. We consider four types of international investors: foreign direct investors, equity investors, international bank lenders, and purchasers of foreign government bonds (see Table 3.1).

TABLE 3.1
Expected Responsiveness of International Investors to Host Country Change in Central Bank Independence

Asset	*Liquidity (as a stock)*	*Policies Affecting Financial Returns*	*Access to Local Information*	*Lobby or Leave?*	*Expected Responsiveness to Central Bank Independence*
Foreign direct investment	Low, limited response to change in policy climate	Sectoral; regulation of profit repatriation; tax	High, less need for signals easily read from abroad	Lobby to salvage sunk costs	Low
Equity shares	Low-Mod. (high as a flow)	Sectoral; capital account regulations	Low, investors unlikely to have direct access, need signals	Hard to lobby; investors face collective action problems	Low-Mod.
Debt (loans)	Low, terms of loan and maturity are fixed	Macroeconomic	Low-Mod., commercial banks with international retail operations should be a source	Lobby	Low-Mod.
Debt (bonds)	High	Macroeconomic, capital account openness	Low, need signals	Leave	High

Foreign Direct Investment

Foreign direct investors should not be very responsive to changes in the general macroeconomic policy environment, which is what change in central bank independence signals. Foreign direct investments cannot be quickly liquidated, although they can be abandoned. Foreign direct investors will find their influence over policy limited once they have invested in physical plant.[12] The interests of foreign direct investors vis-à-vis recipient countries are likely to be somewhat heterogeneous, depending on the sector they operate in and their point along the investment-recovery time line. They should be most sensitive to changes in the regulatory environment for foreign corporations, in sectoral policies, and in trade restrictions.[13] Trade freedom guarantees profit repatriation opportunities through under- and over-invoicing even if capital account regulations otherwise limit it. Foreign direct investors have a physical presence in the host country. Generally speaking, they are closer to local information sources and have less need than arm's length investors to rely on signals of policy direction that are more easily observed from afar, such as central bank independence. If the policy environment changes, foreign direct investors are likely to lobby to try to protect their sunk costs. Their responsiveness to signaling via change in central bank authority should be low.

Foreign Equity Shares

International equity investment involves no time commitment. International equity investments are very fungible compared with foreign direct investments.[14] They are usually more liquid than commercial bank loans. Yet the decision to divest at any given moment can be expensive, because returns vary and risk is shared by investor and borrower. International equity investors are fairly responsive to changes in the policy environment and have more need to rely on signals of change in the policy environment than do foreign direct investors. Yet their responsiveness to central bank independence should only be moderate because, as already noted, they are more concerned with sectoral than with overall macroeconomic policy.[15] An important exception occurs when international equity investors hold shares in financial sector institutions. Equity investors in general should be very sensitive to regulation of the capital account, especially as it affects their repatriation and liquidation options. It is possible that equity investors would read central bank independence as a signal of the capital account policy environment.

Foreign investors purchasing equity shares in developing country corporations rely on signals to forecast returns because acquiring access to local information is costly. But these investors are likely to search for signals specific to particular sectors. Individual investors' responsiveness to market signals should also be high because the number of investors is large. But the number of individual shareholders makes organization to pressure governments an unlikely strategy for protecting investments. The relatively large number of actors and the premium on speed would make bilateral or multilateral bargaining over policy with the host-country government a poor strategy for equity investors.[16] As Frieden emphasizes, asset specificity is the prime determinant of asset-holders' choice of strategy in response to threatened changes in the investment environment. The less specific the assets are, the more likely it is that the investor will chose to exit rather than try to influence the course of change.[17]

Apart from investment in the financial sector, equity investors' interest in the overall macroeconomic environment as signaled by central bank independence should thus be moderate. Central bank independence may induce some response to the extent that equity investors view it as a signal of commitment to a liberal capital account policy.

Debt: International Bank Loans

Debt is extended for a fixed time period: bonds or bank loans typically commit principal for at least several years. International sovereign loans involve explicit negotiation of a contract, usually specified in lender-country currency. Interest rates are often variable over the life of loan, but the time frame is less flexible. Borrowers may repay early, but lenders may not demand early repayment. Although loans can be resold, the extent of the market for them varies, as it does with all assets. The secondary market for developing country loans has never been very liquid; this spurred loan conversion to bonds through the Brady program.[18]

Commercial bank lending involves relatively few actors with relatively homogeneous interests; syndications (formal groups of international banks) may specify terms of seniority and subordination for individual member institutions. As a comparatively small group often facing large exposure, commercial bank lenders can afford to be less responsive to market signals than equity or government bondholders. In other words, moral hazard operates in the case of bank lending.[19] The promise of home government support induces greater risk-taking than market conditions warrant. Typically international banks facing borrower country default receive third-party assistance for efforts to secure the promise of repayment as debt is rescheduled.[20] Through the organization of market or government actors or multilateral intervention, "conditionality" is applied. International or multilateral organizations make loans or loan-term renegotiation conditional on borrower governments' committing themselves to a particular set of policies.[21]

To the extent they feel a need to respond to market signals, bank lenders should be concerned with the overall macroeconomic policy environment signaled by central bank independence. International bank lenders are more likely than international equity investors to have a local presence. Local information could be channeled through correspondent banks in the borrowing country or, in some cases, through branches or subsidiaries operating in the country. Yet this local presence generally does not generate information used by loan officers to the extent expected.[22] This gives greater weight to the need for signals about the macroeconomic policy environment, such as central bank independence, that can be observed from abroad.

Despite this paucity of local information and a concern with the macroeconomic policy environment, the likelihood of market actor or third party intervention and the relatively low liquidity of secondary loan markets both lower international banks' responsiveness to market signals, such as central bank independence.

Debt: Foreign Government Bonds

On the far end of the responsiveness continuum from foreign direct investors lie investors in foreign government bonds. As financial assets, the specificity of bonds and bank loans is a function of market demand. In the post–World War II era there was virtually no international demand for government bonds issued by developing countries until the 1980s. The market boomed in the 1990s.[23] In contrast, demand for repackaged and resold international bank loans was virtually nonexistent in the 1980s; it revived slightly in the 1990s.[24]

Holders of foreign government bonds must respond to market signals because there is no comfort in numbers. International bondholders are much more numerous than international bank lenders. The likelihood of home government intervention or of successful organized action to pressure issuing governments for policy change is low. Evidence from the 1930s, when bond sales dominated international investment, supports this conclusion. In fact, bonds were floated by a relatively small number of syndicates and then sold through "traveling salesmen" to small public investors.[25] The collective action problems arose from the dispersion of owners, not issuers. The issuing syndicates did not have their own money at stake and were only partially motivated by trying to maintain their reputations with bond purchasers. Bondholders' committees were formed to help creditors present a unified front in negotiations with debtors, both in the 1860s in Britain and in the 1930s in the United States. Because of the large number of owners involved, these committees appear to have suffered more from collective action problems than did the loan renegotiation committees representing bank lenders in the 1980s.[26] Cooperation among the bond committees of different nations, especially across the Atlantic, also appears to have been less frequent than cooperation among loan syndicates in the 1980s.

International government bondholders should be especially concerned with macroeconomic conditions and have no special advantage in obtaining local information; they look for signals of the future policy environment. Other things equal, holders of foreign government securities are more likely than any other international investors to be responsive to central bank independence as a signal of creditworthiness. The signals the market relies on may change as time proves them more or less accurate. But in the early 1990s the conventional wisdom was that inflation induced by a government's deficit spending was less likely to the extent that the government relinquished the prerogative for unlimited borrowing from the central bank. The more authority the central bank had in determining interest rates and money supply growth, went the average mutual fund manager's thinking, the less likely these policy instruments were to be used by politicians in accord with their electoral concerns, rather than to further the goal of price stability. Earlier, in the heyday of bond lending between the two world wars, international advisory committees also frequently suggested the creation of central banks or strengthening their independence in addition to the kinds of stabilization policies typically sought by creditors.

The evidence suggests that, other things equal, trying to signal creditworthiness via central bank independence should be least effective when foreign direct investment is the predominant form of "north-south" capital flow and most effective when the predominant form is investment in developing country government bonds. One important determinant of the effectiveness of signaling cuts across asset type. The relationship of the global supply and demand for international resources shapes the need for capital-scarce countries to compete for capital. If global capital supply greatly exceeds demand, as it did in the 1970s, the need to signal creditworthiness is lower.

Financial Regulation

The likelihood that politicians will try to signal creditworthiness via central bank independence is a decreasing function of financial regulation in three ways. When the restrictions on international capital mobility are fewer, national financial markets are more integrated and global financial markets are more encompassing. In general, the more encompassing global financial markets are, the greater the competition for investment.

Although the international investors' preferred signals of creditworthiness may vary, when one—such as central bank independence—is in vogue with international investors, capital mobility dictates that the politician desirous of attracting and keeping capital cannot ignore it. The more international financial integration is the more mobile international financial resources are in general. The need for creditworthiness will grow with international financial integration. Cerny highlights this point when he argues that international financial integration has led to the development of the "competition state," vying for capital.[27]

Yet the claim of growing global openness is controversial. While there is little doubt that governments have dismantled many post–World War II regulatory barriers to international capital movement over the last twenty years, considerable controversy surrounds the quantitative measurement of international capital mobility and international financial integration. In the early 1980s Feldstein and Horioka found a high correlation between changes in national savings and investment rates which they took to be a sign of low capital mobility. Many criticized the Feldstein-Horioka findings.[28] There is a stronger theoretical rationale, critics argue, for using interest rate convergence as a measure of international financial integration. Analysts find different degrees of integration depending on the type of interest rates compared.[29] Currency variability aside, it appears that interest rates *are* increasingly convergent.[30]

The volume of international financial transactions has certainly grown and investors' decision frameworks are increasingly international.[31] This is true of investors in both capital-rich and capital-scarce countries. One study concludes, "capital moves in and out of [developing] countries, both legally and by evasion of controls, with much greater ease than one would expect."[32] In fact, while one would expect foreign investors in developing countries to follow the capital allocation choices of resident nationals, the latter increasingly mimic the portfolio decisions of foreign investors in their countries. In middle-income developing countries the determinants of domestic and international investment are increasingly similar.[33]

Nonetheless, there are important cross-national and cross-regional differences in the extent of international financial openness that facilitate or hinder international capital mobility. The likelihood that government politicians in a particular country will take actions that augment central bank independence increases with the reduction of restrictions on domestic and international financial transactions. Developing countries have historically imposed controls on cross-border capital movements.[34] In the 1980s a growing number of developing countries have opened their financial systems by liberalizing capital flows, though to varying extents.[35] National capital account regulations, therefore, are an important determinant of the possibilities for capital mobility. The need for creditworthiness in middle-income developing countries rises with the deregulation of international financial transactions.

In addition, domestic financial deregulation creates a very particular pressure for creditworthiness noted in Chapter 1. When domestic financial regulations and controls on international capital flows limit the investment options of country nationals, governments can sell debt at relatively low interest rates. Internationally isolated and "repressed" financial markets can create artificially high demand for government securities.[36] Especially when other sources of government revenue are low relative to government expenditures, as is typically the case in developing countries, the cost of raising funds through the sale of government bonds is very important.[37] When financial markets are deregulated and become increasingly internationally integrated, politicians no longer enjoy a captive market for government securities. Domestic deregulation also reduces possibilities of raising revenue through seignorage.[38] When the government has to compete with myriad other investment vehicles to sell its securities, the value of central bank independence rises because it can serve as a signal to investors. A recent comment by Donald Brash, governor of the Bank of New Zealand, captures this phenomenon. Observers herald the Bank of New Zealand as one of the most independent central banks in the world in the 1990s. Questioned about the possibility that even with its great statutory autonomy the bank could be weakened by the appointment of a compliant governor or by pressure on an incumbent hoping for reappointment, Brash said, "The openness of the system, combined with the discipline of the financial markets, make it unlikely that any government would take the risk."[39]

Politicians' Tenure Security

National leaders' tenure security will also affect the decision to pursue creditworthiness. As noted in Chapter 2, theory about the impact of time horizons and tenure security on governing politicians' preferences about monetary policy and monetary institutions is contradictory, while empirical evidence is limited. For OECD countries, theory suggests that the effect of time horizons and tenure security on central bank independence is indeterminate without specification of governing party preferences. This is consistent with Simmons's empirical results from a study of the relationship between time horizons, monetary policy, and preferences for capital inflow. On the basis of evidence for Western countries during the interwar years Simmons argues that stable, right-wing governments are more likely to be "monetary internalizers," seeking international capital inflows at the cost of domestic policy flexibility, than unstable, left-wing governments.[40]

For non-OECD countries, Cukierman and Webb's empirical work suggests that central bank independence is a positive function of politicians' time horizons, regardless of party preferences.[41] The importance of party preferences in OECD countries and their irrelevance outside the OECD world is logical. In most non-OECD countries party systems are only recently beginning to play a consistent and important role in national politics. To explain monetary policy choices in developing countries, Haggard and Kaufman focus on the extent to which party systems, in authoritarian or democratic environments, are "aggregative" or fragmented. "Aggregative party systems are those in which governments can consistently mobilize electoral support through one or two broadly based centrist parties."[42] Fragmented systems are "more likely to generate coalition governments held together by extensive, and costly, side-payments." Aggregative party systems are likely to yield stable, relatively low inflation because they limit the need for side-payments and the strain these can place on fiscal resources. They also encourage policy continuity, "diminish the freedom of maneuver of opposition forces outside of the broad center," and lengthen political leaders' time horizons.

The rule for developing countries between 1945 and 1990 is that national leaders insecure in their positions are likely to want to maintain policy flexibility because it provides greater potential for vote-buying and because the benefits of creditworthiness may accrue for the succeeding leadership.[43] Rising economic literacy in developing countries could reduce this rule's general applicability if electorates understand and value the role of the politician–central bank relationship in sustaining capital flows. For example, Carlos Menem's reelection as president of Argentina in 1995 depended in part on convincing voters that he would be able to sustain a credible commitment to investors. He pursued somewhat expansionary fiscal policy, but did not contemplate encroaching on the central bank or eliminating the currency board. Partisanship is likely to become necessary in explaining the impact of tenure security as democracy becomes institutionalized in developing countries. One can then expect a rise over time in the number of instances in which tenure insecurity leads politicians to increase central bank independence in order to protect gains threatened by electoral successors.

Objective Balance of Payments Conditions and the Need for Creditworthiness

In the midst of widespread default on international bonds in the 1930s, the U.S. Securities and Exchange Commission commented: "The willingness of the issuer to negotiate with representatives of the bondholders and eventually to agree to readjust its default generally has two motivations: a desire to restore the prestige and reputation of the nation and a desire to borrow more money."[44] An indisputably important determinant of the extent to which politicians seek international creditworthiness is their countries' need for international financial resources. A nation's balance of payments situation, specifically debt, export capacity, and foreign exchange reserves, is likely to reflect this need. Several caveats are in order, however. Quantitative indicators of the balance of payments can be highly misleading; large current account deficits may be voluntarily financed in one country, while small deficits may signal a loss of confidence in another. Furthermore, politicians' perceptions of the need for balance of payments support may not be fully objective. History, as well as countervailing contemporary pressures, intervenes, creating varying degrees of separation between objective and subjective evaluations.

Conclusion

This chapter has outlined a theory that politicians' decisions to cede discretion to their nation's central bank should be an increasing function of the need for creditworthiness. One measure of such need lies in a nation's balance of payments accounts. But the story is more complex. Politicians are more likely to use central bank independence to signal global financial markets the greater the role of portfolio finance in financial intermediation between capital-rich and capital-scarce countries. This occurs because the expected effectiveness of signaling via central bank independence varies with the predominant structure of "north-south" financial intermediation. The supply of financial resources, another characteristic of international financial markets, also shapes politicians' perceptions of the potential effectiveness, and therefore value, of trying to signal the need for international creditworthiness. If the global supply of financial resources greatly outstrips demand, the need to compete for capital and for creditworthiness is less.

Politicians are also more likely to use central bank independence to signal international financial markets the more secure they are in office and the less their country restricts domestic and international financial transactions through government regulation. Tenure security is important because the impact of central bank independence on creditworthiness involves a time lag. Government politicians insecure about their tenure in office will have short time horizons in office and are likely to accord low value to central bank independence and the creditworthiness it can bring. The potential political cost of ceding discretion over monetary policy is higher when politicians must fight to win the electorate's support. If there is any chance that monetary policy flexibility will allow weak governing politicians to buy greater support, the cost of ceding discretion over monetary policy is very high. This rule may change with democratic institutionalization and rising economic literacy among the electorate in developing countries. In any case, government regulation of financial transactions is important because it weakens the impact of global financial pressures.

This argument highlights the role of politicians' perceived need for creditworthiness in shaping their decisions regarding central bank independence. If politicians perceive the need as low, the likelihood of an increase in central bank independence is low. If they perceive the need as high, the likelihood of an increase in central bank independence is greater. Many factors can influence politicians' perceptions of the need for creditworthiness. The argument developed here emphasizes the most obvious: the objective balance of payments conditions and the extent to which market forces shape the government's financial situation. The argument also emphasizes politicians' tenure security. Furthermore, conditions in global financial markets will shape expectations about the effectiveness of acting to signal improved creditworthiness via treatment of the central bank. Politicians will only choose to signal creditworthiness via their actions toward the central bank if they expect the signal to be effective.

This book's theoretical claims may be briefly characterized relative to broad themes in the political economy of developing countries. These pages tell a subtle story about forces shaping central bank independence that is consistent with arguments stressing the conditions set by international financial institutions in order to explain the policy choices of developing countries. It is also broadly consistent with arguments linking international economic conditions to the relative capacity of different domestic sectors, such as the financial sector, to influence government actions. Quite simply, hard-money coalitions, often centered around domestic financial actors, have more leverage over government when financing is scarce. The argument is also second cousin to theories of state action stressing the structural power of capital. It is both more and less political than arguments explaining policy choice by virtue of the sectoral composition of a national economy. It is more political because politicians' perceptions are central, but it is less political because the assumption is that the globalization of finance will move politicians' perceptions inexorably toward a consistent concern with their nation's creditworthiness. The impact of economic ideology on politicians' perceptions of the need for creditworthiness is secondary to material conditions manifest in global financial markets. Similarly, for the domain of developing countries as a whole, arguments stressing party politics and/or regime type alone have little relevance for explaining trends in central bank independence in the second half of the twentieth century.

Four

Central Bank Independence in the 1990s

> The intellectual case for independent central banks is more or less won.
>
> —*The Economist*

> I am convinced there is objective reality in my impression that central banks are in exceptionally good repute these days.
>
> —Paul Volcker

THIS CHAPTER surveys the remarkable global rise in central bank independence in the 1990s.[1] It also explores the extent to which cross-regional variation in this global trend corroborates the argument that politicians are more likely to cede discretion to central banks when the need and value of competing for international creditworthiness is high.

Between 1990 and 1995 at least thirty countries, spanning five continents, legislated increases in the statutory independence of their central banks. A list of the countries increasing de jure central bank independence and, in some cases, measures of increase in legal independence (based on the 1992 coding criteria of Cukierman, Webb, and Neyapti, hereafter referred to as Cukierman et al. [1992]) are presented in Table 4.1.[2] This dramatic trend occurred at the same time that portfolio flows became the fastest-growing form of capital inflow for developing countries, global demand for international financial resources rose relative to supply, and financial deregulation in developing countries, especially of international transactions, proceeded rapidly. The global trend in central bank independence in the early 1990s is consistent with the competition to signal creditworthiness engendered by the liquidity of portfolio finance, increasing demand for international financial resources as formerly Communist countries begin rapid infrastructure expansion, and lowering of government barriers to financial transactions.

The trend toward central bank independence has been most pronounced in Europe, but it is also evident in Latin America. Change in Asia and the Pacific has been moderate and in the Middle East and Africa, minimal. If the argument laid out in Chapter 3 is correct, regions

TABLE 4.1
Changes in Statutory Central Bank Independence, 1989–1994

Countries with Charter Change	*Date*	*Regional Averages*
Argentina	1992	
Chile	1989	
Colombia	1992	
Ecuador	1992	
Mexico	1993	
Venezuela	1992	
Latin American Average Level, 1990–1994		.55
Latin American Average Increase in 1990s over 1980s		.19
Albania	1991	
Belarus	1994	
Bulgaria	1991	
Czech Republic	1993	
Estonia	1993	
Hungary	1991	
Kazahkstan	1993	
Latvia	1992	
Lithuania	1994	
Poland	1991 and 1992	
Romania	1991	
Russia	1993	
Slovak Republic	1993	
Ukraine	1992	
Central and Eastern Europe Average Level, 1990–1994		.45
Central and Eastern Europe Average Magnitude Increase in 1990s over 1980s		.26
Belgium	1993	
France	1993	
Greece	1993	
Italy	1992	
Portugal	1992	
Spain	1994	
Western Europe Average Level, 1990–1994		.46
Western Europe Average Magnitude Increase in 1990s over 1980s		.33
Algeria	1991	
Egypt	1992	
Turkey	1989	
New Zealand	1989	
Pakistan	1993	
Vietnam	1992	

Note: Coding of charters based on charter coding and data reported in Alex Cukierman, Steven B. Webb, and Bilim Neyapti, "Measuring the Independence of Central Banks," *World Bank Economic Review*, 6, 3 (September 1992).

with the largest rates of increase in central bank independence should also be regions with the greatest need for international creditworthiness. Using interest rates on private international credits, Table 4.2 shows that Latin American and Central and Eastern Europe were the regions facing the highest rates.

If we turn to the variables that should enhance the impact of need for creditworthiness on central bank independence, the cross-regional variation is generally consistent with the theory. In absolute numbers the two regions with the largest increases in central bank independence, Europe and Latin America, sold more bonds to foreigners than did the other regions. Their short-term debt roughly captures objective need for creditworthiness. This debt, measured as trade and suppliers' credits, was large. It is difficult to capture regional differences in financial regulation and politicians' time horizons in quantitative terms. The capital account openness measure used here as an indicator of overall financial regulation is based on coding of International Monetary Fund (IMF) reports on national exchange restrictions. Capital account openness is greatest in Latin America, which experienced the second-greatest increase in central bank independence. Yet Europe, which saw a larger increase in central bank independence than Latin America, continued to have relatively high capital account regulation.[3]

This chapter is not intended as a strong test of the argument laid out in Chapter 3. However, the data on cross-regional variation in the increase of central bank independence are consistent with the argument, at its broadest level. Other possible factors contributing to central bank independence in different regions, especially Europe, are also noted.

The Maastricht Treaty for European integration, and its impact on expectations about capital mobility, created impetus for the revision of central bank law in Western Europe, where the trend toward increased legal independence has extended to a relatively large number of countries, representing a significant portion of regional GNP. Maastricht heightened politicians' awareness of the need to compete for international capital. In Eastern and Central Europe it is difficult to distinguish among concern over inflation stabilization, capitalist growth, and foreign capital inflow as motivating central bank independence.

The trend toward legal independence has also been dramatic in Latin America. Latin American countries need investment capital to retool for export-oriented production, and many are trying to recover from recent histories of poor international financial management that make their need for international creditworthiness even greater. Portfolio investment is an important source of balance of payments finance in the region. Most of the larger countries in Latin America, measured in

TABLE 4.2
Cross-Regional Indicators of Legal Central Bank Independence (CBI) and Signaling Likelihood, 1990–1992

	Africa	*Asia*	*Latin America*	*Central and Eastern Europe*
Bonds Outstanding (U.S. millions)[a]	140	2,060	2,851	4,727
Interest on Private International Loans[a]	most loans are concessional	7.2	8.3	8.4
Suppliers / Trade Credit Outstanding[a]	1,259	4,622	*N.A.*	13,283
Capital Account Openness (0 = lo; 11 = hi)[b]	5.1	6.9	6.3	8
Domestic Financial Market Regulation (1 = lo; 3 = hi)[c]	3	2	1	1.0
No. of Observations of CBI Increase and Average Magnitude of Increase[d]	2 (*N.A.*)	3 (.07)	5 (.19)	15 (.26)

a. Data from World Bank, *World Debt Tables* (Washington, D.C.: World Bank, various years).

b. From regulations in IMF, *Exchange Arrangement and Exchange Restrictions* (Washington, D.C.: IMF, various years).

c. Based on author's country surveys.

d. Based on legal coding in Alex Cukierman, Steven B. Webb, and Bilim Neyapti, "Measuring the Independence of Central Banks," *World Bank Economic Review*, 6, 3 (September 1992), and author's coding of post-1989 legal changes.

terms of GNP, have revised or are debating revising their central bank legislation in the direction of increased independence.

The need for special efforts to attract international investment is low in the majority of Asian countries, and there have been relatively fewer moves toward central bank independence in this region. Domestic and international financial transactions remain relatively heavily regulated. The proportion of countries that have recently increased central bank authority is lowest in the Middle East and Africa. In Africa this is partly because two different currency boards substitute for central banks in thirteen countries. The relatively weak trend toward central bank reform in Africa also corresponds to the minimal incentive to seek approval from international capital markets for countries considered too poor to receive nonconcessional finance. Middle Eastern countries, though facing growing economic troubles, enjoy good international creditworthiness as indicated in the low interest rates international lenders charge them (see Table 4.2).

Western Europe

On the western side of the former Iron Curtain new central bank charters were promulgated with striking alacrity in the early 1990s. Portugal passed two laws, one in 1990 and a second in 1992, leading to a staged increase in central bank independence. The 1990 legislation gave the Bank of Portugal, previously an administrative arm of the government, the right to collaborate in setting monetary and exchange rate policies. Legislation in 1992 gave the bank independence in setting monetary and exchange rate policies and in the regulation of financial markets and institutions. This law also abolished the free overdraft account the government held with the central bank and limited lending by the Bank of Portugal to 10 percent of budgeted government expenditure. Legislation also lengthened the legally stipulated term of office for the central bank governor.[4]

Throughout 1993 debate surrounded proposals for a new Bank of Spain statute. Informally, government leaders encouraged increases in central bank autonomy even prior to resolution of that debate. For example, in a meeting occasioned by Spain's devaluation of its currency, the Bank of Spain president informed Prime Minister Felipe Gonzalez that he was prepared to accompany the devaluation with a drop in interest rates. Gonzalez reportedly replied that such a move would have to be entirely at the discretion of the central bank.[5] The prime focus of debate over legal revision was the provision for the appointment of the central bank's governing officials, including concern about term length and regional representation. Legislation stipulating greater independence was finally passed in 1994. It lengthened the governor's term of appointment and tightened the grounds for his or her dismissal. The new statute also shifted responsibility for monetary policy formulation more clearly to the central bank. Terms of central bank lending to the government were also made more stringent.

In Greece, Ministry of Economics officials met with IMF representatives to work out details on how best to legislate central bank independence. As of January 1994, when new central bank legislation went into effect, the Greek government lost its right to obtain direct financing from the central bank. The charter also stipulates increases in central bank authority in the areas of terms of government appointment and dismissal, monetary policy, and bank objectives.

The central bank of Turkey, under Rusdu Saracoglu, unilaterally began to operate with increased autonomy from the government. Saracoglu was part of the team advising former Prime Minister Turgot Ozal on economic liberalization in the late 1980s. He was appointed to the central bank in 1987 and struggled to increase central bank authority both de jure and de facto throughout his tenure in the central bank. In 1989 he succeeded in obtaining a protocol restraining Treasury borrowing from the central bank.[6] Commented Saracoglu, "In recent years the independence of the Central Bank has improved markedly. True we are no Bundesbank, not even close. On the other hand, the increased public awareness regarding the Central Bank's independence combined with conscientious behavior on the part of politicians are gradually reducing the impact of elections on the conduct of monetary policy."[7] But Saracoglu's efforts were never enshrined in a new central bank statute. De facto independence did not survive the heightened political uncertainty surrounding government changes in the mid-1990s.

In Italy, despite the progress toward central bank independence achieved through the so-called divorce of 1982, more autonomy for the central bank had been sought for years prior to the 1992 legislation that accorded the Bank of Italy autonomy in setting interest rates.[8] That legislation also gave the bank complete autonomy to intervene in foreign exchange markets. Prior to the change, the Italian Treasury set both interest and foreign exchange rate policy, usually on recommendation of the central bank. Although there had been no Bank of Italy financing of the government for several years in spite of a large deficit, 1992 legislation legally limited Treasury overdrafts with the central bank to 14 percent of the expected increase in government expenditure.[9]

Belgium passed legislation in March 1993 abolishing the Ministry of Finance veto over central bank affairs and preventing Treasury borrowing from the Bank of Belgium. The legislation fell short, however, in failing to include a clear stipulation of monetary stability as the central bank's sole objective.

In mid-1993 France also passed legislation increasing the autonomy of its central bank, considered one of the least independent in Western Europe. Late in 1992 central bank independence became part of the party platform of the French right. In December, with uncertainty surrounding the franc's value, opposition politician Giscard d'Estaing proclaimed that legislating central bank independence "would, in the current situation, be the best political and technical signal of our will to have, from now on, a sound currency policy."[10] "The international markets carefully monitor the independence of central banks," stated Giscard on another occasion.[11] As electoral competition rose in anticipation of the March 1993 elections, the governing party also embraced the concept of speedy action to increase central bank independence. Minister of Finance Michel Sapin expressed favor for immediate legislation of central bank independence as "an elegant way to challenge what could be the policies pursued by another majority."[12]

The legislation put forth by the newly elected neo-Gaullist Prime Minister Edouard Balladur in April 1993, and passed later that year, shifted control over monetary policy from the Treasury to a Monetary Policy Council composed of appointees drawn from a list made up by institutions that included the judiciary and the parliament. The Bank of France governor and deputy governors, previously appointed with no fixed term, were now, under the 1993 legislation, appointed for a fixed six-year term with dismissal only by recommendation of the general council of the bank in the case of gross misdemeanor. After demands by the Ministry of Finance that it be given bank supervisory rights if control over exchange rate parities and rules were passed to the central bank, the latter were left under the purview of the Treasury. Legislation defined the goal of the Bank of France as the pursuit of price stability within the framework of government policy and, though debated, a definition of price stability was not stipulated.[13] The new legislation also restricted the terms of central bank lending.

Debate over changing central bank legislation even spread to Great Britain in the mid-1990s; politicians and policy elites have hotly debated the legal status of the Bank of England. An independent commission of private bankers, academicians, and European central bankers issued "a new mandate for the Bank of England" entitled "Independent and Accountable." This title reflected popular concern that an independent central bank would not be consistent with democratic governance.[14] Some British central bankers expressed skepticism about increasing legal independence in the absence of popular support for it.[15]

Fear of losing international financial resources lurks underneath the proximate legal motivation for politicians to increase central bank independence in Western Europe. The price of failing to do so is exclusion from Maastricht, which would reduce capital inflows. Maastricht mandates institutional convergence to equalize the playing field and prevent unequal access to foreign capital within Europe, and also to act as a vaccine against inflation. In middle-income countries, such as Portugal, Greece, and Spain, the need to beat inflation and to attract foreign capital are intertwined.

Central and Eastern Europe

New central banks have been created and old ones strengthened throughout Central and Eastern Europe. Under the guidance of international advisers, one of the first steps in financial market development has been the revision of central bank legislation. The International Monetary Fund, the World Bank, the Bank for International Settlements, U.S. AID, the European Bank for Reconstruction and Development, and the U.S. Treasury Department, reflects one observer, "are all shoveling in . . . talk as quickly as they can."[16] In many countries of the region central bank development has been an incremental process, with annual change in central banking law.

Many of the former republics of the Soviet Union have enacted new central bank charters. These have had varying impact on actual central bank authority.[17] In many cases the legislation is extremely vague, leaving considerable room for political interference in central bank actions. More important, in situations such as that of Belorussia, where the state or state-owned enterprises spend 85 percent of national income, the practice of independent monetary policy is virtually impossible, despite legal provision of independence. Belorussian legislation, for example, forbids extension of credit to national or local government. It also stipulates monetary stability as the central bank's primary objective. Legal independence is less than ideal in a number of ways; monetary policy is subject to government approval. But the impact of law fades in the shadow of the credit demands of industrial, agricultural, and banking constituencies that dominate and, in some cases, *are* the government.

This situation has certainly prevailed in Russia. An effort to increase the legal independence of the central bank was made because international credibility called for it. But prior to the constitutional changes of December 1993, with a central bank governor responsible to parliament and a parliament dominated by credit-hungry entrepreneurs, restrictive monetary policy was an impossibility despite legal provisions to the contrary. The law stipulated monetary stability as the central bank's primary objective. It also restricted central provision of credit to the government, although the restrictions were weak compared with those of many others in the region. Credit is "limited" to the difference between current government income and expenditure. The constitution approved increased independence for the Russian central bank in December 1993 by giving the president authority to nominate and recommend dismissal of the bank governor subject to parliamentary approval.[18] The constitution now enshrines the goal of monetary stability. But the central bank is still vulnerable to "undue pressure" from the Duma.[19] In 1995 the Duma refused to ratify Tatiana Paramonova's appointment as central bank governor because, as acting governor, she stood fast against legislative pressure. Most Russian politicians do not view the country's need for international creditworthiness as a high priority. Foreign investors fall over one another trying to gain a foothold in the country and in their enthusiasm weaken incentives for economic reform. Multilateral aid to Russia responds more to geopolitical considerations than to Russian leaders' economic choices.

Another obstacle to the effectiveness of legal stipulations of independence in this region is the financial weakness of the commercial banking sector and the requirements of government debt service. In Uzbekistan new central bank legislation limits bank lending to the government to credits of less than three months, but other legislation stipulates that the central bank must service all government debt. The situation in Kazakhstan is similar. The statute provides for independence in some ways. Legislation charges the central bank with maintaining the internal and external value of the currency, and limits the term of credit extended to the government to three months. Nonetheless the statute also allows the government to fill the board of the central bank with political appointees, provides no protection from arbitrary dismissal for the governor,[20] and calls for the central bank to manage and service government debt.

Armenia reveals a virtually identical story. Legislation stipulates that the central bank protect the internal and external stability of the currency. But the law affords little actual autonomy in monetary policymaking, in part because it provides for a combination of central bank board members nominated by the central bank governor and by the government. Credit to the government is limited to one-year maturities and a total not to exceed 25 percent of expected annual government revenue, but the central bank is required to service government debt.

New legislation is under consideration in Ukraine; existing legislation is confusing because of contradictory provisions in the central bank statute and banking law. Again, legislation prohibits the central bank from providing credit to the government but requires it to service government debt. The governor of the central bank enjoys no protection from arbitrary dismissal. As the bank governor V. A. Yuschenko commented in 1994, "existing legislation does not yet establish a civilized relationship between the National Bank of Ukraine and government structures."[21]

The Baltic countries include two in which currency boards protect central banks from the kinds of political pressures for expansionary central bank action that government elites tolerate in many other former Soviet republics.[22] The prime minister of Estonia notes that while currency board–type monetary policies may limit central bank flexibility, they "deflect political pressures" and "preclude colossal mistakes, which at the present stage of transition is much more important [than flexibility]."[23] Estonia adopted a quasi-currency board regime for exchange and monetary policy. The monetary base is backed by gold and hard currency.[24] In addition, legislation protects independence by prohibiting central bank provision of credit to the government and by shielding the governor and board from arbitrary dismissal. Indeed the Estonian central bank governor Siim Kallas survived several changes of government. Estonia boasts that its currency board and central bank independence account in part for its great success in attracting foreign direct investment.[25] Lithuania adopted a currency-board system in mid-1994 in part to prevent the kind of political interference with the central bank that lay behind the dismissal of the bank governor and much of the board in 1993.

Poland, which led regional liberalization, freed its central bank to formulate and conduct monetary policy without parliamentary approval of detailed credit plans in 1990. A Monetary Policy Committee, composed of central bankers, makes monetary policy. An annual outline of monetary policy must be presented to the cabinet for informational purposes. The 1990 legislation charged the Bank of Poland with advising the government on budget policy appropriate to maintain monetary stability and limited lending to government to 2 percent of the government's budgeted expenditures.[26] Legislation charged the bank both with protecting currency stability and with supporting the government's overall economic objectives. Legislation in 1991 increased the bank's supervisory authority over commercial banks.[27] Legislation the next year eliminated the cap on central bank lending to government and made deficit financing subject to negotiation between the minister of finance and the Bank of Poland. This placed a greater burden for maintaining independence on the negotiation and leadership skills of the Bank of Poland governor, Hanna Gronkiewcz-Waltz. She lived up to the challenge, successfully withstanding political pressures for expansionary policy.[28] The governor is appointed by parliament and can be recalled on unspecified grounds.

When it became apparent in 1993 that different levels of development in the Slovak and Czech Republics, compounded by nationalistic divisions, made maintenance of a single central bank, currency, and monetary policy difficult, legal change created a separate central bank in each republic.[29] The Slovak parliament labored hard beginning in February 1993 to write legislation that would both comply with constitutional stipulations on economic policy and guarantee central bank independence. Law gave the Bank of Slovakia the sole objective of currency stability and prohibited it from annual lending to the government of more than 5 percent of national government revenue in the previous year, with a three-month limit on government credit maturities. The law demands that monetary policy be formulated in conjunction with the government, however. The central bank governor is subject to presidential recall, but is legally protected from arbitrary dismissal.[30]

The Czech Republic promulgated new central bank legislation in 1993, making the already strong Czech Central Bank even more legally independent. Legislation charges the central bank with the sole goal of price stability,[31] grants complete autonomy in monetary policy formulation and a formal advisory role in government budget policy, and prohibits the bank from lending the government more than 5 percent of the previous year's government revenues and from extending credit with more than a three-month maturity. The central bank governor and board are subject to presidential recall only if criminally sentenced or incapacitated.[32] The governor's term is six years, exceeding the terms of office of the nation's president and lower house representatives.

Slovenia loosely copied German and Austrian central banking legislation in writing and ratifying a new law in 1992 that provided for the central bank's independence from the government. Observers explicitly heralded the legal change as an effort to attract foreign investors.[33] The legislation sets currency stability as the central bank's primary goal and limits its credit to the government to 5 percent of planned government revenue or 20 percent of the government budget deficit. The governor and board members are appointed to six-year terms but are subject to parliamentary recall.

Legal changes made the Bank of Hungary formally independent of the government in 1991, with further legislation in 1992 and 1994. The law is equivocal about central bank autonomy in the formulation of monetary policy. In contrast to Poland, a monetary policy council composed of an equal number of central bank and political appointees determines monetary policy.[34] The central bank governor is appointed to a six-year term and since 1991 can be recalled only for gross misdemeanor. (The central bank governor and four deputies were dismissed in 1991, days before legislative changes went into effect providing greater protection from arbitrary dismissal.) Central bank lending to government is limited annually to 3 percent of planned government revenue, excluding receipts from privatization, and credits of one-year maturity. The bank's legally stipulated goal is principally to maintain the domestic and foreign value of the currency, but the law also charges the bank to support the government's economic program.[35] Although Hungary's legislation does not make it one of Eastern Europe's more independent central banks, the nation does have a provision unique among the region's central bank laws that instructs the Bank of Hungary to "warn the government and, if need be, turn to parliament and the public," if it "deems that the economic policy or practical activities of the government endanger the stability of the economy."[36]

Both the Polish and Hungarian statutes have the unusual feature of giving the central bank a legally stipulated role in the government's budget policy formulation. Ethiopia is the only other country in the world according its central bank such legal authority. Given the tremendous importance of budget policy in shaping macroeconomic stability, especially in a developing country context, this provision is arguably more important than the celebrated "New Zealand clause" legally stipulating a level of price stability. Authority in the budget process is crucial to the maintenance of price stability in an uncertain political environment where the temptation for politicians to follow expansionary, crowd-pleasing fiscal policies is great.

Bulgaria and Romania also passed legislation in 1991 increasing the independence of their central banks. Three missions from the IMF Central Banking Department helped to formulate a new central bank statute for Bulgaria.[37] According to this statute the central bank is not subject to government directives on monetary policy, nor are there direct representatives of the government on the central bank board. The central bank's legally defined primary goal is internal and external currency stability. Central bank credit to the government can have no more than a three-month maturity, and total credit may not exceed 5 percent of expected current-year revenues and certain other government–central bank assets, including reserves. Nonetheless parliament sanctioned a ten-year government credit in 1992. Five of the nine members of the central bank board are nominees of the central bank governor. Parliament appoints the governor, who is, however, legally protected from arbitrary dismissal. Even so, the central bank governor Vulchev, appointed in 1991, was forced to resign in 1992 after public attacks orchestrated by opponents of his tight money policy.

Romanian legislation provides for significantly less independence than in Bulgaria and many other Eastern European countries. Romanians modeled their central bank law on the legislation that guided French central banking prior to 1993 reforms. The legislation is relatively vague. It provides for central bank credit to the government to cover "temporary deficits" up to 10 percent of the total government budget or twice the sum of central bank reserves and capital, with no maturity provisions. The central bank governor and board are chosen by parliament and enjoy no protection from arbitrary dismissal.

Albania also enacted new central banking legislation, with provisions for a surprisingly independent central bank. The central bank governor is appointed on recommendation of the central bank board for a six-year term, longer than that of any political office, and is protected from arbitrary dismissal. Six-month advances to the government may not exceed 10 percent of the previous year's government revenue. The law stipulates that the central bank's primary goal is maintaining internal and external currency stability. However, the provision for the executive branch to appoint a majority of central bank board members potentially compromises independence.

The need for international financial resources and international creditworthiness has been great in Eastern and Central Europe in the 1990s. In many cases legal protection for central bank independence was a condition of multilateral financing. Newfound nationhood and a strong desire to emulate Western institutions are also behind the trend toward legal protection of central bank independence in the central and eastern part of Europe. But de jure independence is not de facto independence. In many cases the demands of concomitant political and economic liberalization still constrain central bank practice. Great uncertainty faces government leaders in these fledgling democracies. For many of these leaders, the importance of protecting the central bank from the pressure of credit-hungry financiers and industrialists in order to maintain international creditworthiness pales in comparison with the demands of building and maintaining a political mandate to remain in office. These cases, where democracy is barely institutionalized, illustrate the importance of politicians' tenure security in their prioritization of central bank independence.

Latin America

Five Latin American countries enacted new central bank legislation between 1989 and 1992: Chile, Argentina, Venezuela, Colombia, and Mexico. In Chile, the departing Pinochet government granted the Banco Nacional de Chile significant new legal authority in December 1989. Pinochet's concern was to protect Chile's economic progress, including international creditworthiness, against the potentially poor judgment of successor governments. Legislation gave the central bank two objectives: price stability and management of international payments. It created a new central bank board, prohibited the central bank from extending credit to the government or purchasing government paper, and permitted the minister of finance to attend, but not vote at, board meetings. The statute made the central bank the final authority on monetary policy. It also increased central bank authority in governor appointment procedures. Although Pinochet had hoped to fill the board with personal allies prior to leaving office, negotiations with the united opposition, represented by Alejandro Foxley, led to a compromise. Of the new five-member central bank board, Pinochet chose two members, the opposition chose two, and a fifth was chosen by consensus of both parties. The five were appointed for staggered terms so that no more than one new member would be replaced every two years.[38]

Between 1989 and 1992 the Peronist government of Argentina also drew up several plans to give the central bank more independence in handling monetary policy. A 1989 conditional loan agreement with the IMF included provisions for increased central bank independence.[39] Congress finally approved a new central bank law in mid-1992.[40] Among other things, it promised to end an era of virtually unlimited central bank financing of government deficits by restricting legal central bank lending to the government to 10 percent of the value of the central bank's total public debt holdings.[41] The new statute lengthened the governor's term of office, gave the central bank the primary objective of preserving monetary stability, and made it the final authority over monetary policy.

The new Colombian constitution of 1991 included a commitment to future legislation of increased central bank independence. Congress approved a new central bank statute in December 1992. Under this new statute the central bank's sole objective became maintaining the currency's purchasing power.[42] The statute also increased central bank independence in the areas of term of governor appointment, formulation of monetary policy, and methods of government finance.

The Venezuelan government also approved a new central bank statute in December 1992. This statute gave the central bank complete independence in the formulation of monetary policy. This authority was deftly exercised following the announcement of an impeachment order for President Carlos Andres Peres in May 1993. The central bank president, Ruth de Krivoy, immediately raised interest rates in a successful effort to prevent capital flight.[43] The new statute also tightened requirements for central bank financing of the government and increased central bank authority through changes in the terms of governor appointment. Nonetheless, Venezuela's vast oil wealth tends to reduce the priority most politicians place on the goal of international creditworthiness. In practice, government mishandling of the domestic financial sector in the mid-1990s has severely compromised Venezuelan central bank autonomy.

In Mexico, President Carlos Salinas sent new legislation to the legislature in May 1993 that was designed to increase the autonomy of that country's central bank, the Banco de México. The new statute, passed into law in December 1993, mandated that the bank follow the sole objective of preserving the purchasing power of the peso. It also restricted government borrowing from the central bank to finance its deficits and changed appointment procedures for the central bank governor and board members. The statute stipulated that the governor and board members be selected for fixed, staggered terms by the nation's president (subject to Senate approval) and be dismissed only for severe breach of duty. For Salinas, Mexico's international creditworthiness was a strong consideration in introducing changes in the statute. Note that although major politicians were leaving the scene in both the recent Mexican and the Chilean cases of central bank statute change, uncertainty was low. Law proscribed Pinochet and Salinas from competing in upcoming elections. Because chances of reappointment were close to zero, pressure to manipulate the central bank for personal political gain was minimized.[44]

Even in strongly antiliberal Brazil, the country's constitution, rewritten in the 1980s as part of Brazil's democratic transition, opened the door to unspecified reform of the central bank. Since then, there have been a variety of proposals to increase central bank autonomy. Enhancement of central bank independence was an important part of fiscal reform legislation presented to the Brazilian congress in 1992. This proposal would have replaced the top monetary policymaking body, the National Monetary Council, on which the central bank has only one vote of seventeen, with a new council dominated by the central bank.[45] This aspect of the fiscal reform package did not survive congressional debate. However, in August 1993 there was again high-level murmuring about the need to increase central bank independence. After several years of haranguing on the subject by economist-turned-parliamentarian José Serra, Finance Minister Fernando Henrique Cardoso publicly conceded the importance of trying to increase central bank autonomy from government. As a candidate for the national presidency in 1994, Cardoso made a call for central bank independence part of his campaign platform. By early 1995 President Cardoso's administration was drafting new central bank legislation for congressional review.

Throughout Latin America central bank independence came after considerable progress had already been made in stabilizing inflation and consolidating democracy. From the point of view of official creditors, such as the Inter-American Development Bank, improvement in governance institutions was the second stage in the fight to build healthy economies in the region. Most Latin American elites gave the fight for international creditworthiness high priority in the 1990s for several reasons. The debt crisis imposed high-risk premia. Capital account and domestic financial liberalization increased the global integration of Latin American financial markets. Both the incentives and the value expected from manipulating the central bank for personal political gain fell. And the role of international bond financing raised the expected effectiveness of signaling creditworthiness via central bank independence.

Asia and the Pacific

Perhaps the most well known and dramatic case of increased central bank independence since 1990 is in the Asian and Pacific region. A new and globally unique central bank statute went into effect in New Zealand in February 1990.[46] It had four main components: complete freedom from political interference in the operation of monetary policy; the stipulation of a single central bank goal, price stability; a legally specified inflation target; and a link between the governor's tenure and inflation performance.[47] No other central bank in the world legally specifies an inflation rate and makes this a performance criterion for central bank personnel. The only chink in the central bank's armor left by this legislation is a provision for parliamentary revision of the inflation target.[48] The business weekly *The Economist* explicitly links investor interest in New Zealand with the uniquely independent Bank of New Zealand.[49]

Several other countries in the Asian-Pacific region have seen an increase in central bank authority in recent years, although the trend has been less pronounced than elsewhere. In anticipation of change in the legal status of the central bank, debate has heated up in Australia. Looking to New Zealand, reformers have proposed complete independence from the federal government and the stipulation of inflation control as the bank's sole objective.[50]

In Pakistan, after a period in which the central bank had suffered significant decline, the World Bank began working with the government in 1991 to strengthen this primary financial institution.[51] A September 1993 presidential ordinance, part of Prime Minister Moeen Qureshi's economic reform program, allowed the State Bank of Pakistan to recruit staff without federal government clearance, gave it new power to control the money supply and regulate commercial banks, and set limits on deficit financing of the government.[52] There were modifications to this ordinance after Benazir Bhutto took over from Moeen Qureshi in late 1993. These reduced the governor's term of office and gave the government the right to name new board members. Opponents of these changes warned that the change would create difficulties in the country's negotiations with the IMF. They argued that an independent central bank would increase the IMF's confidence that the government would abide by the loan agreement.[53] The Bhutto government was quick to defend itself publicly, emphasizing that the bank retained the important power to limit credit to the federal and provincial governments.

Elsewhere, in 1991 the IMF began helping the State Bank of Vietnam become a central bank with the tools to control money and credit.[54] In Sri Lanka in that same year the central bank regained de facto autonomy, lost under the previous government. A previous victim of political pressure, the Harvard-trained economist Neville Karunatillake, returned to the governorship of the Central Bank of Sri Lanka on the condition that there would be no political interference in the bank's operations. Prime Minister D. B. Wijetunge, also the finance minister, appears to have honored his side of the bargain.[55]

There have even been tentative nonlegal moves toward increased independence in South Korea and Japan. During his one-year tenure as governor of the Bank of Korea from 1992 to 1993, Cho Soon was able to raise the central bank's status by exercising a strong and independent voice on monetary policy and single-mindedly pursuing low inflation and financial liberalization. He also called for revision of the Bank of Korea charter.[56] Tolerated for a while, Cho Soon eventually engendered sufficient concern among government politicians to warrant his dismissal. The union of Bank of Korea workers had worked hard to raise public consciousness of, and support for, central bank independence. Union members protested Cho Soon's dismissal, and his successor at the central bank promised to continue giving top priority to stabilizing the value of the won.[57] Many observers criticized the nation's May 1993 draft financial reform legislation for its omission of provisions for increased central bank autonomy.[58]

Japan's central bank governor in the early 1990s, Yasushi Mieno, exercised considerable independence and frequently raised the ire of Liberal Democratic Party leaders.[59] He restructured the Bank of Japan internally in 1990, a year after being appointed.[60] This restructuring, involving increased research capacity, a stronger international department, a more efficient payment system, and a new management structure, was "designed to show the central bank's independence from the finance ministry."[61] In a style consistent with Japanese politics, instead of pressing for legal freedom, the Bank of Japan is "employing a flanking strategy . . . that involves turning information gathering into regulatory and policy-making power."[62]

In general the trend toward increased central bank independence has been less pronounced in Asia than in regions, such as Europe and Latin America, in which middle-income developing countries seek to ensure their ability to compete successfully for international capital. Given interest rates paid on private international credits and its relatively low levels of external debt relative to exports of goods and services evident in Table 4.2, Asia as a region has had considerably less need to be concerned with competing for international capital and creditworthiness than Latin America or Central and Eastern Europe. Financial regulation has also remained high, mitigating international financial pressures.

Middle East

The push for central bank independence in the Middle East has been limited. In Algeria central bank independence was decreed as part of a broad package of economic liberalizations implemented in January 1991. Concern with international creditors' views of Algeria was part of the context in which these changes occurred. Legislation made the Banque d'Algérie independent of government, accorded it power to autonomously set monetary policy, and gave it a lead role in structuring international financial transactions.[63] The Iranian central bank, Bank Markazi, moved unilaterally to detach itself from the government in 1991 by rejecting its previous role as guarantor of foreign loans. The Iranian political leadership tolerated, if it did not encourage, this move,[64] and one of the objectives of the 1994–1999 five-year economic plan was more central bank independence in the formulation of monetary policy.[65] Although it is difficult to pinpoint precise motives for specific changes in central bank independence without deep knowledge of the particular context, it is plausible that these changes in central bank independence also reflected concerns over international creditworthiness. In Egypt a new banking law passed in June 1992 shifted authority over the banking sector from the Ministry of the Economy and Foreign Trade to the Bank of Egypt. Observers viewed this as an important move toward increased authority and ultimately greater independence for the central bank.[66]

The Middle East and Northern Africa is a region in relatively low need of international creditworthiness (see Table 4.2). Debt relative to exports is low and interest rates are low, reflecting the favor of international creditors. The relatively small moves toward central bank independence in the region have come in countries with weaker than average balance of payments.

Africa

As in so many other ways, Africa, the "lost continent" of the 1990s, has remained outside the central bank reform movement. The issue of central bank independence has arisen in relatively few African countries. Among these are Namibia and South Africa. In the Namibian case the role of the IMF was crucial. As part of an IMF and United Nations Development Program assistance package, the Bank of Namibia was run in 1990 by an official of the Dutch central bank. Largely owing to the government's unwillingness to "incur the IMF's displeasure, he enjoyed several victories in his efforts to increase Namibian central bank autonomy."[67] In South Africa, provision for central bank independence in the new national constitution was heatedly debated throughout 1993. Both the transitional and the permanent constitutions included strong provisions for central bank independence.

African external debt is very high, but much of this reflects official credit extended on concessional terms. Although South Africa and Nigeria are important exceptions, most countries in Africa suffer limited access to international market finance, a situation that makes creditworthiness a minor concern. Relatively little increase in central bank independence should not surprise us.

Conclusion

The pattern of regional variation in the extent of increase in central bank status worldwide in the 1990s is consistent with variation in the need to compete for capital and creditworthiness. Latin American political elites have viewed the need to compete for creditworthiness as high, and legal central bank independence reflects this. The percentage of countries in the region showing an increase is relatively high. As Table 4.1 indicates, these increases in Latin America raised its average for legal central bank independence to .55, among the highest of any region. Central and Eastern Europe also had a very high percentage of countries which increased legal independence, again reflecting a great need to compete for international creditworthiness. Western Europe began the 1990s in a position of relatively high legal independence; many countries lagging in legal independence had changed their statutes by mid-decade. The average level of legal central bank independence remained low in Asia and the Middle East, where the need to compete for creditworthiness was relatively low.

TABLE 4.3
London Eurodollar and Interbank Interest Rates

Year	*Interest Rate*[a]	*Year*	*Interest Rate*[a]
1970	8.5	1982	13.7
1971	6.6	1983	10.2
1972	5.5	1984	11.8
1973	9.2	1985	9.1
1974	11.0	1986	7.0
1975	7.0	1987	7.6
1976	5.6	1988	8.4
1977	6.0	1989	9.3
1978	8.7	1990	8.5
1979	12.0	1991	6.3
1980	14.4	1992	4.2
1981	16.1		

Source: Data from IMF, *International Financial Statistics* (Washington, D.C.: IMF, various years).

a. Rate is for one-year Eurodollar loans in London through 1980. The 1981–1992 rate is the London interbank offer rate.

The number of efforts to increase central bank authority in the early 1990s marks a significant change over earlier trends. As we saw in Table 1.1, this represents a rate of legislated increase in central bank independence many times greater than in any other decade since World War II. The evaluation of central bank independence based on the coding of legal documents provides only a partial picture of trends in central bank authority. Yet cross-temporal global trends evident in this data accord with internationally determined change in the need to compete for creditworthiness. For example, rising liquidity and loan "pushing" characterize the 1970s, a period in which the legal data indicate a relatively great decrease in central bank independence. Table 4.3 provides data on interest rates in the London Eurodollar and interbank markets that give an indication of the relationship between global supply and demand for international financial resources. For example, interest rates are relatively low, as in the 1970s, when supply exceeds demand.

This variation between decades also helps us begin to separate concern over inflation from the need to compete for international capital as motivations for central bank independence. There appears to be a much closer temporal connection between the rise of portfolio finance (and the need to compete for capital associated with it) and central bank independence than there is between inflation and central bank independence. Inflation was very severe in developing countries in the 1970s and 1980s, yet central bank independence decreased in the 1970s and changed little in the 1980s.

Despite the utility of quantitative indicators of legal independence, it is important to remember that they may miss important elements of central bank discretion and authority. The limited quantitative data presented here fall short of providing a full understanding of the extent to which political elites facing complex domestic politico-economic pressures give priority to the need for international creditworthiness. In an effort to gain a fuller empirical picture of the connection between the need for and value of competing for international creditworthiness, on the one hand, and central bank authority, on the other, the following four chapters present detailed histories of central bank authority in specific developing countries.

Five

The Politics of Changing Central Bank Authority: Thailand

APPROACHING central bank authority from an international perspective suggests that, globally, changes in central bank authority should occur in broad temporal waves as international financial integration increases, as the relationship between supply and demand of international financial resources varies, and as predominant forms of international investment change. But as the cross-regional variation evident in Chapter 4 suggests, governing politicians' views of the need to compete for capital are influenced by domestic as well as international factors, including national balance of payments constraints, national regulation of financial transactions, and national politicians' tenure security. The perception of the need to compete for capital internationally is related to objective conditions; but it is not easily judged through simple quantitative indicators. Yet if central bank status changes partly in response to the need to compete for capital internationally, this should be evident in studies of change in the authority of central banks in particular countries over time. This and the following three chapters examine change in central bank authority in four developing countries. These case studies explore the extent to which changes in politicians' perceptions of the need and value of competing for capital internationally have affected central bank authority.

The four countries, Thailand, Mexico, South Korea, and Thailand, were chosen from the set of newly industrializing countries because they represent a wide range of experiences and contexts. The countries were chosen independently of any knowledge of variation in their need to compete for capital internationally or in their level of central bank authority.[1] Together the country histories include many instances of change in the need to compete for capital internationally and change or nonchange in central bank authority. The analysis pools observations across countries in Chapter 9.

Recall the argument that the need to compete internationally for capital is more likely to lead politicians to increase central bank independence the greater the objective need for balance of payments support and creditworthiness, the greater the expected effectiveness of signaling (a function of the extent of foreign investment in the form of securities, particularly bonds, and the supply and demand of international financial resources), the greater politicians' tenure security, and the lower a country's regulation of national and international financial transactions. In the country histories a combination of quantitative indicators and qualitative evaluation is used to identify these factors and their impact on politicians' actions vis-à-vis central banks.

Factors shaping political elites' perceptions of need for creditworthiness are complex. We can expect some correlation with objective conditions. Although some balance of payments crises are more easily corrected than others, I use "import coverage" (month's worth of imports covered by central bank reserves) to indicate actual balance of payments pressure. Data on foreign exchange reserves used in calculating import coverage are also included. The average interest rate on new private international credits to each country, minus the London interbank or Eurodollar interest rate, is a measure of international creditors' evaluation of national creditworthiness.

Data on annual stocks of foreign investment in the form of bonds indicate the relative effectiveness of signaling creditworthiness via central bank independence, as outlined in Chapter 3. The nominal or real stock of foreign investment is less important than the changing relative composition of foreign investment in any given country. Rapid increase in any particular form of international liability in any given country suggests the relative predominance of that mode of international financial intermediation globally. The relationship of global supply and demand for financial resources is assessed qualitatively and on the basis of interest rates on Eurodollars and interbank loans in London presented in Table 4.3. For each of the four country studies, financial regulation and politicians' tenure security are evaluated qualitatively as part of the historical narrative. In general, financial regulation is a relatively minor part of the story of the changing need and value of competing for international creditworthiness and varying central bank status, because levels of regulation are fairly consistent over time. Financial regulation is a more important part of the explanation for the temporally fixed cross-national variation in the need for international creditworthiness and central bank independence evident in the four countries highlighted here. This static cross-national comparison is explored in Chapter 9; the emphasis in this and the following three chapters is on explaining change over time within a single country.

Given the problems, discussed in Chapter 2, that are associated with measuring central bank independence through quantitative coding of legal statutes, particularly in developing countries, the country profiles use more traditional and contextual measures of power. Central bank independence is low when there is conflict between the central bank and the government which is not resolved in the central bank's favor, and/or when policy falls far from the central bank's preferred position and/or when it is clear that the central bank de facto follows executive branch directives.[2]

Table 5.1 presents data indicating change over time in Thailand's objective need for balance of payments support and international creditworthiness. Data on the composition of foreign investment, from which the relative weight of different assets is evident, are presented in Table 5.2.

The Thai government has regulated domestic and international financial transactions very little, especially compared with other middle-income developing countries. The capital account has been comparatively and consistently open in Thailand since the 1950s. Foreign exchange allocation was regulated by the central bank from 1942 to 1947, when liberalization began.[3] Remaining controls on exchange allocation, which consisted of a system of multiple rates for different types of activities, were eliminated in the mid-1950s. After 1957, provision of selective, preferential credit was the exception rather than the norm, as in many other middle-income developing countries. In general, relatively unrestricted domestic and international financial transactions increased the incentive for central bank independence. Regulation was relatively and fairly consistently liberal from 1957 until the present, with a marginal increase in the mid-1970s.[4]

The Central Bank: From Weak to Strong

There are three turning points in Bank of Thailand history: 1959, 1973, and 1982. The first and third are associated with an increase in the need to compete for international creditworthiness. They mark the beginning of periods of increased central bank authority. The year 1973 marks the beginning of a period of decline in central bank authority and is associated with a decline in the need to compete for international creditworthiness.

Weak Central Bank Authority, 1948–1957

As the Bank of Thailand began operations during the postwar administration of Field Marshal Plaek Phibunsongkhram (1948–1957),[5] its governorship turned over an average of every two years. Turnover was virtually the same for the Ministry of Finance. Conflict between

TABLE 5.1
Indicators of Thailand's Need to Compete for International Capital

Year	*Import Coverage*	*Foreign Exchange Reserves (U.S. millions)*	*Average Annual Interest on Private Credit Minus the Eurodollar or Libor Interest Rate*[a]
1946	15.24	72	
1947	7.35	68	
1948	11.58	139	
1949	6.22	100	
1950	9.75	170	
1951	10.80	245	
1952	9.26	235	
1953	6.94	191	
1954	6.39	166	
1955	6.79	189	
1956	6.66	203	
1957	6.15	209	
1958	5.92	194	
1959	5.75	204	
1960	6.87	256	
1961	8.39	339	
1962	8.97	408	
1963	8.88	461	
1964	9.62	545	
1965	10.09	624	
1966	10.89	808	
1967	10.04	893	
1968	9.37	905	
1969	8.36	869	
1970	7.30	790	
1971	6.86	736	–2.5
1972	7.25	896	–0.6
1973	6.63	1,132	*N.A.*
1974	6.42	1,681	–2.0
1975	5.87	1,605	–0.4
1976	5.80	1,725	1.5
1977	4.51	1,735	2.5
1978	4.42	1,974	2.2
1979	3.01	1,794	0.1
1980	2.02	1,552	–0.6
1981	2.01	1,671	–2.4
1982	2.12	1,513	–2.8
1983	1.82	1,561	–1.2
1984	2.18	1,890	–1.3
1985	2.80	2,157	–1.5

TABLE 5.1 *(cont.)*

Year	*Import Coverage*	*Foreign Exchange Reserves (U.S. millions)*	*Average Annual Interest on Private Credit Minus the Eurodollar or Libor Interest Rate*[a]
1986	3.58	2,736	–1.4
1987	3.60	3,906	–1.6
1988	3.60	5,997	–1.9
1989	4.41	9,461	–1.4
1990	4.76	13,247	–1.5
1991	*N.A.*	*N.A.*	1.4
1992	*N.A.*	*N.A.*	2.9

Source: Calculated from IMF, *International Financial Statistics* (Washington, D.C.: IMF, various years), and World Bank, *World Debt Tables* (Washington, D.C.: World Bank, various years).

Note: The *World Debt Tables* changed the definition of the numerator in 1980. *N.A.*–Not available.

a. Libor–London interbank offer rate.

the government and the bank was relatively great, with the Bank of Thailand usually on the losing side. This was most obvious during the governorship of Dej Santivong (see Table 5.3). The early 1950s was a period of deficit financing and heavy government involvement in production and distribution. As is evident in the 1952 annual report of the Bank of Thailand, Dej opposed deficit spending and blamed the government's heavy investment in economic activities, which he felt should be the province of the private sector.[6] When Phibun ordered the central bank to revalue the baht vis-à-vis the pound sterling in 1952, Dej refused on the grounds that this would hurt exports, and resigned.

Another major conflict arose in 1953, leading to Phibun's dismissal of the deputy governor of the bank, Puey Ungphakorn. Phibun wanted the central bank to make foreign exchange available at rates highly favorable to commercial banks. The Bank of Thailand protested, fearing the loans would be used in financial arbitrage, and issued a prohibition on commercial bank sale of foreign exchange at subsidized rates. One bank, with highly placed military supporters, violated this prohibition. The resulting cabinet-level hearing resolved to fine the bank but also to dismiss the Bank of Thailand official who had issued the prohibition.[7]

During this time the need for international creditworthiness became objectively greater, as Table 5.1 indicates. The extent of import coverage, for example, fluctuated greatly. Steep declines in months' worth of imports covered by central bank reserves occurred in 1946, 1949, and

TABLE 5.2
Foreign Investment in Thailand (stock of investments, in U.S. millions)

Year	*FDI*	*Bonds*	*Equities*	*Loans*
1954				3.7
1955				4.5
1956	2.4			28.1
1957	2.4			24.1
1958	3.3			13.9
1959	3.4			19.5
1960	2.4			30.1
1961	6.0			26.8
1962	7.5			51.6
1963	20.6			43.6
1964	18.1			65.0
1965	28.4			29.7
1966	27.0			18.0
1967	43.0			40.0
1968	60.0			30.0
1969	51.0			60.0
1970	43.0			85.0
1971	39.0			93.0
1972	63.0			163.0
1973	65.0			117.0
1974	157.0			238.0
1975	71.0			276.0
1976	69.0			389.0
1977	91.0			561.0
1978	45.0	57.0	5.0	908.0
1979	42.0	137.0	3.0	1,562.0
1980	146.0	35.0	39.0	2,341.0
1981	249.0	28.0	10.0	2,009.0
1982	174.0	37.0	24.0	1,755.0
1983	327.0	88.0	14.0	1,872.0
1984	346.0	116.0	33.0	2,481.0
1985	163.0	854.0	41.0	2,385.0
1986	263.0	126.0	96.0	1,863.0
1987	352.0	(154.0)	499.0	1,833.0
1988	1,105.5	87.0	444.0	1,660.0
1989	1,775.0	63.0	1,424.0	3,097.0
1990	2,444.0	(478.0)	440.0	4,164.0
1991	2,014.0	(118.0)	37.0	5,011.0
1992	2,116.0	295.0	455.0	4,487.0

Source: IMF, *International Financial Statistics* (Washington, D.C.: IMF, various years).

Note: FDI–Foreign direct investment.

TABLE 5.3
Change of Government, Regime Type, and Central Bank Governor in Thailand

Prime Minister	*Regime*	*Bank of Thailand Governor*
Plaek Phibunsongkhram (1938–44)	MILITARY	Viwat-anachaichaiyan (1942–46)
Kuang Aphaiwong (1944–45)	SEMI-DEM.	
Thavee Bunyaket (1945)		
Seni Pramoj (1945–46)		
Kuang Aphaiwong (1946)	DEMOCRATIC	Serm Winijaikul (1946–47)
Pridi Banomyong (1946)		
Thawal Thamrongnawasawat (1946–47)		
Kuang Aphaiwong (1947–48)	MILITARY	Laeng Srisomwongse (1947–48)
Plaek Phibunsongkram (1948–57)		
		Viwat-anachaichaiyan (1948)
		Laeng Srisomwongse (1948–49)
		Dej Santivong (1949–52)
		Serm Winijaikul (1952–55)
		Kasem Srihpayak (1955–58)
Poj Sarasin (1957)		
Thanom Kittikachorn (1958–59)		Jote Guna-Kasem (1958–59)
Sarit Thanarat (1959–63)		Puey Ungphakorn (1959–71)
Thanom Kittikachorn (1963–73)		
Sanya Thammasak (1973–75)	DEMOCRATIC	Bisudhi Nimmanhaemin (1971–75)
Seni Pramoj (1975)		
Kukrit Pramoj (1975–76)		Snoh Unakul (1975–79)
Seni Pramoj (1976)		
Thanin Kraivichien (1976–77)	MILITARY	
Kriangsak Chamanan (1977–79)	SEMI-DEM.	
Prem Tinsulanond (1979–87)		Nukun Prachuabmoh (1979–82)
		Kamchorn Sathirakul (1982–88)
Chatchai Shunhanan (1988–91)	DEMOCRATIC	
		Chavalit Thanachanan (1988)
Anand Panyarachun (1991–92)	MILITARY	Vijit Supanit (1988–)
Suchinda Krapayoon (1992)		
Anand Panyarachun (1992)		
Chuan Leekpai (1992)	DEMOCRATIC	
Barnharn Silapaarcha (1995)		

1953. (Although these are sharp declines in the Thai context, import coverage still remained fairly high compared with that of other developing countries.) From annual increases of international reserves of 45 percent in 1950 and 25 percent in 1951, reserves declined or increased only minimally between 1952 and 1958.

Increased Central Bank Authority after 1959

The initial weakness of Thailand's central bank authority contrasts sharply with its steady growth after 1957. Thailand's declining international reserves in the mid- and late 1950s (see Table 5.1) gave President Sarit Thanarat a strong desire for recognition from the International Bank for Reconstruction and Redevelopment and the U.S. government. The rise in central bank independence coincides with Sarit's desire to improve Thailand's international creditworthiness.

In terms of the relationship between supply and demand of international investment, the 1950s were not an era of tremendous liquidity and availability of commercial loans. But the World Bank was coming into its own as one of the new Bretton Woods institutions purveying loans around the world. World Bank missions to developing countries engaged in serious study and recommendations for economic policy and institution building. These missions brought the promise of loans and left a reform blueprint. Although conditionality was not as explicit as it became in the context of IMF stabilization loans in the late 1970s, those who wanted access to World Bank loans had to show signs of commitment to comply with bank suggestions.

Accompanying the objective increase in Thailand's need for international creditworthiness, partially indicated in Table 5.1, was a change in the time horizon of political leaders, stemming from increased tenure security. Phibun was replaced by Marshal Sarit Thanarat. Both the Phibun and Sarit regimes were military, but after coming to power through a military coup in 1958 Sarit was able to wipe out the many competing military factions that had plagued the Phibun era.

During the Phibun administration the military was divided into three principal factions, one under Phibun, a second under General Phin Chunhawan and Police General Phao Sriyanond, and a third under Marshal Sarit. Political opposition to the military regime also came from the Democratic Party, a major force in the National Assembly. Between 1948 and 1951 Phibun's government was challenged by three coup attempts.[8] After 1951 Phibun only managed to stay in power by playing the Sarit and Pao factions off against each other.

Financial demands by Phibun's government were a direct source of central bank–government conflict. Sarit, when he came to power, managed to secure his leadership and reduce the patronage costs of remaining in power by eliminating competing factions. Sarit also developed illicit means for increasing the spoils of office-holding without demanding that the central bank print more money. The elimination of rival factions brought an increased measure of elite political stability to Thailand. Sarit could be much more secure about his tenure in office than his predecessor had ever been. Greater tenure security increased the value of improving Thailand's international creditworthiness.

Central bank governor Puey, appointed by Sarit in 1959, exploited the political leadership's desire for international support. He used his personal ties to international credit organizations as leverage with military leaders.[9] Puey occasionally threatened to resign when he could not secure government cooperation; these threats were powerful because in international circles Puey was perceived as the "only honest Thai," and international financiers would not do business with Thailand unless he was involved.[10] Stifel notes that to achieve its goals the Bank of Thailand "skillfully mobilized the support of foreign aid donors as a powerful lever in their internal political effort."[11]

Puey used the political elite's concern with international creditworthiness to greatly increase the central bank's authority. On the few occasions when open disagreement arose between the Bank of Thailand and the military, the military backed down. The most public source of disagreement was over the role of military personnel on the boards of commercial banks. After Puey made a public speech subtly condemning the practice of generals sitting on bank boards, at least one field marshal resigned as a bank board member. In another instance Puey tried to encourage two generals on the board of a failing bank to intervene; they refused and the bank, the Thai Development Bank, became insolvent. Chagrined, the generals reportedly apologized to Puey for their obstinateness.[12]

The authority of the central bank under Puey is also evident in debate over the locus of responsibility for fiscal policy. The government proposed the creation of a new committee to handle fiscal issues, especially those internationally related. Puey's response was that such policy lay clearly under the jurisdiction of the Bank of Thailand. "I did not see any use for the new committee," Puey recalls, "and if this committee was appointed [I said] I would have no choice but to resign . . . nobody ever mentioned the committee for fiscal policy again."[13]

International Liquidity and Unstable Democracy: Central Bank Weakening

The beginning of democratic government in the mid-1970s marks a second turning point in Thai central bank history. The uncertain political environment created by the democratic opening decreased political leaders' tenure security and their assignment of value to maintaining international creditworthiness. Uncertainty also increased politicians' desire to wrest authority over financial and monetary policy from the central bank in order to increase their arsenal of political weapons.

Objective conditions did little to counterbalance these pressures. The flood of oil revenues into the Euromarket also decreased the importance of maintaining international creditworthiness. International loan rates were low, and banks pushed loans wherever they could. Annual increase in total international lending rose from 27 percent in 1972 to 56 percent in 1974.[14] The need to maintain international creditworthiness declined as resources became easier and less expensive to get. Thailand's international reserves, which had shrunk annually from 1969 to 1971, rose 21, 24, and 42 percent annually in 1972, 1973, and 1974, respectively. Meanwhile the nation continued to enjoy high creditworthiness in international financial markets as indicated by the comparatively low interest rates charged by private international creditors. For example, as is evident in Tables 5.1, 6.1, and 7.1, in 1971 the average interest charged on private international loans to Thailand was .4 percent below the rate on one-year Eurodollar deposits in London, while Mexico and Korea paid 1.2 percent over the Eurodollar London rate.

Sarit's successor, Marshal Thanom Kittikachorn, governed—as Sarit had—with military backing under an interim constitution. But Thanom did not enjoy Sarit's success in controlling either the outbreak of military factionalism or civilian pressures to accelerate the drafting of a new constitution. A new constitution was promulgated in 1968 legalizing political parties, which had been banned for ten years, and creating a semi-parliamentary system; parliamentary elections were held in 1969. Thirteen parties were organized.[15]

The military continued to be the primary force in politics, but disputes between military leaders constantly threatened Thanom's leadership and provided further openings for the civilian opposition. This factionalism came to a head in 1971 with a military coup; the new government dissolved the legislature, revoked the constitution, and banned political parties and meetings.[16]

Civilian backlash against military rule intensified; in what is known as the "October Revolution" the monarchy intervened, forcing Thanom to resign. A new constitution was invoked and the parliamentary system was reinstated in 1974. January 1975 elections yielded a multiparty coalition government under the leadership of M. R. Kukrit Pramoj of the Social Action Party, after a Democratic Party coalition suffered a no-confidence vote. The unstable base of this coalition and the governments that followed forced politicians to use cabinet appointments as rewards for political support. For example, Boonchu Rojanastien, appointed finance minister in 1978, was a leading party politician who sought to further his political ambitions at the expense of central bank authority.

The renewed need for Thai political leaders to engage in patronage politics in order to maintain power created incentives to capture the central bank as a source of funds to generate political support. While political uncertainty created incentives for political leaders to undermine central bank authority, the era of easy money internationally undermined a potential bulwark against these pressures. The World Bank, for example, encouraged Thai borrowing.[17] The rise of international liquidity and ease of access to international loans undercut what had been an important source of Bank of Thailand authority in the 1950s and 1960s.

The roles of the central bank and the Ministry of Finance in the adoption of selective credit for agriculture in the 1970s reveals the changed balance of power between the central bank and the government.[18] The private banks opposed the program, arguing that the loans were too risky, in large measure because the banks did not have the capacity to effectively evaluate potential rural borrowers.[19] The program posed a similar problem for the Bank of Thailand, which did not have an agricultural credit division to supervise the program. A group with this responsibility was set up within the bank, but initiative and control over the program lay with the Ministry of Finance.[20] "The Ministry of Finance said we had to do it," notes Chavalit Thanachanan, a high-level Bank of Thailand staffer at the time, about this program.[21]

The increase in government regulation indicated by this preferential credit program was roughly simultaneous with the decrease in central bank independence. Nonetheless, the general excess of international financial resources compared with demand, Thailand's strong balance of payments position, and high creditworthiness as indicated by interest rate data in Table 5.1 were more proximate reasons for Thai politicians' decision to rescind de facto central bank independence than was the extent of financial regulation.

The weakness of the Bank of Thailand in the 1970s, compared with the 1960s, is also evident in other episodes beyond the squabble over agricultural credit. Criticism of the central bank governor Snoh Unakul for his handling of the Raja Financial Company, for example, was an important factor leading to his resignation. The Raja Company, on the verge of failure, used its connections to convince several military officers to pressure for a government bail-out.[22] The Ministry of Finance supported this move. Snoh was forced to choose between acceding to a bail-out he felt would compromise the central bank and resigning.[23] When asked in retrospect about Bank of Thailand preferences regarding Ministry of Finance actions during this time, Finance Minister Boonchu commented that Bank of Thailand officials disagreed with the Ministry of Finance, but had no recourse.[24]

In 1976 the democratic period ended with the military's installation of Thanin Kraivichien as prime minister and the appointment of a new legislature. Opposition to military government from civil servants, liberal parties, and violent protest by the Communist Party of Thailand posed threats to Thanin's tenure that continued to create incentives for political manipulation of the central bank. Discord within the military added uncertainty to the situation. In 1978 a military faction of "young Turks" led another coup, resulting in the installation of General Kriangsak Chamanan. A new national constitution was promulgated in 1978 that theoretically increased the power of the parliament.[25] Parliamentary elections in 1979 saw a wide dispersal of votes among multiple parties; this made parliamentary politics highly unstable. In addition to uncertainty surrounding parliamentary reaction to and support for executive branch actions, growing fragmentation of power among army generals made gaining military support more difficult.[26] The incentives created by this uncertain political environment were not conducive to restoration of Bank of Thailand authority.

In a detailed study of economic policymaking, Doner and Laothamatas suggest that Kriangsak's efforts to shore up his political position by dispensing government jobs to key politicians led to changes in the budget process that resulted in a total loss of central bank or finance ministry control over military and state enterprise spending.[27] Central bank authority also declined.

Kriangsak's appointment of Boonchu as minister of finance typifies the way that government leaders' tenure insecurity may undermine central bank authority, if there are no countervailing pressures. Kriangsak himself held the Ministry of Finance position at first because he could not find a suitable candidate. He correctly feared the power that the appointment of Boonchu would give the Social Action Party (SAP) within his coalition government. Boonchu had made full finance ministry control over other economic policymaking bodies of the executive a condition for accepting the job. The Social Action Party pressured hard for Boonchu to be given the position; but many of Kriangsak's supporters objected that Boonchu had orchestrated the private banks' to refusal to bring new foreign loans into the increasingly credit-squeezed Thai economy. Nevertheless Kriangsak did not feel he could afford to alienate the SAP.[28] Once appointed finance minister, Boonchu tended to use government funds to gain political support for himself and his party. This was not conducive to central bank authority.[29]

The Need for International Creditworthiness and Renewed Central Bank Status

After 1979 Thailand's need for external creditworthiness began to rise again. In 1979 and 1980 Thailand suffered significant decline in import coverage. The level of import coverage reached in 1980, only two months' worth of imports covered by total central bank reserves, was the lowest in post–World War II Thai history. The early 1980s also saw Thailand's ratio of external debt to exports of goods and services more than double. The need to compete for international capital was on the rise generally after 1982, as global liquidity dried up. International loans became scarce and expensive, especially compared with the 1970s. In Thailand, foreign investment in the form of bonds also rose steeply in 1979 (see Table 5.2).

Although one would expect these events to be associated with a rise in central bank authority, evaluation of Thailand in the 1980s suggests that the impact was not immediate. From 1979 to 1982 the central bank found itself in frequent conflict with the finance ministry over austerity-related measures and was often on the losing side. The central bank governor appointed in 1982 enjoyed rising respect in international circles, however, and a tenure in office only exceeded in Thai history by Puey in the 1960s. As part of its effort to restore Thailand's access to international credit, the Prem government made an effort to insulate the central bank from the political pressures under which it had operated since the democratic opening beginning in the late 1960s.

Influencing political leaders' subjective perceptions of the need for international creditworthiness was the uncertainty surrounding General Prem Tinsulanond's grip on power. Prem's initial political support came from a four-party coalition. As in the 1970s, the rigors of governing through a coalition in a semi-democratic environment continued to create incentives to manipulate the central bank for short-term political gain. Prem's emphasis on restoring Thailand's credibility with international creditors facilitated the increase in central bank authority, but monarchical support for the Prem government could only go so far in counterbalancing pressures from coup attempts and unexpected elections that led to government–central bank conflict.

The Thanin-Kriangsak period preceding Prem was viewed as one of crisis in which foreign direct investment had declined and agricultural exports stagnated. After several years of strong growth in the mid-1970s, international reserves contracted in 1979. The change was dramatic: from 22 percent growth in 1979 to 3 percent contraction in 1980. International lending also began to shrink after many years of steady increase. Beginning in 1973 inflation rates had begun to climb. The Bank of Thailand began experiencing difficulty attaining foreign loans. "The country's traditionally strong reputation among foreign lenders," note Doner and Laothamatas, "seemed to be weakening."[30]

In early March 1980 Army Commander-in-Chief Prem Tinsulanond was appointed prime minister by the king and was later elected by the lower house of the legislature to succeed Kriangsak, who resigned after years of mounting political trouble. Prem had a reputation for incorruptibility and enjoyed the support of key military factions, a coalition of political parties, and the king. In 1981 Prem faced a coup attempt that he put down with support from the monarchy and its loyalists. Prem put down a second coup attempt in 1985 and faced unanticipated elections in 1983, 1986, and 1988.[31]

The rigors of maintaining the support of a party coalition to help confront military insurrection made the finance ministry, in particular, susceptible to pressures that created tension with the central bank.[32] In 1985, for example, the minister of finance "was a primary target for a no-confidence motion in the Parliament."[33] Even before this, and despite a generally shared outlook on price stability and an overall increase in central bank authority, there were a number of conflicts between the central bank governor, Nukun Prachuabmoh, and Finance Minister Somaii Huntrakul over the extent of sacrifice necessary to achieve inflation control.[34]

In one instance of conflict Nukun wanted to float both savings and loan rates, while Somaii wanted to cushion the blow to borrowers and keep the ceiling on loan rates.[35] In the end, the finance ministry position prevailed. In another case, the Bank of Thailand imposed an 18 percent ceiling on commercial bank credit increases, which caused a credit crunch seriously affecting small- and medium-sized industry. There was heavy criticism from business, the media, and the finance ministry; and the measure was reversed. Trouble also arose between the central bank and finance ministry when the Bank of Thailand made a public statement opposing Thailand's planned purchase of several F-16 fighter planes on the grounds that the purchase would strain the national budget. Somaii criticized this public discussion of budget policy by the Bank of Thailand. Conflict also surrounded policy toward troubled financial institutions, of which there were many in this period. The Ministry of Finance position was generally that the central bank should extend soft loans. The Bank of Thailand felt this was unsound policy.

Other conflicts, with less clear macroeconomic policy motivations, also occurred. For example, the Bank of Thailand proposed a savings insurance scheme which Somaii opposed. The finance minister's threat of resignation led the cabinet to table the Bank of Thailand proposal. Another source of friction between the central bank and the Ministry of Finance concerned the supervision of commercial banks. Believing Bank of Thailand supervision to be lax, Somaii assigned personnel from the finance ministry's Fiscal Policy Office to work with Bank of Thailand supervisors on a regular basis.

Somaii eventually dismissed Nukun, abruptly, in the wake of a bank collapse that drew considerable media attention. Somaii brought in a close associate, Kamchorn Sathirakul, to run the central bank. Open conflict arose again when Pramual, a Social Action and Chart Thai Party politician with close ties to Boonchu, became minister of finance. The conflicts between Pramual and Kamchorn were typically over the finance ministry's expansionary macroeconomic policy preferences. In one case the Bank of Thailand simultaneously removed interest rate ceilings and restricted credit expansion; Minister of Finance Pramual opposed the measures because they would slow growth. He also accused the bank of colluding with private banks in setting interest rates and promised the public he would not allow this in the future. Many interpreted this statement to mean that the Bank of Thailand would not be allowed to independently formulate and implement monetary policy.[36]

Although both personality clashes and the difficulties of trying to keep Prem's coalition partners content caused considerable conflict, the Bank of Thailand was marginally more autonomous under Prem than it had been under Kriangsak. Kamchorn lasted six years as governor, during which he was able to partially regain the central bank's traditional veto power over national fiscal policy. The political leadership's emphasis on restoring Thailand's international creditworthiness allowed Kamchorn, as Puey before him, to use his links to international creditors such as the World Bank as leverage in policy debates with the government. One high-level Bank of Thailand staffer recalls, "We had our policy preferences, which were similar to the IMF's, but we had to ask the IMF to impose them because of opposition from outside government."[37] Kamchorn's coup de grace came when Pramual negotiated the terms of entry into the Thai financial market of five foreign banks without consulting the Bank of Thailand. Kamchorn left the governorship in a media uproar over Pramual's lack of respect for central bank independence.

The trend toward restored central bank independence, however, has continued. The most recent era includes the short preretirement governorship of Chavalit Thanashanan and that of his successor, Vijit Supanit. Vijit was a central bank insider; his appointment was viewed as a sign that the Ministry of Finance, where the nomination for governor typically originates, intended to support Bank of Thailand autonomy.[38] This period spans the end of the elected Chatchai government and the militarily installed Anand government. In the early 1990s, as Tables 5.1 and 5.2 indicate, debt, interest rates and portfolio foreign investment in Thailand all rose. In this context it is not surprising that Anand's government showed great respect for central bank independence, to the point of supporting discussion of charter changes that would legally secure greater autonomy.[39]

Conclusion

Change in the status of the Bank of Thailand appears to be connected with changes in governing politicians' perceptions of the need to increase international creditworthiness. While the extent of government financial regulation remained relatively low and open after 1957, changes in politicians' security, in objective indicators of balance of payments trouble and the stock of creditworthiness, and in the composition of foreign investment, appear to have influenced the likelihood of change in central bank status as expected. Sarit increased central bank independence in 1957. He was more secure in his position and stayed in power longer than his predecessor; he also wanted to improve Thailand's balance of payments position. The democratic opening in 1973 lowered governing politicians' tenure security. This, combined with a relatively sound balance of payments, excessively easy international credit, and the tremendous favor creditors found in Thailand (evident in interest rates in Table 5.1), led to a decline in central bank status. This situation was partially reversed when the supply of international financial resources contracted in the 1980s and Thailand's balance of payments position deteriorated. After several years of consolidating his power, Prem gained the political security that finally permitted him the luxury of increasing central bank independence in 1982.

Chapter 2 outlined the arguments typically made to explain central bank authority. These are based on law, sectoral strength, political institutions, government financial needs, ideology, and leadership capabilities. The explanation derived from the need to compete for international creditworthiness draws on several of these factors, combining the need for government finance with aspects of the arguments based on sectoral strength and political institution. The competing arguments, based on law, personality or leadership capability, and ideology, are not supported by Thai central bank history.

Legal Arguments

If law were the primary determinant of central bank authority, we would expect to see a decrease or an increase in conflict between the central bank and the government, and conflict resolution closer to or further from the central bank's ideal point, after changes in legislation affecting central bank independence. The Thai central bank statute itself has not been rewritten since it was promulgated in 1942, although several other legal changes clearly impinge on central bank independence. The most important are the commercial banking acts promulgated in 1962 and 1979 and the government budget law enacted in 1959. Measures of central bank independence based on central bank statutes do not capture changes in authority implied by legislation in related areas. Legal coding of central bank statutes, following the Cukierman et al. (1992) criteria, reveals no change in Bank of Thailand authority between 1950 and 1990.

Even the pattern of changing authority implied by legislation in the related areas of commercial banking and government budgeting corresponds only weakly to the pattern of change in central bank authority as evident in government–central bank conflict. The Government Budget Procedures Act of October 1959 discontinued Bank of Thailand financing of the government through overdraft mechanisms.[40] The Commercial Banking Acts of 1962, 1979, and 1985 are other pieces of legislation that increase central bank supervisory power vis-à-vis the commercial banks.[41] The dates of these changes correspond roughly to eras in which central bank authority rose. Whether they are cause or effect of political leaders' decisions to respect central bank authority is hard to determine.

Puey, the central bank governor appointed in 1959, had strongly supported the end of overdraft financing of the government because he believed it compromised central bank autonomy. The timing of the Government Budget Procedure Act reflects both Puey's appointment and Sarit's interest in increasing Thailand's international creditworthiness, which led to his choice of Puey.

The 1962 Commercial Banking Act also strengthened the Bank of Thailand by providing new tools for banking supervision and control of credit. The timing and formulation process of this legislation illustrates how financial law follows politics, rather than the other way around. Both Puey and his colleagues in the multilateral credit agencies saw increasing the central bank's supervision and control of commercial banking as crucial to the bank's ability to increase and sustain its authority. Maintenance of price stability, a key to international creditworthiness, requires the ability to control credit, among other things. Puey drafted this legislation, but rather than imposing new commercial bank regulations unilaterally, Puey was careful to involve the commercial banks through consultation with the Thai Bankers Association.[42] Government sympathy for the central bank facilitated central bank–private bank collaboration. Had political leaders been less internationally oriented and more nationalist and/or populist, central bank–private bank collaboration could easily have become politicized, stirring popular opposition to the central bank and increasing the potential for government interference.[43]

Another major legislative change increasing the legal scope for central bank action was the 1979 Commercial Bank Act. Its timing corresponds with a period in which objective conditions suggested increased need for international creditworthiness. But the legislative change can hardly be interpreted as causing the modest increase in central bank authority that began after 1982. The legislation was controversial. The political environment of hesitant and sporadic progress toward liberalization was not conducive to close central bank–private bank consultation over regulatory reform. When the policy was announced, private banks were angry over the lack of prior consultation; this damaged central bank credibility with domestic bankers for several years. The 1985 commercial bank law reform came at a time when the central bank was gradually winning the campaign to restore lost autonomy.

Decrease in central bank authority is not associated with any legal change in Thailand. Legal protection of central bank independence and growing political support for central bank autonomy may be mutually reinforcing, but law alone will not prevent politically motivated encroachment on central bank authority—especially not in a developing-country context, where the role of law is uncertain. Lack of variation in the Bank of Thailand statute contrasts sharply with instability in the legal framework overall: Thailand had thirteen constitutions and seven constitutional amendments in the fifty years from 1932 to 1982.[44]

In cross-national comparative terms, as briefly noted in Chapter 2, there is also some reason to doubt the validity of a legal approach to central bank authority. The Bank of Thailand's position in the international rankings of central bank independence, based on the coding of its legal statute, falls significantly below where it would be placed based on a conflict-oriented evaluation.

Leadership and Ideology

Puey Ungphakorn is the kind of governor who comes to mind when the argument is made that central bank authority rests on the quality of its leadership. He had integrity; he was cautious and judicious. He perfected the art of moral suasion in the conduct of bank regulation. Tales are told that he had informants who would provide information on bankers' conduct; if reports of "inappropriate behavior" (excessive drinking, extramarital affairs) reached Puey, subtle reprimands were delivered. This practice increased Puey's reputation of integrity, because it was thought that only a man above moral reproach himself would dare to employ such practices.

But leadership qualities are an unsatisfying explanation of institutional capability. Moe and Wilson's complaint about students of the American presidency applies well to leadership-focused studies of central banks. "Scholars have long insisted in seeing the presidency in highly personal terms, as an institution built around a single person whose personality, skills, experiences, ideology, and decision-making style are the prime determinants of presidential behavior." But this does not allow us to "build genuine theories of presidential behavior."[45]

The two criticisms of quality-of-leadership explanations raised in Chapter 2 are also borne out in the context of Thai history. These concern the endogeneity of strong leadership in two senses. The first issue is how and why strong central bank leaders are selected. Puey brought experience in, and contacts with, multinational credit institutions to the job. These were outstanding aspects of his resumé; he was one of the only Thais with such a background. His professional record indicated he could be a strong central bank leader. It is hard to imagine that Puey's leadership potential was not part of the reason Sarit asked him to be governor of the Bank of Thailand. Second, Sarit's support for central bank autonomy and for the governor personally facilitated the development of Puey's leadership capabilities. It is also difficult to imagine that the politician-finance ministers of the 1970s, such as Boonchu, would have tolerated Puey-style leadership tactics.[46]

For similar reasons ideology also rings hollow as an explanation for variation in central bank authority in the Thai context. It begs the question of why political leaders chose or tolerated central bank governors of particular ideological leanings. The answer proposed here is that when the need for international creditworthiness is great, political leaders want fiscally conservative central bankers as effective interlocutors with investors.

Six

The Politics of Changing Central Bank Authority: Mexico

As in the discussion of Thailand, the history of central bank politics in Mexico helps us to evaluate the importance of competing for international creditworthiness in our search for explanations of changing central bank authority. Again, the likelihood that the need for creditworthiness will lead politicians to increase central bank status changes with conditions in international financial markets, which alter the anticipated benefits of trying to increase creditworthiness via central bank independence; with politicians' tenure security; with objective indications of balance of payments trouble and creditworthiness; and with the extent of national financial regulation.

There are five turning points in Mexican central bank history: 1934, 1954, 1972, 1983, and 1993. Two, 1934 and 1972, are associated with a decrease in the need for international creditworthiness and with declining central bank authority. In the 1970s international liquidity and "loan-pushing" undermined central bank autonomy because they reduced the need and value of competing for international capital and creditworthiness. Mexico, like Thailand, saw a decrease in central bank authority in the 1970s. The years 1954 and 1983 both mark increases in the need for external credit that created propitious conditions for an increase in central bank authority. These periods of increased central bank authority in Mexico coincide roughly with periods of increase in Thailand, reflecting similar pressures and opportunities emanating from international financial markets: a growing opportunity for multilateral and international commercial bank borrowing in the 1950s and the relative tightening of international credit in the 1980s. In Mexico, 1954 and 1983 were also years of extreme balance of payments difficulty, which fell early in the six-year Mexican presidential cycle. In these instances, Mexican politicians still had four and five years, respectively, of their government terms ahead of them. The 1993 Mexican statute change illustrates how growing portfolio investment and global competition for capital, especially in a context of financial deregulation and ballooning short-term debt, create incentive for political leaders to signal their creditworthiness via institutional change. As in Thailand, Mexican government regulation of domestic and international financial flows has been relatively constant, until recently. Prior to the 1990s variation in the impact of the need for international creditworthiness on central bank status corresponds more to politicians' tenure security, characteristics of international financial markets, and objective indications of balance of payments and creditworthiness than to change in financial regulation.

Declining Central Bank Authority in the 1930s

The decline in Mexican central bank authority that took place over the course of the 1930s reflected the limited effectiveness expected of efforts to increase international creditworthiness. This era in Mexican central bank history illustrates the principle that no matter how open a country's capital account, conditionality, implicit or explicit, does not work if the promise of new investment is not credible. Mexico has a long history of relatively unrestricted currency exchange, reinforced in the 1930s by President Lazaro Cárdenas's consideration and dismissal of exchange controls. Objectively speaking, Mexico's need for international investment was also relatively high in the 1930s. Domestic savings were low and domestic investment needs high. Central bank reserves were drained by efforts to support the peso's value in the face of capital flight and "dollarization" (ratio of dollar to overall demand deposits in local banks). Yet the value of adopting policies and institutions aimed at building international creditworthiness was severely discounted all over the world in the 1930s as international investment and credit dried up. Mexico's own international debts were large enough, and the history of negotiations with creditors so long and unsuccessful, that hope of renewed access to international credit was remote.[1] An exhaustive study of Mexican attitudes toward foreign creditors in the 1920s and 1930s concludes: "By 1932 relations with the [foreign] bankers were so distant that Mexico decided to give up on them and direct their attention in the search for more resources towards the oil companies. . . . Then, with external sources exhausted, Mexico issued 504 thousand pesos in 1933 and 333 thousand pesos in 1934 of internal bonds, although this tactic succeeded only by pressuring several banks into buying them."[2]

Political uncertainty and the power of populist appeals in the aftermath of a partially labor- and peasant-based revolution also decreased the relative importance President Cárdenas accorded international creditworthiness. Cárdenas came to the presidency in late 1934, facing an uncertain political environment. It was not clear whether former president Calles could be forced to cede his behind-the-scenes control of the Mexican presidency. Cárdenas faced potential threats from within the political elite and a growing challenge from society, workers in particular, in reaction to the policies of Calles. While there had been virtually no strike activity in Mexico in 1932, there were over two hundred in the year preceding Cárdenas's inauguration. Cárdenas took on the monumental job of trying to consolidate his power and that of the institution of the presidency by weakening the military and building a new labor- and peasant-supported political party. The latter task, in particular, mandated government access to central bank financing for vast, popularly oriented spending programs.

The financial pressures stemming from Cárdenas's effort to build labor and peasant support created incentives to make the central bank a subservient financier of an expensive process of political consolidation. There was little hope of significant international financing that could have counterbalanced the incentive to restrict central bank authority.

For most of Mexican central bank history, governor turnover has followed the six-year presidential cycle. Periods of central bank weakening coincide with presidential terms that saw more than one central bank governor. During the Cárdenas presidency Eduardo Suárez, a Cárdenas ally, replaced Gonzalo Robles as central bank governor. Other important indicators of declining central bank authority during the Cárdenas regime are also apparent. Over the course of several years the Banco de México went from being able to obtain a written agreement from the government on lowering deficit financing to being forced by the government to cover deficit spending in amounts far beyond legal limits.

Cárdenas found expansionary policies necessary to consolidate a partly peasant- and labor-based political hegemony. An authoritative central bank interfered with those plans. Gonzalo Robles, named the first governor of the Banco de México in 1935, resigned after less than a year, along with a number of other cabinet-level officials opposed to Cárdenas's populist state intervention, particularly his agrarian reform. One of Cárdenas's prime concerns in considering a replacement for Robles was the ability of a central bank governor to be subservient to the president, through the Ministry of Finance and its head, Eduardo Suárez. After laying plans for controlling the central bank with Suárez, Cárdenas appointed Luis Montes de Oca governor of the Banco de México.[3]

One of the first tasks Suárez assigned Montes de Oca was revision of the Banco de México charter.[4] Rhetoric aside, the intent of the charter was debilitating for the central bank; it legalized increased government borrowing, in part by permitting central bank investment in government paper. Previous restrictions on central bank credit provision to the government were emasculated by explicit exemptions for six types of government financing operations. Foreign banks and businessmen with interests in Mexico expressed concern that the new legislation was not compatible with inflation control and peso stability. The U.S. embassy in Mexico City reported to the State Department its belief that the legislation spelled the end of Banco de México's ability to resist presidential requests for credit.[5]

The 1936 charter revision is interesting for what it reflects about the balance of power on the charter-writing subcommittee between those interested in preserving or increasing central bank authority to pursue monetary stability and those interested in giving a legal foundation to Cárdenas's desire for increased central bank subservience. The history of implementation of the 1936 amendment is even more revealing. The charter included a four-month transition period for gradual implementation that was repeatedly extended by executive decree as the reality of government desire for central bank finance increasingly conflicted with even the relatively permissive stipulations of the charter. In effect, the 1936 amendment was never implemented.

Even before the ink was dry on the new legislation it was clear that government demands for central bank financing were going to far exceed what most Banco de México board members felt was healthy.[6] During 1937, the Banco de México board of directors became increasingly concerned about deficit financing of the government. A small subcommittee was appointed to write a report outlining the dangers inherent in the prevailing situation; this report was presented to Minister of Finance Suárez along with recommendations for change in government policy. As a result, the government signed an agreement stating its intention to limit deficit spending. In the face of political pressures motivating large government spending Cárdenas essentially ignored the limitations in this agreement, as he had ignored the limitations included in the 1936 charter.[7] A second report requesting deficit-reducing efforts was sent by the Banco de México board to the president in 1938. It too was ignored.[8] In 1938 the 1936 central bank law was retroactively revised, bringing the central bank's legal authority into line with the political and financial reality of the Cárdenas administration. One of its most important changes made the Minister of Finance head of the central bank board of directors.

Seeking International Loans and Strengthening the Central Bank in the 1950s

The second major change in Banco de México history came in the 1950s, as central bank authority rose under the governorship of Rodrigo Gómez. Although governor turnover is not necessarily a reliable measure of central bank autonomy, in Mexico periods of increased central bank authority coincide with the two instances in which a central bank governor remained in his post for more than one presidential term *(sexenio)*. Rodrigo Gómez remained central bank governor through the three *sexenios* comprising the presidencies of Adolfo Ruiz Cortines, Adolfo López Mateos, and Gustavo Diaz Ordaz. Depletion of the foreign exchange reserves Mexico had built up during World War II and the rise of international development lending created pressures and opportunities supporting the growing authority of the central bank under Gómez. Although Mexican political leaders of the 1950s faced several political challenges, the six-year pattern of regular presidential succession and the political hegemony of the ruling party, PRI, was well institutionalized compared with the 1930s.[9] The tenure security of political elites and their technocrats was long, and the costs of nationalist, populist economic policies seemed high, given the balance of payments problems and the unfavorable international interest rates Mexico faced (evident in Table 6.1), an exceptionally open capital account relative to other developing countries, and the opportunity to obtain significant loans from the World Bank.

Objective indications of a growing need for international credit and creditworthiness are evident in data for the early 1950s. Balance of payments trouble had been building since the late 1940s. In 1947, as Table 6.1 indicates, reserves covered less than 0.5 (months' worth of imports). Coverage reached 2, still low in comparative terms, and fell to under 1 again in 1951. Similar trends are reflected in the reserves data. Reserves fell 26 percent in 1951, recovering in the following year only to fall again in 1953.

The 1954 devaluation is an important part of the context of this second shift in Mexican central bank authority. It highlights both the nature of Mexican economic policymaking and the role of international financiers' influence.[10] The devaluation negotiations established a direct relationship between the central bank governor and the minister of finance, on the one hand, and the IMF, on the other, with no presidential intermediation. The finance ministers of this era and the governor of the central bank consciously used presidential interest in securing new international credit for Mexico, and their own relationships with international creditors, to strengthen institutional authority.

Speaking for financial technocrats in general, Antonio Ortiz Mena notes that "we go to the IMF to make us do what we know we have to do. . . . this helps us control public opinion."[11] In the 1950s and 1960s, the efforts of Gómez and Ortiz Mena brought the settlement of Mexico's old debts, sale of Mexican government paper to foreign governments, and new bilateral and multilateral credits. The search for these new sources of external finance "imposed very strong discipline" and greatly strengthened the authority of the central bank and the finance

TABLE 6.1
Indicators of Mexico's Need to Compete for International Capital

Year	*Import Coverage*	*Foreign Exchange Reserves (U.S. millions)*	*Average Annual Interest on Private Credit Minus the Eurodollar or Libor Interest Rate*[a]
1945	1.80	52	
1946	0.91	43	
1947	0.45	26	
1948	0.95	36	
1949	2.02	74	
1950	1.92	89	
1951	0.96	66	
1952	1.70	115	
1953	1.02	69	
1954	2.47	147	
1955	3.74	276	
1956	3.60	322	
1957	2.84	273	
1958	2.39	225	
1959	3.23	271	
1960	2.64	261	
1961	3.17	301	
1962	3.02	288	
1963	3.52	364	
1964	3.00	373	
1965	2.50	325	
1966	2.76	369	
1967	2.23	325	
1968	2.20	359	
1969	2.20	381	
1970	1.88	385	0.4
1971	2.74	550	1.2
1972	3.23	731	1.4
1973	2.79	888	0.6
1974	1.90	960	–0.6
1975	2.13	1,168	2.2
1976	2.36	1,187	1.4
1977	3.48	1,592	2.2
1978	2.64	1,786	1.7
1979	1.86	1,871	0.2
1980	1.66	2,688	1.8
1981	1.85	3,709	0.3
1982	0.66	828	1.3
1983	5.68	3,795	1.5
1984	7.40	7,269	0.5

TABLE 6.1 *(cont.)*

Year	*Import Coverage*	*Foreign Exchange Reserves (U.S. millions)*	*Average Annual Interest on Private Credit Minus the Eurodollar or Libor Interest Rate*[a]
1985	4.21	4,906	0.7
1986	5.66	5,667	2.2
1987	11.08	11,758	0.2
1988	2.99	4,885	0.8
1989	2.92	5,946	0.5
1990	6.64	9,446	0.8
1991	*N.A.*	*N.A.*	2.9
1992	*N.A.*	*N.A.*	3.2
1993	*N.A.*	*N.A.*	*N.A.*

Source: Calculated from IMF, *International Financial Statistics* (Washington, D.C.: IMF, various years), and World Bank, *World Debt Tables* (Washington, D.C.: World Bank, various years).

Note: The *World Debt Tables* changed the definition of the numerator in 1980. *N.A.*–Not available.

a. Libor–London interbank offer rate.

ministry to define how to make Mexico attractive to international creditors. It should be pointed out, says Ortiz Mena, that the "international banks worked with us because they liked what we were doing . . . if we did it any other way the doors would close."[12] The most difficult challenge, he reports, was to maintain the authority to control spending when international reserves were in excess.

In addition to strengthening direct ties between the central bank and international creditors, the 1954 devaluation also set an important precedent for central bank and Finance Ministry authority *over* the president. The devaluation was worked out by Minister of Finance Antonio Carillo Flores and central bank governor Rodrigo Gómez with the IMF. It was announced as a virtual fait accompli to President Ruiz Cortines.[13] In historical perspective this constitutes a highly unusual departure from the traditions of the Mexican presidency. The precedent the president set by accepting the central bank and Ministry of Finance lead on this issue significantly strengthened the central bank–finance ministry role in economic decision making thereafter.

Rodrigo Gómez was appointed head of the Banco de México by newly elected president Ruiz Cortines in 1954 on the recommendation of his mentor, Finance Minister Carillo Flores. Rodrigo Gómez remained as central bank governor until his death at the end of the Díaz Ordaz administration in 1970. During his long tenure, Mexico experienced a remarkable period of low inflation and high growth known as the era of "stabilizing development." Relations between the central bank and the Ministry of Finance were exceptionally close, both under Finance Minister Carillo Flores and his successor, Antonio Ortiz Mena. One sign of the authority of the Banco de México under Gómez is the bank's success in divorcing itself from responsibility for the operations of the agricultural development banks established by Cárdenas. The U.S. embassy in Mexico City reported that "the President was persuaded by the Bank of Mexico . . . that [it] should cease serving as a virtually inexhaustible source of funds for the credit operations of the agricultural banks."[14]

When Ortiz Mena became chief economics adviser to the campaign of López Mateos in 1957, he discussed the evils of popular sentiment in favor of government control of the central bank with the president-elect.[15] "The central bank should serve as our conscience, to tell us when we go astray," Ortiz Mena argued.[16] In keeping with this belief, when López Mateos appointed Ortiz Mena finance minister in 1958, he became the first Mexican finance minister to refuse to take on the chairmanship of the central bank board.

Jointly, the head of the central bank, Gómez, and Minister of Finance Ortiz Mena exercised a virtual monopoly on major macroeconomic policy decisions. Price stability was their main goal and, although the central bank had no legal role in the budget process and there were no legal limits on government borrowing from the central bank, they successfully dictated the limits on government programs and policies necessary to protect that goal.[17] They also managed to obtain a change in charter stipulations regarding governor appointment procedures. Although central bank law changed, in reality the president continued to control selection of the central bank governor.

International Liquidity and Central Bank Denouement

A tremendous influx of oil export proceeds and foreign loans in the 1970s, combined with a left-wing challenge to the PRI's legitimacy, coincided to bring an end to the halcyon days of Mexican central bank authority in the 1950s and 1960s. In 1970, as Table 6.2 shows, Mexico contracted foreign loans at double the rate of 1969; borrowing held steady for a few years only to double again in 1972, after which it expanded steadily until 1982. Mexican debt relative to exports of goods and services outstripped that of most other middle-income developing country borrowers. Was this a sign of rising or falling need for international creditworthiness? As Tables 6.1, 7.1, and 8.1 indicate, Mexico borrowed in 1971 at rates comparable to those of Korea, lower

TABLE 6.2
Foreign Investment in Mexico (stock of investments, in U.S. millions)

Year	*FDI*	*Bonds (Disbursements)*	*Equities*	*Loans*
1954	105			63
1955	112			56
1956	118			107
1957	132			165
1958	100			243
1959	81			224
1960	(38)			363
1961	120			352
1962	127			401
1963	118			426
1964	102			755
1965	214			370
1966	183			128
1967	130			295
1968	227			208
1969	297			418
1970	323			893
1971	306			928
1972	277	115		986
1973	383	126		1,881
1974	564	10		2,562
1975	502	178		3,940
1976	544	166		4,443
1977	476	1,049	1,146	4,363
1978	662	648	603	6,645
1979	1,033	*N.A.*	(306)	8,759
1980	1,678	236	(57)	9,278
1981	2,155	*N.A.*	845	12,095
1982	1,489	*N.A.*	844	13,353
1983	425	*N.A.*	(583)	8,236
1984	382	*N.A.*	(610)	4,937
1985	491	43	(984)	14,177
1986	1,523	0	(816)	12,029
1987	3,246	0	(397)	8,542
1988	2,594	0	1,676	5,934
1989	3,037	0	438	3,653
1990	2,637	975	5,359	12,082
1991	4,762	1,122	9,267	13,188
1992	5,366	1,157	14,095	12,717

Source: IMF, *International Financial Statistics* (Washington, D.C.: IMF, various years). For bonds (disbursements), see World Bank, *World Debt Tables* (Washington, D.C.: World Bank, various years), disbursement tables.
Note: FDI–Foreign direct investment; *N.A.*–Not available.

than those of Brazil. Import coverage fell, but foreign reserves did not contract during the period (see Table 6.1). In fact, in 1971 Mexico's international reserves grew faster than they had in all but two of the previous twenty-one years. In sum, in Mexico, as in other countries, the growth of the Euromarket in the late 1960s pushed the supply of international financial resources far beyond demand. Easy money internationally undermined an important rationale for central bank independence. For Mexico, in addition, the promise of oil helped preserve its reputation as a good credit risk internationally despite high debt-to-export ratios.

Mexican political leaders had little reason to be concerned with the impact of their nation's economic policy processes and outcomes on international financiers, because oil guaranteed easy access to international loans. President Luis Echeverría was free to be consumed with meeting the leftist challenge to his party's semi-authoritarian monopoly on political representation. (Table 6.3 lists Mexican presidents, regime type, and central bank governors by years of tenure.) Concern with growing income inequality and the authoritarian side of PRI governance led to student demonstrations during the 1968 Olympic games in Mexico City. These demonstrations were violently suppressed by the government, creating further discontent with the ruling party. Early in Echeverría's term his role in overseeing the police action against students and workers in 1968 became public knowledge. To general partywide concerns about legitimacy in the aftermath of the 1968 events was added Echeverría's own personal drive to improve his popularity. In 1971, a deeper than anticipated recession scared the president into a major policy shift designed to buy back popular support for himself and his party. Echeverría announced that Mexico would move from stabilizing development to "shared development." In the absence of counterpressures from international financial circumstances, pressure from the left gave Echeverría incentive to pursue policies requiring deficit financing by the central bank.

Central bank president Ernesto Fernández Hurtado and Finance Minister Hugo Margáin did everything possible to convince Echeverría to scale back his plans to use public spending to stimulate growth. When Margáin protested to Echeverría that certain spending could not be authorized because reserves were insufficient, he was summarily dismissed. Echeverría declared that "economic policy is made at Los Pinos" (the presidential mansion) and turned the office of the presidency into a shadow economic cabinet which persistently fought other economic policymaking institutions. Fernández Hurtado, director of the Banco de México at the time, found his institution's policy preferences subordinated to the president's spending plans.

TABLE 6.3
Change of Government, Regime Type, and Central Bank Governor in Mexico

President	*Regime*	*Banco de México Governor*
Lazaro Cárdenas (1934–40)	ONE-PARTY DEMOCRACY	Gonzalo Robles (1935)
		Luis Montes de Oca (1935–40)
Manual Avila Camacho (1940–46)		Eduardo Villaseñor (1940–46)
Miguel Aleman (1946–52)		Carlos Novoa (1946–52)
Adolfo Ruiz Cortines (1952–58)		Rodrigo Gómez (1952–70)
Adolfo López Mateos (1958–64)		
Gustavo Díaz Ordaz (1964–70)		
Luis Echeverría Alvarez (1970–76)		Ernesto Fernández Hurtado (1970–76)
Jose López Portillo (1976–82)		Gustavo Romero Kolbeck (1976–82)
		Miguel Mancera (1982)
		Carlos Tello (1982)
Miguel de la Madrid (1982–88)		Miguel Mancera (1983–)
Carlos Salinas (1988–1994)		
Ernesto Zedillo (1994–2000)		

Echeverría wanted to fire Fernández Hurtado for his opposition to government economic policy, as he had Margáin. Margáin's replacement in the Ministry of Finance, José López Portillo, argued forcefully that Echeverría should keep the central bank director to avoid the destabilizing impact his resignation would have on an already unstable economic environment. Although he wanted to leave the governorship, Fernández Hurtado was asked to remain in the position. Fernández Hurtado's successor in the following *sexenio*, Gustavo Romero Kolbeck, concluded, "None of us had the pants to resign when we should have."[18]

From 1973 to 1976 central bank governor Fernández Hurtado's policy advice was repeatedly dismissed. "Those years were terribly hard," he recalls; "I had to go in front of the press after my positions were rejected and say that the policies were good and wouldn't add to inflation or lead to devaluation, when I knew that wasn't true. I had to do this in order to try to preserve public confidence in the central bank."[19]

López Portillo's fear of the impact of the resignation of a central bank governor on economic stability lessened as he succeeded Echeverría in the presidency. There was considerable hubris in López Portillo's attitude, perhaps stemming in part from Mexico's foreign exchange bonanza. López Portillo's conflicts with central bank governor Romero Kolbeck were bitter, particularly over the issue of devaluation. "I was a victim of the Banco de México's dependence on the executive," states Romero. López Portillo refused to even contemplate devaluation. After several meetings in which Romero argued the necessity of the move, López Portillo told him he wasn't going to meet with him again. "Don't even ask for an appointment with me," the president reportedly said. "I won't grant it. I am not going to leave office as a 'devalued' president."[20] Yet contact was necessary if López Portillo was to personally oversee Banco de México policy implementation. He instructed the central bank governor daily on what to do with the exchange rate. One day he called for an appreciation, over Romero's strong protest.[21] But with the country awash in foreign exchange, there seemed little need to heed central bank advice. This incident resulted in Romero's resignation.

Miguel Mancera replaced Romero Kolbeck at the central bank, only to find that the president had plans for bank nationalization and exchange controls. Rather than try to fight a losing battle with the president behind the scenes, Mancera chose a more public strategy. He wrote, published, and distributed a treatise against exchange controls. When López Portillo went ahead with his plans anyway, he replaced Mancera with Carlos Tello, an ideologically unorthodox economist who was one of the architects of bank nationalization and the concomitant exchange controls. The nationalization in September 1982 marked the culmination of the second major period of declining central bank authority in Mexico.

Competing for Creditworthiness: Rebuilding Central Bank Authority

The September 1982 measures also marked the end of Mexico's foreign exchange bonanza. After this, the urgent need for foreign exchange and international creditworthiness became the primary criterion against which government decisions were judged. Foreign exchange reserves contracted more in 1982 than they ever had in post–World War II Mexico. Table 6.1 also shows that foreign exchange reserves fell to 0.66 of a months' import cost, a level close to the postwar low of 0.45 in 1947. In the context of contraction in global financial markets, even projected oil wealth could not prevent high debt-to-export ratios from taking their toll on Mexican creditworthiness. Tables 5.1, 6.1, 7.1, and 8.1 show that the average interest rate for private credits to Mexico in 1982 was 1.3 percent over the London interbank offer rate (Libor) while it was, –2.8 percent relative to Libor for Thailand and –0.7 and –2.1 percent for Brazil and South Korea, respectively.

The nationalization measure engendered extreme business opposition and drove several prominent businessmen into the arms of the PRI's prime competitor party, the PAN. In addition to Mexico's urgent need for international creditworthiness, the partisan nature of this challenge to Mexico's political leadership prompted measures to circumscribe government and lessen the future possibility of such an unexpected and seemingly arbitrary exercise of government power. The year 1983 marked the beginning of a steady increase in Mexican central bank authority that culminated in a charter change promulgated ten years later, in 1993. Miguel de la Madrid reappointed Miguel Mancera as central bank governor in 1983, and like Rodrigo Gómez in the 1950s and 1960s, Mancera's tenure as central bank governor spanned three *sexenios*.

Salinas continued the de facto policy of support for central bank independence and authority as part of a multifaceted effort to increase foreign financial inflows, even though by some objective measures the need for international creditworthiness was declining. Import coverage reached unprecedented highs for Mexico in 1987 (eleven months), but short-term debt was creeping back up from its 1985 low and the country still faced relatively high international loan rates, especially compared with those of Asian middle-income countries (compare Tables 5.1, 6.1, 7.1, and 8.1). While growth of new foreign direct investment in Mexico was uneven, foreign equity and bond investment began to boom during Carlos Salinas's administration (Table 6.2).

The Salinas administration also saw the first substantial change in Mexican financial regulation in decades, induced in part by the North American Free Trade Agreement financial sector negotiations. The NAFTA-related reforms included substantial deregulation of the domestic financial market, reprivatization of the banks that had been nationalized in the wake of the crisis, and the opening of the financial sector to foreign competition.[22] U.S. banks had long sought freer access to the Mexican market, and the negotiation of the North American Free Trade Agreement provided them an entry point. Despite the strong external pressure and the Salinas administration's interest in seeing the NAFTA succeed, the newly privatized banks were able to win a gradual phase-in of the entry provisions and certain market-share restrictions. However, the financial crisis of 1994–95 resulted in an acceleration of the NAFTA liberalization timetable.[23]

Given financial deregulation, the dramatic rise in bond investments, and rapidly growing short-term debt, signaling government commitment to investor-friendly policies became increasingly important to

Mexican political leaders, who were almost single-mindedly concerned with foreign capital inflow. When it looked as though the cornerstone of Salinas's effort to attract foreign capital, the North American Free Trade Agreement, might fail due to U.S. congressional opposition, Salinas pushed through a statutory increase in central bank authority as a partial substitute. Salinas saw both measures as ways to signal the PRI's future commitment to policies favorable to foreign capital, even after he left the presidency. Salinas's term was ending, and he was ineligible for reelection. Political manipulation of the central bank could thus not have helped extend Salinas's own term of office. Salinas sought instead to make an institutional change that would help future governments, likely to be PRI-dominated, compete for international creditworthiness.[24]

The proposed central bank statute changes passed the Mexican legislature easily.[25] Representatives of the small Mexican political parties of the left objected to the proposal on the grounds that it would reduce the likelihood of economic policies favorable to the poor. Other observers saw the increase in central bank independence as a positive move in the process of political liberalization, contributing to reductions in the power of the presidency.[26]

The new statute made three changes. It stipulated securing the stability of the peso's purchasing power as the central bank's primary goal. The new legislation also prohibited the extension of central bank credit to the government. Finally, the statute provided for terms and conditions of appointment for the central bank governor and board "that would be conducive to exercising autonomy." The statute provides for recall of these personnel only on grounds of *"falta grave"* (grave fault). This is actually a weaker provision than those in many other recently changed central bank statutes, where recall can only occur on the basis of judicial sentencing or extended incapacitation.

The 1994 peso crisis illustrates the limited impact of increased legal independence.[27] Salinas succumbed to political pressures to expand economic activity prior to the August 1994 elections. On top of growing overvaluation, off the books lending through para-state organizations such as Nafinsa heightened the need for the central bank to tighten monetary policy throughout 1994. Yet two factors prevented Mancera from accomplishing this tightening; they signal the continued weakness of the Mexican central bank despite the 1993 charter change. First, tightening would have contravened the wishes of leading PRI officials and Salinas associates. Second, the weakness of the private banking system precluded monetary tightening that would have dangerously increased the banks' liquidity problems.

Conclusion

The history of the politics of Mexican central banking highlights the complexity of international financial influence as it relates to political leaders' prioritization of their need to compete for international creditworthiness. The nature of predominant forms of international investment and the global relationship between supply and demand for international investment are important determinants of the extent to which objective balance of payments considerations translate into a perceived need for creditworthiness and a decision to try to improve creditworthiness via central bank independence. In the 1930s international financial market conditions heavily foreclosed the possibility that international lenders might have leverage over debtor countries. This coincided in Mexico with domestic political conditions that made a nationalist, populist economic strategy appealing to political leaders trying to consolidate their hold on government. Similarly, in the 1970s, permissive international financial conditions significantly lowered the costs to political leaders of responding to leftist pressure with policies that would, under other international financial market conditions, have lowered international creditworthiness. The rise in international portfolio investment in Mexico, growing short-term debt, and financial deregulation made Salinas's move to increase central bank independence in 1993 predictable.

As in the Thai context, problems arise with alternative arguments about longitudinal variation in central bank authority that are based on legal stipulations, leadership qualities, or ideology. Mexican central bank history strongly suggests that legal change follows *from* increase in central bank authority, with a considerable lag. The increases of the 1950s and the 1980s both led in the following decades to changes in the Banco de México statute. Specifically, the 1962 statute change made the governor an appointee of the central bank board rather than of the executive branch. It also changed the legal delineation of the central bank's role in the monetary policy process. The original statute had no provision for a central bank role in policy formulation; the altered statue provided for the government to seek central bank advice before undertaking monetary policy decisions. But once again, Mexican central bank history suggests that legal stipulations do not prevent decline in central bank authority.

Mexican central bank history also illustrates the ways in which central bank leadership capabilities are shaped by presidential preferences. Regardless of whether Ruiz Cortines knew that Rodrigo Gómez would be a strong leader when he chose him, Ruiz Cortines's own weaknesses in economic knowledge and his virtual delegation of economic policymaking to the central bank and Ministry of Finance *allowed* both Rodrigo Gómez and Antonio Ortiz Mena to become strong leaders. The tenure of Miguel Mancera also illustrates the problems in the leadership quality argument vis-à-vis central bank authority. All the central bank leadership capability in the world could not have kept López Portillo from nationalizing the banks and imposing exchange controls.

In general, differentiating between market force explanations and those based on ideology is difficult. Worse still, in this book emphasis is on politicians' perceptions of market dictates. While Mexican central bank history demonstrates that the president's preferences constrain the central bank governor, it is harder to distinguish between the role of ideology and markets in shaping the president's preference formation. The cost and benefit of economic strategies associated with different ideologies varies with market pressures. In a time of global depression, such as the 1930s, internationalist economic policy has little pay-off and nationalist policy conversely little cost. In the 1930s in Mexico Cárdenas could pursue the economic implications of his national populist ideology at relatively little cost. Similar interaction between ideology and market conditions is evident in Mexico in the 1970s. Echeverría did not begin his administration with clear populist economic policy preferences, but the prospects of oil windfall and loan bonanza helped push him in that direction, with obivous consequences for central bank independence. Mexican central bank history lends credence to the intuition that, in the last instance, markets shape ideology more than ideology shapes markets.

Seven

The Politics of Changing Central Bank Authority: South Korea

The history of central banking in Korea is another case that aids our exploration of the extent to which variation in the need for international creditworthiness corresponds to change in central bank independence. Several factors stand out in evaluating Korea's need for international capital and creditworthiness since World War II. First, as is evident in Table 7.2, trends in foreign borrowing in the 1950s are different from those in the other three countries examined. Foreign borrowing rises fairly steeply beginning in 1954 in Mexico and Brazil and in 1956 in Thailand; in constrast, foreign borrowing falls off in Korea in 1954 from comparatively high levels in 1952–53. This shift reflects U.S. and allied loans to Korea during the Korean War. The relatively sharp decline in foreign lending between 1953 and 1955, a time when lending to other developing countries was rising, coincides with the beginning of serious encroachment on central bank autonomy. The largely geopolitical determinants of capital inflow led the Korean leadership to discount the role of economic policy in attracting capital, even though the need to compete for international capital was objectively high by some indicators (see Table 7.1).

Foreign borrowing was modest in the 1970s compared with that in Latin America. Even as Korea's relative favor with international creditors fell slightly in 1971–72 (as measured by interest rates shown in Tables 5.1, 6.1, 7.1, and 8.1) and Korea experienced several years of decline in foreign exchange and import coverage, the strength of Korean exports, the ease of foreign borrowing, and Korea's extensive capital controls limited political elites' perceptions of the need to compete for international capital. Korea also weathered the debt crisis well. As Table 7.1 indicates, debt-to-export ratios remained modest, especially by Latin American standards. Through the late 1980s objective indicators of the need to compete for international capital remained low. Import coverage was scant, but so was the country's international debt. Korea enjoyed extremely favorable interest rates on international loans. In accord with leaders' low prioritization of the need to compete for capital internationally, Korea's failure to increase central bank authority is notable throughout the 1970s and 1980s. In

TABLE 7.1
Indicators of South Korea's Need to Compete for International Capital

Year	*Import Coverage*	*Foreign Exchange Reserves (U.S. millions)*	*Average Annual Interest on Private Credit Minus the Eurodollar or Libor Interest Rate*[a]
1951		37	
1952		81	
1953	3.73	107	
1954	5.20	106	
1955	3.33	95	
1956	3.02	97	
1957	3.10	114	
1958	4.60	145	
1959	5.74	146	
1960	5.41	155	
1961	7.79	205	
1962	4.74	167	
1963	2.78	130	
1964	3.83	129	
1965	3.58	138	
1966	3.95	236	
1967	4.18	347	
1968	3.18	388	
1969	3.62	550	
1970	3.53	584	–1.8
1971	2.01	401	1.2
1972	2.29	481	2.1
1973	2.35	829	0.2
1974	0.48	276	–1.8
1975	1.28	777	1.4
1976	2.68	1,962	2.7
1977	3.28	2,955	2.3
1978	2.19	2,736	1.0
1979	1.72	2,910	–0.6
1980	1.57	2,912	–0.3
1981	1.20	2,619	–2.5
1982	1.36	2,744	–2.1
1983	1.02	2,230	0.0
1984	1.07	2,723	–0.9
1985	1.09	2,829	–0.5
1986	1.25	3,301	0.3
1987	1.04	3,566	0.0
1988	2.86	12,340	0.6
1989	2.93	14,978	–0.8

TABLE 7.1 *(cont.)*

Year	*Import Coverage*	*Foreign Exchange Reserves (U.S. millions)*	*Average Annual Interest on Private Credit Minus the Eurodollar or Libor Interest Rate*[a]
1990	2.49	14,459	0.4
1991	*N.A.*	*N.A.*	1.4
1992	*N.A.*	*N.A.*	2.9

Source: Calculated from IMF, *International Financial Statistics* (Washington, D.C.: IMF various years), and World Bank, *World Debt Tables* (Washington, D.C.: World Bank, various years).

Note: The *World Debt Tables* changed the definition of the numerator in 1980. *N.A.*–Not available.

a. Libor–London interbank offer rate.

1987–88 there was an unsuccessful movement to provide a statutory basis for increased Bank of Korea independence. Financial regulation remained consistently great from the 1950s through the early 1990s.[1] Throughout the period studied here this high level of government financial regulation mitigated the impact any need for creditworthiness might have had on central bank status.

Eroding Central Bank Authority, 1956–1962

The contemporary Korean central bank is based on legislation drafted by two advisers from the Federal Reserve Bank of New York. Officials of Korea's Chosen Bank, which had been the state bank in the era of Japanese colonialism, circulated a draft central bank law to the National Assembly and various government ministries in 1948. The Ministry of Finance drafted an alternative bill in early 1949 that included much less autonomy for the proposed central bank. The government then decided to invite foreign experts to write the legislation. Arthur I. Bloomfield and John P. Jensen wrote a charter for the new Bank of Korea stipulating independence and the primary goal of maintaining price stability, proposals fairly far from the Ministry of Finance's ideal.[2] The charter was modified slightly, but not significantly, by the legislature. The main debate was over the constitutionality of the Bank of Korea legislation; the Korean constitution reserved responsibility for monetary, financial, and foreign exchange policy for the government, that is, the Ministry of Finance.[3]

The ink was hardly dry on this legislation when finance-hungry Korean government politicians began to abrogate the law, firing central

TABLE 7.2
Foreign Investment in South Korea (stock of investments, in U.S. millions)

Year	*FDI*	*Bonds*	*Equities*	*Loans*
1952				70.3
1953				85.8
1954				30.0
1955				8.5
1956				12.9
1957				20.2
1958				*N.A.*
1959				(13.0)
1960				(9.8)
1961				(0.7)
1962	0.6			(3.3)
1963	4.8			77.8
1964	(0.8)			17.2
1965	0.3			18.2
1966	13.0			185.0
1967	11.0			264.0
1968	1.0			392.0
1969	(3.0)			518.0
1970	66.0			617.0
1971	42.0			651.0
1972	59.0			601.0
1973	117.0			598.0
1974	99.0			777.0
1975	47.0			1,172.0
1976	70.0			1,523.0
1977	80.0	60.0		1,652.0
1978	71.0	34.0		2,382.0
1979	28.0	6.0		3,038.0
1980	6.0	31.0		2,568.0
1981	86.0	14.0	39.0	3,603.0
1982	62.0	13.0	*N.A.*	3,216.0
1983	65.0	176.0	*N.A.*	3,391.0
1984	109.0	309.0	21.0	3,514.0
1985	234.0	861.0	121.0	3,611.0
1986	435.0	262.0	39.0	2,901.0
1987	601.0	(151.0)	38.0	2,836.0
1988	871.0	(511.0)	29.0	1,796.0
1989	758.0	(59.0)	30.0	1,263.0
1990	715.0	431.0	380.0	940.0
1991	1,160.0	3,116.0	*N.A.*	2,033.0
1992	550.0	3,414.0	2,328.0	966.0

Source: IMF, *International Financial Statistics* (Washington, D.C.: IMF, various years).

Note: FDI–Foreign direct investment. *N.A.*–Not available.

bank presidents who did not provide them money on demand. The prime motivation for the government's encroachment on central bank authority beginning in 1956 was the need to raise campaign financing to compete successfully with an ever-growing political opposition. Perhaps the single most important indication of the uncertainty President Syngman Rhee faced is the fact that his own party's vice-presidential candidate lost in the 1956 elections, and Rhee was forced to govern with an opposition party vice-president from 1956 to 1960.[4]

In the minds of Korea's political leaders at this time, the demands of securing power outweighed any concern with the reaction of international financiers to particular changes in economic policy or economic policymaking institutions. The influence of international financiers was limited for objective reasons as well. Patterns in foreign lending were closely tied to geopolitical concerns. Initially this meant that foreign loans and aid were abundant. Korea's political leadership took the U.S. loan and aid program for granted and made the correct assumption that Korea's security importance to the United States would outweigh any disgruntlement with Korean economic policies. The United States did monitor efforts to amend the original central bank charter and saw them as dangerous to Korea's future economic health.[5] Diplomatic suggestions were made to the Korean government, but no specific pressure was ever exercised with regard to central bank authority.

When U.S. loans and aid declined (see Table 7.2), it was clearly because the United States considered South Korea relatively secure against Communism. Because lending rose and fell in response to U.S. security concerns, over which the Koreans had little control, Korea still had little incentive to seek creditworthiness. The Korean political leadership's largely correct perception of the delinkage between international financing and domestic economic policy in the late 1950s and early 1960s was a condition that helped encourage the wanton disregard for legally stipulated central bank independence. Other indicators of the objective need to prioritize competition for international investment also suggest permissive conditions. As Table 7.1 shows, import coverage was high (by Korean standards) and growing from 1956 through 1961.

Although the political leadership changed between 1956 and 1962, the governments of this period shared a strong opposition to central bank independence that is clearly reflected in governor turnover rates. In this period there were six different Bank of Korea governors (see Table 7.3). The Liberal Party government, in particular, sought to use the central bank in efforts to raise campaign financing. Direct requests to the Bank of Korea to aid the Liberal Party in its fund-raising efforts were a prime source of conflict between the government and the central bank at this time.

TABLE 7.3
Change of Government, Regime Type, and Central Bank Governor in South Korea

President	*Regime*	*Bank of Korea Governor*
Rhee Syngman (1948–60)	SEMI-DEM.	Ku Yŏng-Sŏ (1950–51)
		Kim Yu-Taek (1951–56)
		Kim Chin-Hyŏng (1956–60)
Chang Myon (1960–61)		Bae Ŭi-Hwan (1960)
		Chu Ye-Yŏng (1960–61)
Park Chung Hee (1963–79)	MILITARY	Yu Ch'ang-Sun (1961–62)
		Min Pyŏng-To (1962–63)
		Lee Chŏng-Hwan (1963)
		Kim Se-Ryŏn (1963–67)
		Sŏ Chin-Su (1967–70)
		Kim Sŏng-Hwan (1970–78)
		Shin Pyŏng-Hyŏn (1978–80)
Choi Kyu-Ha (1979–80)		Kim Chun-Sông (1980–82)
		Ha Yŏng-Ki (1982–83)
		Choi Ch'ang-Rak (1983–86)
		Park Sŏng-Sang (1986–88)
Roh Tae Woo (1988–93)	SEMI-DEM.	Kim Kŏn (1988–92)
		Cho Sun (1992–93)
Kim Young Sam (1993–)		Kim Myŏng-Ho (1993–96)
		Lee Kyung-Shik (1996)

The second governor of the Bank of Korea, Kim Yu-Taek, both refused to provide loans to the Liberal Party and rebuffed the "invitation" to become a member of the party's central committee.[6] In order to increase its control over the bank, the Liberal Party leadership, through the Ministry of Finance, proposed amending the central bank charter to give the minister of finance veto power over decisions of the Monetary Board. (The Monetary Board's relationship to the Bank of Korea was intended to be like that of the Federal Reserve Board to the Federal Reserve banks.) Kim Yu-Taek called one of the authors of the original statute, Bloomfield, to Korea to investigate and report in defense of the bank's independence as originally stipulated. This report was not made public, but was circulated within the government, angering many cabinet and party officials. When this tactic failed to deter government politicians, Kim broke with protocol and issued a public denunciation of the minister of finance. The government's State Council voted to force Kim to resign.

The bank's fourth governor, Bae Ŭi-Hwan, also clashed with the government over Liberal Party financing and proposals to change the central bank statute.[7] Bae was extremely critical of what he saw as president Syngman Rhee's use of the Bank of Korea as his "personal cash register."[8] He also strenuously opposed government proposals to change the central bank charter, arguing that the Bank of Korea needed more, not less, statutory independence. His swan song was a newspaper article alluding to corrupt campaign financing practices involving the banking system and suggesting that the Monetary Board was irresponsible in hesitating to admit its knowledge of the corruption. Bae went on to argue that this type of corruption could only be avoided if the Bank of Korea were allowed genuine political independence. He was forced to resign shortly thereafter.

This scenario of conflict between the central bank director and the government was repeated a third time during the governorship of Yu Ch'ang-Sun. In this case the Liberal Party had raised funds through manipulation of the stock market, which led to a minor financial crisis known as the "Padong stock market scandal."[9] Yu managed to convince the Monetary Board to refuse government requests that the central bank continue providing funds to help cover up the manipulation and calm financial markets. Shortly thereafter, in December 1961, the Ministry of Finance presented a central bank charter amendment to the cabinet for approval. Governor Yu had not been consulted about the amendment; he resigned in protest.

The governorship of Min Pyŏng-To was also curtailed by conflict with the government, which included a proposal to remove bank supervisory authority from the central bank,[10] the sudden end of central bank authority over foreign exchange policy, and the contract of a foreign loan concluded by the government without consultation of the central bank.[11]

Although, de facto, the Bank of Korea never exercised the full authority granted it under its original charter, the amendment promulgated May 24, 1962, formalized the central bank's political weakness. Under this amendment the minister of finance was given veto power over all Monetary Board decisions. The minister of finance was also given authority to oversee the Bank of Korea's bookkeeping. The Bank Supervisory Office of the Bank of Korea was turned into a separate entity placed under direct Monetary Board jurisdiction. The policy scope of the Monetary Board was also reduced from covering both exchange and credit policy to simply covering credit policy. This left a central bank that over the next several decades did little more than implement credit policies in line with policies designed by the Economic Planning Board and the Ministry of Finance. In fact, the bank was commonly called the "Namdaemun *branch* of the Finance Ministry," referring to the Seoul district in which the bank is located.

The Central Bank Remains Weak

Over the two decades following the 1962 charter revision there was little change in the Bank of Korea's authority.[12] Political stability ceased to be a problem during the Park regime, the need for international creditworthiness remained low, and capital account regulations implied a consistently low level of openness, creating little incentive for change in central bank authority. Korea suffered oscillation in international reserves and some change in the relative interest margin to London interbank rates. But the growth in the supply of international financial resources compared with demand, strong government regulation of financial transactions, Korea's relatively low levels of indebtedness and successful transition to export-led growth, especially compared to that of many Latin American countries, combined to keep politicians' perceptions of the need for international creditworthiness low. Even though Korea suffered economic troubles concomitant with the oil price hikes of the 1970s, a variety of factors vitiated the need for political leaders to be concerned with making domestic institutional changes in order to secure international creditworthiness.[13]

In accord with this low concern for international creditworthiness, the history of central bank politics in the two decades after 1962 reveals only minor instances of further challenge to Bank of Korea authority, counterbalanced by sporadic, also minor, Bank of Korea backlashes. For example, there was open debate again in 1968 about the locus of authority over commercial bank supervision. The central bank governor, Sŏ Chin-Su clashed with the minister of finance over a proposal to transfer some responsibility to the central bank; the latter backed down and as a result resigned.[14] Some transfer of bank supervisory authority to the central bank occurred, but this authority was repeatedly challenged in the following years.

Several years later the Bank of Korea was on the losing side of a controversy over details of the 1972 Emergency Decree.[15] The debate concerned the level below which savings in the informal financial sector would be exempt from confiscation. For a number of reasons the Bank of Korea wanted to maximize the squeeze on the informal sector, with a low exemption point. The minister of finance and others wanted to minimize political fall-out and sought a higher level that would maximize the number of individuals exempted. The minister of finance prevailed.

In the mid-1970s President Park Chung Hee cut Bank of Korea salaries, which had been high compared with those of other government employees, and thus contributed to low morale and a small exodus of some of the best central bank personnel. The story circulates that this move was Park's response to his wife's complaints about how well-off the neighboring central banker's household appeared. Specifically, Park investigated the nonsalary perquisites of Bank of Korea employment and eliminated many of them.[16]

After this blow to Bank of Korea capacity came a small compensating victory. Governor Shin Pyŏng-Hyŏn successfully lobbied the minister of finance in the late 1970s to grant the Bank of Korea power to formulate, though not necessarily implement, quarterly credit programs.[17] Perhaps more significant, in 1981 the bank obtained a promise from the Ministry of Finance to permit the central bank autonomy in its own operational budgeting. This was a right accorded the central bank by law in the Bank of Korea statute but not followed in practice.[18]

The issue of bank supervision arose again in the early 1980s. In 1982–83 Minister of Finance Kang Kyŏng-Shik presented the governor of the Bank of Korea, Ha Yŏng-Ki, an amendment proposing to remove bank supervision rights from the central bank. Ha managed to block the amendment but had to resign as a result.

While there was no international financial pressure on Korean political leaders to increase central bank authority in the 1970s, there were domestic pressures *against* doing so. The Korean government had developed a system of industrial and government finance dependent upon extensive state control. As a subordinate arm of the government the central bank played an important role in this system. The Bank of Korea oversaw the commercial banks' implementation of credit distribution plans drawn up by the Economic Planning Board in accord with overall industrialization goals.[19] Furthermore, the central banks' implementation of credit and interest rate controls limited development of the financial sector. This kept demand for money high; high money demand was crucial to government finance through seignorage.[20]

A Failed Independence Movement, 1987–88

The year 1987 marked the beginning of a complex several-year effort to increase central bank authority that ultimately failed. The movement had popular origins and became caught up in the hesitant rebirth of party politics. As Table 7.1 indicates, the push for central bank independence coincided with a very large rise in foreign exchange reserves and a return to import coverage levels not sustained for more than a year since the late 1960s. Domestic actors in favor of increased central bank authority therefore did not enjoy the option of seeking support for their movement from increasingly influential international financiers.

The issue of central bank independence was brought to public debate by a small group of Bank of Korea employees as part of the Korean democracy movement. Central bank independence, they argued, should be a necessary corollary of democratization.[21] For slightly different reasons large-scale industrialists also joined the call of Bank of Korea employees for central bank independence.[22] Bank of Korea directors, as opposed to employees, also argued for increased central bank authority but recommended different tactics. They suggested that authority could not simply be restored to the central bank by constitutional decree and called for quiet negotiation for modification of the existing central bank charter, rather than public mobilization for constitutional change.[23] Bank of Korea directors wanted to eliminate the finance minister's voting rights on the Monetary Board, to make the governor of the central bank, rather than the finance minister, chair of the Monetary Board, to increase central bank policy jurisdiction to foreign exchange and nonbank financial markets, to eliminate the Ministry of Finance's role as central bank auditor and its right to appeal Monetary Board decisions, and to shift responsibility for recommendation of the central bank governor from the Ministry of Finance to the president.[24]

The debate over tactics for ensuring central bank independence became caught up in party politics and the campaign leading up to the 1987 presidential and 1988 congressional elections. The National Assembly held hearings in August 1987. The Bank of Korea governor Park Sŏng-Sang argued for increased authority and Minister of Finance Sakong Il, testified against it.[25] Sakong Il argued that the government's overall responsibility for economic performance and social welfare mandated that it have control over important policies such as monetary policy. He also noted that evidence from other countries suggests that there is no guarantee that increased statutory independence of a central bank will bring monetary stability. Sakong Il further claimed that Ministry of Finance intervention in central bank affairs in Korea was minimal.

All major parties included the promise of increased central bank independence in their campaign platforms. The party of the incumbent president, Roh Tae Woo, was the Democratic Justice Party. The formerly united opposition party, the Democratic Party, split into the left-leaning Peace Democratic Party, led by Kim Dae Jung, and the more centrist Democratic Party for Unification, led by Kim Young Sam. Followers of the late president Park Chung Hee also formed a new opposition party during this electoral campaign: the relatively conservative New Democratic Republican Party led by Kim Jong Pil. The Democratic Justice Party argued that constitutional revision was not necessary. In its view, amendment of the existing Bank of Korea law would be sufficient. The opposition Peace Democratic Party and Democratic Party for Unification adhered to the position that constitutional revision was necessary. The New Democratic Republican Party, perhaps because there were a number of former government bureaucrats among its leadership—such as former finance minister Kim Yŏng-Hwan—argued for little deviation from the status quo.

After winning the presidential election, Roh Tae Woo announced that the guarantee of central bank independence would be a primary concern during the first year of his term. In July 1988 the three opposition parties announced a joint proposal for a new Bank of Korea law that largely echoed the preferences of the central bank directors.[26] The main changes proposed were that the chairmanship of the Monetary Board should be held by the central bank governor rather than the finance minister and that authority over nonbank financial institutions and foreign exchange matters should be passed from the Ministry of Finance to the Bank of Korea.

The government, through the Democratic Justice Party, responded to the opposition proposal with a proposal of its own.[27] This proposal conceded that the chairman of the Monetary Board should be the Bank of Korea governor and that the president, rather than the minister of finance, should choose the Bank of Korea governor. But the proposal suggested that all bank supervision authority should be transferred from the central bank to the Ministry of Finance and reiterated that ultimate authority for monetary policy should lie with that ministry.[28]

The two most important points of debate between the Bank of Korea and the opposition parties, on the one hand, and the Ministry of Finance and the government party, on the other, concerned who should have authority over financial institution supervision and whether or not the Bank of Korea needed guarantees of increased independence. Ironically the two sides used similar arguments to defend different positions. The Ministry of Finance's rationale for removing financial supervisory authority from the Bank of Korea was to ensure "checks and balances" of power. Its argument against central bank independence rested on the need for coordination in order to have effective macroeconomic management. The Bank of Korea reversed this logic, arguing that independence provides important checks and balances for executive branch power but that coordination is necessary for effective financial supervision.[29]

Through back-room lobbying the government party persuaded the

Monetary Board to release a letter supporting the government–Ministry of Finance position. Despite holding a seat on the Monetary Board, the Bank of Korea governor was excluded from the letter-drafting process.[30] The letter stated the Monetary Board's belief that authority over monetary policy and financial administration should reside with the Ministry of Finance, although there should be "some restraints" on the minister of finance. The letter suggested that the Monetary Board (which is appointed by the minister of finance) itself elect its chairman, who would then serve concurrently as head of the central bank.[31] This political maneuvering greatly annoyed the central bank employees' union, which issued a statement arguing that the Monetary Board's actions revealed opportunistic motives and complete subordination to the Ministry of Finance. The employees called for the resignation of the Monetary Board.[32]

In responding to the Monetary Board letter, Bank of Korea officials also particularly objected to the possibility that the Ministry of Finance, through its appointment of Monetary Board members, could select the governor of the Bank of Korea.[33] During six meetings over two weeks in late August 1988, the Bank of Korea and the Ministry of Finance were unable to reach a compromise.[34]

In the meantime, the government pressured the opposition parties to modify their support of the Bank of Korea. The opposition New Democratic Republican Party renounced its commitment to the unified opposition proposal and put forward a new proposal much closer to the position of the Ministry of Finance and the governing Democratic Justice Party.[35] By November the other two opposition parties had also decided to more or less support the Ministry of Finance and Democratic Justice Party position.[36] They withdrew this proposal after hearing strenuous objections from the Bank of Korea, however, and fell back on proposals closer to their original pro–central bank stance.[37]

With little hope of relying on opposition party support to help win independence, the Bank of Korea employees turned to the populace, launching a street campaign to collect signatures on a petition supporting the Bank of Korea's proposals for increased authority.[38] Once again the Bank of Korea and the Ministry of Finance held a series of private meetings to try to hammer out a compromise. These negotiations dragged on through the first half of 1989.[39] In May the Ministry of Finance broke off the talks and submitted a unilateral proposal to the governing party. The governing party requested the opinion of the Monetary Board, which reportedly came to shouting and fisticuffs over the issue without being able to break its deadlock. Unable to reach an agreement to support the Ministry of Finance proposal, the Monetary Board recommended dropping the idea of legal change in the Bank of Korea's status.

The 1987–88 Bank of Korea independence movement failed because the government mobilized the power of a semi-authoritarian regime against it. This stance was possible because Korea's economic situation did not demand that political elites assign a high priority to the competition for international capital. Foreign borrowing had been well managed, Korean growth remained strong, and capital controls provided assurances against sudden capital flight.

Conclusion

Korean central bank history highlights the way in which politicians' perceptions of low need and value of competing for international creditworthiness can jeopardize central bank independence. If objective conditions do not put pressure on political leaders to give priority to the competition for international capital, they are free to follow the logic of the domestic political economy. Accordingly, tenure insecurity of government politicians and abundant international aid worked against the institutionalization of Bank of Korea independence in the late 1950s and early 1960s. A variety of factors—heavy government regulation of the financial sector, fairly strong export performance relative to debt, and favorable interest rates on foreign loans (compared with those of other middle-income developing countries)—kept the need to compete for international capital and creditworthiness low throughout the 1970s and 1980s, and central bank status remained poor.

The picture that emerges from Korean central bank history on the relationship between de facto and de jure authority is similar to that emerging from the histories of Thailand and Mexico. To the extent that there is any relationship, de jure change appears to follow from de facto change, as in the 1962 Korean statute reform episode.

It also seems clear in this case that both technical capacity and strong central bank leadership are, to a large extent, a function of the preferences of political leaders. Many of the Korean central bank governors of the late 1950s and early 1960s had as much potential to become strong central bank governors as did Puey in Thailand or Gómez in Mexico, but could not overcome political obstacles. Similarly, while the Bank of Korea attracted highly trained personnel in the 1950s, it became a less desirable place of employment for the best of Korea's young economists as it became more nearly an administrative arm of the Economic Planning Board and the Ministry of Finance.[40]

Foreign portfolio finance is slowly increasing in Korea but plays a smaller role than in any of the other countries examined in Chapters 5–8. As suggested by the forced resignation in 1993 of Sun Cho, one of Korea's most widely respected and powerful central bank governors, the Korean central bank is likely to continue in its current subservient position until the nation's international economic position deteriorates significantly and/or the country finds itself with a well-institutionalized democracy.

Eight

The Politics of Changing Central Bank Authority: Brazil

THERE ARE two identifiable turning points in Brazilian central banking history: 1964 and 1967. Lack of change in the 1970s and 1980s also requires explanation. In 1964, economic crisis and the need for international creditworthiness helped bring about both a military coup and the creation of an official central bank, after two decades of debate over the nature of official financial institutions. As Table 8.1 indicates, restoration of import coverage, growth of Euromarket lending, and export levels that lagged only modestly behind debt took away pressure to maintain international creditworthiness, and with rising debate in the military over economic policy, the newly created central bank quickly lost its promise of authority and independence after 1967. Brazilian creditworthiness measured by an international comparison of interest paid on its international loans (Table 4.3) remained good during the 1970s. In the 1980s, despite higher interest rates on foreign borrowing (by international comparison), rising debt-to-export ratios, and growing short-term debt, Brazilian political leaders did not perceive a great need to compete for international capital (see Table 8.2). Government regulation of the financial sector was significant, and this regulation mitigated the need and value of competing for international capital and creditworthiness.[1] Import coverage remained adequate. Furthermore, the incentive to maintain policy flexibility with which to try to buy political support in the uncertain context of political liberalization provided an important motive *not* to increase central bank authority in the 1980s.

SUMOC: Precursor to a Central Bank

In the 1940s, spurred by developments in the international monetary arena and by a strong desire to avoid a repeat of the inflation experienced early in the decade, government technocrats pressed the issue of creating a central bank.[2] But Brazil's largest commercial bank and longtime state bank, the Banco do Brasil, and the agricultural and commercial elite represented among its owners, resisted.

TABLE 8.1
Indicators of Brazil's Need to Compete for International Capital

Year	*Import Coverage*	*Foreign Exchange Reserves (U.S. millions)*	*Average Annual Interest on Private Credit Minus the Eurodollar or Libor Interest Rate*[a]
1945	7.06	312	
1946	6.83	396	
1947	4.14	420	
1948	4.67	441	
1949	4.33	403	
1950	3.80	348	
1951	1.18	198	
1952	1.25	209	
1953	2.58	284	
1954	1.19	161	
1955	1.54	168	
1956	2.79	287	
1957	1.22	152	
1958	1.24	140	
1959	0.35	40	
1960	0.48	58	
1961	1.52	185	
1962	0.49	60	
1963	0.56	69	
1964	1.46	154	
1965	4.61	421	
1966	2.95	368	
1967	1.02	142	
1968	1.13	200	
1969	3.17	599	
1970	4.05	962	−1.2
1971	4.70	1,450	1.4
1972	9.62	3,836	1.9
1973	10.34	6,030	0.1
1974	4.13	4,874	0.7
1975	3.23	3,653	1.9
1976	5.33	6,101	1.9
1977	6.14	6,787	2.4
1978	9.09	11,406	1.5
1979	5.05	8,342	−0.4
1980	2.42	5,042	−0.9
1981	2.93	5,888	0.1
1982	2.07	3,641	−0.7
1983	3.11	4,355	1.0
1984	9.08	11,507	1.5

TABLE 8.1 *(cont.)*

Year	*Import Coverage*	*Foreign Exchange Reserves (U.S. millions)*	*Average Annual Interest on Private Credit Minus the Eurodollar or Libor Interest Rate*[a]
1985	8.88	10,604	1.3
1986	4.48	5,803	2.2
1987	4.56	6,299	0.2
1988	5.21	6,971	1.5
1989	4.52	7,535	0.5
1990	3.97	7,430	0.5
1991	*N.A.*	*N.A.*	1.5
1992	*N.A.*	*N.A.*	4.1
1993	*N.A.*	*N.A.*	*N.A.*

Source: Calculated from IMF, *International Financial Statistics* (Washington, D.C.: IMF, various years), and World Bank, *World Debt Tables* (Washington, D.C.: World Bank, various years).

Note: The *World Debt Tables* changed the definition of the numerator in 1980. *N.A.*–Not available.

a. Libor–London interbank offer rate.

The Banco do Brasil had been the primary source of funds supporting São Paulo businessmen and, in particular, the government's coffee price support programs since 1906.[3] The political pressure of São Paulo entrepreneurs, coffee planters, and industrialists played a large role in shaping government financing needs and the Banco do Brasil's actions. Over the course of the 1920s, as Brazil's First Republic drew to a close, the Banco do Brasil became a quasi-central bank with the main goal of directly and indirectly supporting first the credit-hungry businessmen of São Paulo, then mostly coffee growers, and later industrialists.[4] The interests of the Banco do Brasil and its owners and clients were so antithetical to those of Brazil's international creditors that a 1923 British loan negotiation team decided that the only way to guarantee that Brazil would follow sound financial policies was for British creditors to buy the Banco do Brasil.[5]

The more practical idea of limiting Banco do Brasil functions and creating a genuine central bank alongside it was first seriously considered in 1931. In that year, as part of British financiers' evaluation of Brazilian creditworthiness, the adviser Otto Niemeyer traveled to Brazil. He wrote a report on Brazilian financial policy that included a detailed statute for a separate central bank which would usurp the Banco do Brasil's central banking functions.[6] While some private bankers supported the proposal, the Banco do Brasil and São Paulo businessmen

TABLE 8.2
Foreign Investment in Brazil (stock of investments, in U.S. millions)

Year	*FDI*	*Bonds*	*Equities*	*Loans*
1949	44.5			31.5
1950	39.1			23.4
1951	63.5			28.8
1952	94.5			28.8
1953	59.9			22.9
1954	51.4			110.2
1955	78.7			109.4
1956	140.0			83.0
1957	179.0			57.0
1958	128.0			172.0
1959	158.0			192.0
1960	138.0			72.0
1961	147.0			361.0
1962	132.0			177.0
1963	87.0			142.0
1964	86.0			125.0
1965	128.0			158.0
1966	159.0			282.0
1967	115.0			193.0
1968	136.0			183.0
1969	252.0			491.0
1970	421.0			1,470.0
1971	535.0			2,069.0
1972	550.0			4,036.0
1973	1,156.0			3,825.0
1974	1,103.0			5,869.0
1975	1,346.0			5,070.0
1976	1,567.0			6,958.0
1977	1,567.0			7,182.0
1978	1,597.0			12,326.0
1979	1,869.0			7,854.0

opposed it and succeeded in getting the report shelved, as they had the 1923 proposal.

The political power of the Banco do Brasil's supporters was based largely on the heavy representation of coffee planters in Congress, which was closed after Getulio Vargas's 1937 coup. In 1945, the government economist Octavio de Gouvêia Bulhões convinced President Vargas to take advantage of the soon-to-end eight-year congressional recess and decree the creation of the Superintendency of Money and Credit (SUMOC) as a precursor to a central bank.[7]

TABLE 8.2 *(cont.)*

Year	*FDI*	*Bonds*	*Equities*	*Loans*
1980	1,470.0			13,128.0
1981	2,142.0			11,232.0
1982	2,647.0			6,583.0
1983	1,456.0			10,895.0
1984	1,559.0			15,963.0
1985	1,348.0	(222.0)	(15.0)	13,221.0
1986	320.0	(460.0)	10.0	13,533.0
1987	1,225.0	(489.0)	61.0	14,368.0
1988	2,969.0	(13.0)	189.0	31,000.0
1989	1,267.0	(364.0)	(57.0)	5,137.0
1990	901.0	(72.0)	584.0	3,072.0
1991	972.0	3,230.0	578.0	15,274.0
1992	1,454.0	1,466.0	*N.A.*	*N.A.*

Source: IMF, *International Financial Statistics* (Washington, D.C.: IMF, various years).
Note: FDI–Foreign direct investment. *N.A.*–Not available.

The Superintendency of Money and Credit was created in 1945 as a "halfway" central bank because of Banco do Brasil opposition to creating a genuine central bank. It was responsible for foreign exchange policy, interest rates, the registration of foreign capital, and commercial bank reserve requirements, and was authorized to conduct open market operations. Essentially, SUMOC was given jurisdiction over policy formulation while the Banco do Brasil continued to be the executor of foreign exchange policy and, to some extent, interest rate policy. The SUMOC statute authorizes the minister of finance to contract with the Banco do Brasil to execute the policies of SUMOC,[8] and stipulates the bank as its financial agent.

The Banco do Brasil also continued to enjoy other privileges that would have made SUMOC control of monetary and exchange policy difficult even if it had more legal authority over policy execution. The Banco do Brasil offered the government virtually costless, limitless automatic overdraft protection. It was also the legally stipulated recipient of mandatory commercial bank reserve requirements while enjoying exemption from such requirements, despite significant commercial banking operations of its own.

Furthermore, SUMOC was housed in the Banco do Brasil building. It had a limited number of personnel, selected from Banco do Brasil staff, and virtually no autonomous technical capacity until a government decree created a statistics department within SUMOC in 1950.[9] SUMOC did not publish its own annual reports but rather was given a few pages in the Banco do Brasil annual report.

These conditions "annihilated . . . SUMOC in the cradle."[10] SUMOC was "confined to the role the Bank of Brazil sought to assign to it."[11] SUMOC spent its first five years promoting mergers among commercial banks during a period of great instability in the private bank sector.

The archeology of SUMOC's failures between 1945 and 1964 is predictable. The directorship of SUMOC changed hands fifteen times in the nineteen years between 1945 and 1964. SUMOC personnel frequently complained to U.S. embassy personnel about their inability to pursue money-stabilizing goals.[12] SUMOC was inevitably caught up in struggles between the minister of finance and the Banco do Brasil president, whose powers in the economic policy process were considered roughly equal. SUMOC was weakest when the Banco do Brasil president and the minister of finance were closely allied. SUMOC initiatives came closest to success when it could count on Ministry of Finance support in the face of Banco do Brasil intransigence. One such instance occurred while Horacio Lafer was finance minister (1953). Lafer clashed seriously with the Banco do Brasil president, Ricardo Jafet, and had to resign. Before that, he provided political protection for SUMOC to raise the issue of its right to solicit information about Banco do Brasil loans and inspect the bank's books. In the end, however, the Banco do Brasil "obtained a half victory that constituted a total defeat for the SUMOC."[13]

The pattern is also evident during Lucas Lopes's tenure as finance minister (1958–59). SUMOC proposed institutional reforms transferring some of the Banco do Brasil's executive authority in the area of monetary and exchange policy to SUMOC. That the proposal could be advanced is testimony to the strong support of the finance minister. Nonetheless it eventually sank into the abyss of growing politico-economic crisis that cost Lopes his job and intensified as the 1960s approached.

SUMOC was the official Brazilian interlocutor with the IMF, but this did little to bolster its authority in a context of strong opposition to IMF conditions from Brazil's political leaders. SUMOC tried to use its ties to the IMF as a lever in debates over government policy and issues concerning its own scope of authority. "Forever worried, like the entire SUMOC group, with external repercussions," during 1958 debate over stabilization Garrido Torres, executive director of SUMOC in 1958, warned of "the weakening of the Brazilian government's position overseas for the negotiation of loans."[14] Ultimately Banco do Brasil dominance of SUMOC created difficulties in SUMOC–IMF relations. The IMF placed greatest confidence in the Brazilian representatives to the

Fund, including Octavio Gouvêia de Bulhões and Francisco Alves dos Santos Filho. Nonetheless the IMF's vote of confidence in these officials was not sufficient to overcome opposition, which stemmed from incentives created by a fragmented party system, to their economic vision.

Debating the Need for a Central Bank

Brazil's nineteen-year debate over central bank legislation, from 1945 to 1964, must be understood in the context of the tremendous political uncertainty facing the nation's political leaders in that period. All the civilian leaders of that era experienced tenure insecurity, as indicated by the frequent changes in government leadership. Creating a central bank implied reducing the scope for action of the Banco do Brasil, Brazil's largest commercial bank and also Brazil's longtime state bank. Until the military coup of 1964 no political leaders had a strong enough coalition either to give up the direct source of government finance the government had in the Banco do Brasil or to incur the political costs of circumscribing Banco do Brasil operations when the bank was backed by powerful industrial and agricultural interests. Coffee exporters, for example, required inexpensive government-subsidized credit from the Banco do Brasil to weather cycles in coffee production and business.

Getúlio Vargas, who had governed Brazil under a dictatorship from 1937 to 1945, won the presidency in free national elections in 1950. To overcome his dictatorial legacy he was determined to prove himself a successful democratic leader. Most important, he had to avoid providing the military with an excuse to intervene. Given the weakness and fragmentation of the Brazilian party system, this required a careful balancing act. Vargas had been elected for a constitutionally defined five-year term with a 49 percent plurality and help from an extremely diverse coalition, including the rural elite–based Partido Social Democrático (Social Democratic Party or SDP), the labor-based Partido Trabalhista (Brazilian Workers' Party or PTB), the Partido Social Progressista (Progressive Social Party or PSP—the personal machine of the populist politician Adhemar), and even a minority group within the União Democrática Nacional (National Democratic Union or UDN—a party linked to one army faction and united largely around opposition to Vargas's dictatorial populism). Although a minority within the National Democratic Union had supported Vargas, the party leadership tried to block Vargas's inauguration on a constitutional technicality. A military tribunal rejected the appeal. No single party had a majority in Congress, and most were represented in Vargas's cabinet.

In this context Vargas pursued a strategy of reconciliation, trying to win full National Democratic Union support. This merely succeeded in alienating the Brazilian Workers' Party and other of Vargas's left-leaning allies. Vargas tried to combine nationalism and orthodoxy in his economic policy in order to maintain the support of as many classes or sectors as possible. For example, to gain support for a much-needed monetary stabilization program in 1953 he appointed Goulart, a politician with a reputation for collaborating with Communists and militant labor leaders, as his labor minister. Ultimately this move led to a demand by the military and the National Democratic Union for Vargas's resignation. Despondent, Vargas committed suicide. His vice-president, João Café Filho, succeeded him for a brief period until new elections brought Juscelino Kubitschek to the presidency in 1956 (see Table 8.3).

Kubitschek's political situation was also tenuous. He was elected with a 36 percent plurality and support from a Democratic Socialist and Workers' Party alliance. As it had done earlier, the National Democratic Union tried, and failed, to block the new president's inauguration. The military staged a "preventive" coup to ensure that Kubitschek could take office. Like Vargas, Kubitschek tried to govern without appealing to a single identifiable party or movement, endeavoring to preserve the broadest appeal possible. Although Kubitschek managed to survive his term, national political instability rose with the election of Jánio Quadros. Quadros ran in the 1960 elections with a National Democratic Union endorsement but tried to maintain distance from the party whenever possible. He ran as an outsider, with an "antipolitician," anticorruption, anti-inefficiency platform. This stance left him without an organized political base when he came to power. He was forced to resign from the presidency within a year of taking office and was succeeded by his vice-president, João Goulart, after a ten-day interregnum during which both pro- and anti-Goulart military factions debated the merits of a coup.

This national-level political fragmentation hindered the ability of any political leader to build a coalition behind bank reform. Armijo's characterization of the 1980s holds equally well for the 1950s: "Political parties were not strong or deep. It was possible to arrange a coalition to block . . . economic initiatives, but not one to pass serious stabilization programs or far-reaching financial reforms."[15] SUMOC officials observed and lamented the need for, and lack of, a strong presidential commitment and political push to get central bank legislation passed.[16]

In this situation domestic political pressures, specifically the incentives stemming from constant uncertainty, swamped the need for international creditworthiness. Brazil's need for international capital rose

TABLE 8.3
Change of Government, Regime Type, and Central Bank Governor in Brazil

President	*Regime*	*SUMOC Director/Banco Central Governor*
Enrico Gaspar Dutra (1946–51)	Democratic	José Vieira Machado (1945–51)
Getúlio Dornelles Vargas (1951–54)		Valter Moreira Sales 1951–52)
		Egidio da Camara Sousa (1952)
		José Soares Maciel Filho (1952–54)
João Café Filho (1954–55)		Octavio Gouvêia de Bulhões (1954–55)
		Prudente de Morais Neto (1955)
		Inar Dias de Figueiredo (1955–56)
Juscelino Kubitschek de Oliveira (1956–61)		Eurico de Aguiar Sales (1955–56)
		José Joaquim Cardoso de Melo Neto (1957–58)
		José Garrido Torres (1958–59)
		Marco de Sousa Dantas (1959–60)
Jánio da Silva Quadros (1961)		Fransisco Vieira de Alencar (1960–61)
João Belchor Marques Goulart (1961)–64)		Octavio Gouvêia de Bulhões (1961–63)
		Julio Augusto Dias Carneiro (1963–64)
Humberto de Alencar Castelo Branco (1964–67)	Military	Denio Chagas Nogueira (1964–67)
Arthur da Costa e Silva (1967–69)		Rui Aguiar da Silva Lerma (1967)
		Ernane Galvêas (1968–74)
Emilio Garrastazu Medici (1969–74)		
Ernesto Geisel (1974–79)		
		Paulo H. Pereira Luna (1975–79)
João Baptista de Oliveira Figueredo (1979–85)		
		Carlos Langoni (1980–82)
		Affonso Celso Pastore (1983–84)
José Sarney (1985–89)	Democratic	Fernão Carlos Botelho Bracher (1985)
		Fernando Milliet de Oliveira (1986)
Fernando Collor de Melo (1989–92)		Elmo de Araujo Camoe (1988)
		Wadico Waldir Bucchi (1990)
		Ibrahim Eris (1990–91)
		Fransisco Roberto André Gros (1991–92)
Hamar Franco (1992–93)		Gustavo Jorge Laboissiére Loyola (1992–93)
Fernando Henrique Cardoso (1994–)		Pedro Sampaio Malan (1993–94)
		Gustavo Jorge Labroissiére Loyola (1994–)

during the 1950s. Import coverage fell 69 percent in 1951, 54 percent in 1954, and 56 percent in 1957 and hovered between 1.18 and 2.79 months (see Table 8.1). But the logic of trying to remain in power in a polarized, unstable democracy weighed much more heavily on politicians' minds than competing for international capital—until import coverage fell below 1 month in 1959 and foreign investment in Brazil virtually ceased in the early 1960s (as is evident in Table 8.2). But that is getting ahead of our story.

In 1946, immediately after the SUMOC was founded as a precursor to a central bank, President Enrico Dutra had charged his minister of finance, Pedro Luís Correia e Castro, with writing thorough-going bank reform legislation that would provide for the establishment of a genuinely independent central bank. As the debate over central bank foundation became prolonged, it became clearer and clearer that SUMOC was inadequate as a central banking institution.

The political debate over bank reform over the next nineteen years was complex, reflecting many cleavages among and within economic groups and political parties.[17] There were at least eight alternative proposals, hundreds of congressional amendments, and several special study commissions.[18] These proposals covered a broad banking reform agenda. Debate centered on the specification of the public and private sector roles in the financial market, the place of foreign capital, the creation of a central bank and its relationship to the Banco do Brasil, the power and composition of the National Monetary Council (CMN) which would replace SUMOC, and the definition of selective credit policy. Roughly speaking, international creditors, national bankers, and the conservative National Democratic Union favored creation of a central bank which would take over many Banco do Brasil functions, although they disagreed on its balance of power with the National Monetary Council and the related issue of the composition of the council. The Workers' Party, together with the industrialists' association Federacão das Industrias do Estado de São Paulo (Federation of Industries of the State of São Paulo or FIESP), favored turning the Banco do Brasil into a central bank and having broad sectoral representation on the CMN.

The original proposal was written by Finance Minister Correia e Castro, who had earlier been a longtime employee of the Banco do Brasil as well as, more briefly, a politician. He was determined to elaborate and implement a plan to eradicate Brazil's century-old inflationary tendency, which had been aggravated by wartime shortages. Ideally, Correia e Castro must have recognized, an independent central bank would have increased the likelihood of success for an orthodox inflation-fighting strategy. But he was not successful. Several years later this institutional lacuna was highlighted by a bilateral development commission. Brazil's inflation-fighting ability, the commissioners wrote, is "weakened by the lack of an effective, independent and nonpolitical body entrusted with the supervision of the banking system and the coordination of monetary and credit policy."[19] Yet the political exigencies of implementing even a short-term stabilization plan were such that they left little political capital with which to try to accomplish institutional reform. The fragmentation and polarization of the national political environment was not conducive to the coalition building necessary to overcome diverse opinions on banking reform.

A second banking reform proposal was introduced in Congress by Daniel Faraco, then a Social Democratic Party deputy from Rio Grande do Sul. Faraco was friend and admirer of two well-known Brazilian proponents of orthodox economic policy at the time: Octavio Gouvêia de Bulhões and Eugenio Gudin. In his proposal he called for the creation of a central bank to replace SUMOC and take over the Banco do Brasil's rediscounting and foreign exchange operations. Although he proposed that the central bank be an independent policymaking entity, Faraco also proposed creation of a National Monetary Council with Ministry of Finance, private bank, and central bank representatives. This reflected the recognition that a future central bank was unlikely to be completely immune from political pressures and that it would be necessary to try to counterbalance Banco do Brasil influence by increasing the role of the Ministry of Finance and private bank representatives in the formulation and implementation of monetary policy.[20]

There was considerable sectoral and party opposition to this proposal, and an alternative was eventually offered by the Workers' Party deputy Camilo Nogueira da Gama in 1959. Despite his labor party affiliation Gama had worked under Minister of Finance Oswaldo Aranha, helping to formulate and implement a monetary stabilization plan. His bank reform proposal therefore reflected a compromise between the Faraco position and the preferences of the more extreme members of the Brazilian Workers' Party. Gama's proposal called for establishment of a large, sectorally diverse National Monetary Council with guaranteed labor representation. In contrast to the Faraco proposal, the new central bank would not have independent policymaking authority; it would execute policy defined by the National Monetary Council. Faracao responded with his second attempt at bank reform legislation, proposing a similar balance of power between the National Monetary Council and the central bank, but significantly narrowing the size and scope of representation on the council.

In 1962 a Workers' Party deputy from São Paulo also submitted an alternate proposal that responded to the attack on the Banco do Brasil implied by the earlier proposals. He proposed that the Banco do Brasil become the nation's central bank. President João Goulart, in turn, commissioned a study of all preexisting reform proposals that concluded that SUMOC should be granted the central banking functions held by the Banco do Brasil at the time. The industry association of São Paulo (FIESP) criticized the weakening of the Banco do Brasil implied in Goulart's proposal, and that proposal was soon met with a counter-proposal by the Social Democratic Party deputy Jose Maria Alkmin, calling again for the Banco do Brasil to become the nation's central bank.

Creation of the Banco Central do Brasil, 1964

Central bank politics in the mid-1960s were no different from the politics of all other economic issues. Growing frustration was felt by the Brazilian military and their political sympathizers. Resolution of the debate over a hypothetical central bank came only when Brazil's international financial situation reached crisis proportions, inducing a military coup. Objectively, the need for international creditworthiness mounted in the late 1950s. Import coverage fell below one month in 1959 for the first time since World War II, and remained below one month on average in 1960, 1962, and 1963 (see Table 8.1). Meanwhile, as Table 8.2 shows, foreign direct investment dipped significantly in 1963 and 1964. Foreign lending to Brazil was more erratic, but declined significantly in 1960 only to reach a record high in 1961 and fall consistently every year thereafter until after the central bank was created in 1965. Corrêa do Lago notes, "Foreign capitalists had, in effect, ceased to be interested in investing in Brazil . . . since 1962."[21]

The two-decade-long stalemate engendered by political polarization and fragmentation only ended with the imposition of military government in 1964. Once political debate within Brazil's polarized party system was circumscribed and power centralized, agreement on central bank legislation was quickly reached. Humberto Castelo Branco's finance minister, Bulhões, maneuvered to impede approval of the Alkmin bank reform proposal and formed an extra-parliamentary five-member commission to write central bank legislation. This proposal was passed to a special congressional commission headed by the Social Democratic Party deputy Ulysses Guimarães. According to this legislation, approved in 1964 after relatively minor debate between the executive and the Congress, SUMOC was replaced by two new bodies: the Central Bank of Brazil and the National Monetary Council.

The Brazil central banking statute passed into law in 1964 achieved an independence measure of .21 on the Cukierman et al. (1992) scale. The statute sets forth a variety of central bank objectives, but does not include price stability among them. The statute does explicitly refer to the central bank as autonomous. Regarding the chief executive officer of the central bank, the charter specifies legislative approval of the governor's appointment, with term length and dismissal at the unconditional discretion of political authorities. The statute provides for the central bank to advise the government on monetary policy but does not endow it with the capacity to influence the budget process or the direction of other government decisions. In the area of central bank financing of the government, the Brazilian central bank statute stipulates that the executive branch may unilaterally decide on the terms and conditions of loans and impose them on the central bank; there is no mention of maximum maturities on loans.

The Brazilian Central Bank: From Creation to Irrelevance

The central bank opened its doors in March 1965. But in the words of one observer, it took "several years before it gathered the necessary staff and operations from other institutions to actually function as a central bank."[22] No sooner had this consolidation occurred than it was undermined by the government's centralizing response to intramilitary debate over economic policy. Although in the following years of military rule, from 1968 until 1979, there were only two central bank presidents, this reflected subservience rather than autonomy.[23] Planning Minister Antonio Delfim Netto's efforts to bring the central bank into his personal political orbit were bolstered by growing access to relatively inexpensive international credit.

The history of central bank authority in this period is closely tied to the history of the National Monetary Council. The idea behind creation of the National Monetary Council was to help insulate the central bank from electoral and party pressures, regional demands, and government officials' salary requests. It was, in essence, meant to be a buffer between the Ministry of Finance and the central bank. The National Monetary Council statute states the intent to strengthen the central bank by creating a monetary authority that would prevent government interference in central bank affairs. The council was created with an eight-member board: the governor of the central bank and three central bank directors, the president of the National Bank of Economic Development (BNDE), the minster of finance, as chair, and two private sector representatives named by the federal president for six-year terms. Although the independence of the National Monetary Council, conceived as similar to the U.S. Federal Reserve Board, was limited by the role of finance minister as its chairperson, the intention was to preserve some independence through the provision of staggered six-year terms of appointment for the four central bank representatives to the council. In addition, the six-year terms of the two private sector representatives were intended to give them more power than their government colleagues, who would be replaced whenever the personnel in the president's office changed.[24] SUMOC had been composed entirely of government officials. The motive for adding private sector representatives to SUMOC's successor institution was to counterbalance the power of expansion-oriented government representatives. Creation of the central bank and the National Monetary Council and their activism was applauded by the Fifth National Bankers Congress in Porto Alegre in November 1964.[25]

The first serious blow to the newly created central bank came in 1967 with the change from one military president to another. There was a month-long debate about whether incoming Arthur da Costa e Silva should replace the central bank governor, even though the central bank statute provided a four-year term. Supporters of leadership continuity pointed out that replacing Denio Chagas Nogueira would abrogate the central bank statute. Furthermore, argued Octavio Gouvêia de Bulhões in a leading magazine, it would undermine "the very reason for central bank existence . . . because it [the central bank] should function as a symbol of continuity in government monetary policy for purposes of external credibility, particularly with international financial organizations."[26] An adviser to the new Brazilian president responded that "every government needs freedom to move in all areas."[27]

Central bank supporters lost, and in late April 1967 Rui Aguiar da Silva Lerma took the helm of the Banco Central do Brasil. In response to criticisms about concentration of power in the central bank's hands, one of Lerma's first moves was to announce a phase of "central bank decentralization." This was accomplished by restructuring the National Monetary Council. Costa e Silva's minister of finance, Delfim Netto, had wanted to create a Development Council to coordinate government economic policy with industrialization plans. Instead, with Costa e Silva's backing, he began to try to transform the National Monetary Council into a powerful government agency through which monetary and financial policy would be formulated and implemented in line with industrialization plans.

After forcing out the previous administration's central bank head, the new administration also forced the resignation of the three central bank directors previously sitting on the National Monetary Council.[28] Not long after this reshuffling there was yet another key personnel change; Delfim Netto removed central bank governor Rui Aguiar da Silva Lerma in favor of Ernane Galvêas. In November 1967 Costa e Silva decreed a change in the National Monetary Council statute and expanded its membership, adding a fifth central bank representative. This gave the central bank a majority on the National Monetary Council, which was part of Delfim Netto's plan to gain firm Ministry of Finance control of the council through the ministry's power to nominate the central bank governor. This legal change was followed by another, reorienting the council's mission toward the formulation of monetary and credit policy in accord with "the real needs of the economy."[29] One observer remarks that 1967 witnessed the "complete disfigurement" of both the central bank and the National Monetary Council.[30]

Delfim Netto gradually expanded the representation of other government ministries and agencies on the National Monetary Council as part of his goal to cement Ministry of Finance control over both public and private financial institutions and all other economic agencies of the government. By 1972 the National Monetary Council included the ministers of industry, agriculture, planning, and interior as well as the presidents of the National Housing Bank and the National Bank of Economic Development. The increase in size and government representation on the National Monetary Council was accompanied by an increase in its scope.[31] As minister of finance Delfim chaired the council which, with its expanded jurisdiction and representation, provided him an ideal entity through which to try to centralize economic control. In a reversal of its original role of insulating the central bank from government pressures, under Costa e Silva the National Monetary Council became an institution that facilitated government control of the central bank and all other economic policymaking agencies.[32]

Delfim's swift and immediate moves against the autonomy of the National Monetary Council and the central bank must be understood against the backdrop of a declining need for international creditworthiness and increasing uncertainty over presidential succession. The 1964 coup was partly motivated by frustration with Brazil's recurring balance of payments problems and lack of access to new international credit. The new economic policy of the military government, of which central bank foundation was a part, helped lay the groundwork for the successful renegotiation of Brazil's short-term international debts and for reestablishment of access to international credit. The central bank's efforts to consolidate its authority were aided by the interest and support of international creditors. The post-1967 years, in contrast, were characterized by easy money, both from exports and from international financial markets awash with liquidity. An authoritative central bank was not necessary to gain access to international financial resources; private bankers were busy urging loans on any developing country that would accept them. As it did in many other developing countries, the growth of international liquidity and Euromarket activity beginning in the late 1960s undermined the ability of the central bank in Brazil to build alliances with international creditors that would allow it to increase its authority vis-à-vis domestic actors.

Since the late 1960s there has been virtually no change in Brazilian central bank authority. Pressure for democratization created political uncertainty in the 1970s. This together with the low need for international creditworthiness due to high reserves, excess liquidity in international financial markets, and relatively manageable debt-to-export ratios in the 1970s created little incentive for strengthening the central bank. In the 1980s there were occasional public and private discussions, often motivated by foreign exchange difficulties and IMF negotiations, about the need for a more authoritative central bank. Despite the rise in need for international creditworthiness in the 1980s and 1990s, relative to the 1970s, Brazil's endemic political instability continued and did not provide political leaders sufficient political capital to allow them to cede authority to the central bank. The fate of Finance Minister Fernando Henrique Cardoso's August 1993 call for a more independent central bank is typical.[33] Even before debate over creating a "central bank or [a] Frankenstein" could take hold, the proposal was buried, at least temporarily, in the political chaos of new and grander corruption scandals plaguing Brazil's political elite.[34] As portfolio investment in Brazil grows (Table 8.2) and short-term debt sky-rockets (Table 8.1), it is not surprising that proposals to increase central bank independence resurface every few months. Central bank reform was highlighted in Cardoso's campaign platform and was high on the agenda of his administration's legislative goals in early 1995.

Current debate about central bank independence in Brazil may chart the future for South Korea. The growing importance of equity investment, particularly as a source of balance of payments financing, has made Brazilian political elites increasingly sensitive to the need to compete for international finance. As Brazilian democracy develops, political elites are increasingly held accountable for their economic policy decisions. Not only must policy respond to public opinion, which appears to be increasingly in favor of central bank independence, but accountability creates incentives for political elites to delegate economic policy responsibility.

Conclusion

Brazilian central bank history emphasizes the importance of politicians' tenure security in coloring their evaluation of the costs and benefits of signaling international creditworthiness via central bank independence. Brazil, like South Korea, has had relatively strict regulation of domestic and international financial transactions; this has also mitigated the need to compete for international creditworthiness. Nonetheless several years of relatively low import coverage occurred in the late 1950s and early 1960s. These were not sufficient to bring an end to the debate over creation of a central bank. It was not until low import coverage persisted, foreign direct investment and foreign lending declined, and a military coup occurred that a genuine Brazilian central bank was created. Objective measures of the need for international creditworthiness combined with an increase in politicians' tenure security finally brought a halt to endless haggling over central bank creation.

After the coup, political security allowed Brazil's new military leaders to take a longer-term view of the benefits associated with an independent central bank. From a more secure political position than that of previous civilian leaders, the military also perceived less political cost in the loss of monetary policy flexibility associated with central bank independence. Prior to the military coup of 1964, political uncertainty lowered the value political elites placed on trying to improve Brazil's creditworthiness. In the phase of central bank creation, high levels of political competition and a large number of legislative impediments severely undermined the prospects of those favoring an independent central bank. After the bank was created, however, lack of political competition and the centralization of political power in a context of relatively low objective need to compete for international capital and creditworthiness had extremely negative consequences for central bank independence.

Nine

Conclusion

THIS CONCLUDING chapter revisits the country histories in light of alternative theories about the politics of central bank independence, presents quantitative evidence constituting an indirect test of the signaling model of central bank independence, and ends by evaluating these findings in light of questions about the desirability and feasibility of central bank independence.

Alternative Arguments

I have argued that in middle-income developing countries central bank indepenence corresponds to politicians' preferences. Politicians favor sharing policy authority with central banks to the extent they give priority to building or protecting their nation's attraction for creditors and investors. Competing arguments include those based on the weight of law, central bank governor leadership capabilities, and ideological trends. Arguments based on sector strength and political institutions are partially encompassed in the argument about international influence developed here.

It is equally clear in Brazil, as in Thailand, Mexico, and South Korea, that behind central bank authority and ideology lie the strategic actions of political elites. In 1967 Delfim Netto could force out a governor with the leadership potential of Puey or Gómez because he wanted to and felt little need to be concerned with the impact on international creditworthiness. The challenging questions concern how and to what extent finance, politics, and law shape changing preferences of political leaders with regard to central bank authority.

One problem with both the legal and the pure sectoral arguments is that while they may explain broad cross-national differences in central bank authority viewed as relatively unchanging over time, they do not point to sufficient variation in explanatory factors to account for change over time. As noted in previous chapters, central bank statutes do not vary as much as de facto central bank authority does. For example, Cukierman et al.'s (1992) legal measure of Brazilian central bank independence does not change at all from 1964 through 1989, although the bank's de facto authority declined dramatically after 1967. The

TABLE 9.1
Political Vulnerability Index for Central Banks

Country	*1950–1971*	*1972–1989*
Thailand	.25	.11
Mexico	.25	.67
South Korea	*N.A.*	.67
Brazil	.50	1.00

Source: Alex Cukierman and Steven Webb, "Political Influence on the Central Bank—International Evidence," paper prepared for the meeting of the American Political Science Association, New York, August 31–September 4, 1994. *N.A.*–Not available.

place of the financial and industrial sectors in Brazil's national production profile also did not change sufficiently over time to account for the variation in central bank authority. A similar misfit between sectoral change and variation in central bank authority is apparent in Thailand, Mexico, and South Korea.

The legal argument also appears inadequate in explaining static, cross-national variation in central bank authority, at least in the four country histories examined here. Average legal independence for the period 1950–1989 yields .21 for Brazil, .27 for both Thailand and South Korea, and .34 for Mexico, based on the Cukierman et al. (1992) codings. Yet it is not clear from the histories that Korea deserves a higher ranking than Brazil in terms of central bank authority. This coding also obscures the serious decline in authority suffered by the Banco de México in the 1970s. Thailand, moreover, appears to deserve a higher ranking than South Korea. Quantitative political measures of central bank independence fit the historical record much better than do legal measures. Cukierman and Webb's measure of central bank political vulnerability calculates the fraction of political transitions followed within six months by a change in the central bank governorship.[1] Their measures of political vulnerability, shown in Table 9.1, find the Bank of Thailand least vulnerable and the Bank of Brazil most vulnerable.

The important point about sectoral arguments highlighted in all four histories is that domestic financiers' influence on central bank independence varies over time with the degree of leverage gained from ties to international financiers in times of need for international creditworthiness and with the scope of sectors' political access. The less competitive the system, the less likely it is that there will be a strong and consistent correspondence between a nation's production profile and a politician's preferences about economic policy and economic institutions.[2] In Brazilian monetary policy the influence of private bankers, enshrined in law by the changes of 1964 and for a time allowed to operate, swiftly eroded when military leaders of a different stripe came to power in 1967. Delfim Netto was the architect of the Brazilian central bank's rapid decline after 1967. While he eventually came to be seen as having very close ties to São Paulo industrialists, he was able to undermine central bank authority rapidly and thoroughly because he had the backing of a military regime and because the country had relatively little objective need for international creditworthiness. Yet intense political competition in a context of fragmentation and a weak party system hindered the success of central bank proposals prior to 1964. In this setting, even the growing leverage gained by proponents of central bank independence as Brazil's international financial situation deteriorated was insufficient to tilt the domestic political scales in their favor.

A purely sectoral argument is a poor predictor of change in central bank authority in the other three country histories as well. As in Brazil in 1967, in Korea after 1956 it was not sectoral demand from expansion-oriented industry or labor that primarily induced political leaders to encroach on central bank authority. In both the Brazilian and the Korean cases an increasingly authoritarian context and the low value of competing for international creditworthiness created space for political elites to pursue a state-centered, rapid industrialization policy that required central bank subordination. Strong expansion-oriented industrialist groups later emerged in both countries, after central bank authority had been undermined.

Later in Korean history partial political liberalization created the opening for a central bank independence movement. The impetus came not from a stronger domestic financial sector but from pro-democracy forces seeking to limit arbitrary state power through every means possible. This movement failed in part because there was no incentive or obvious opportunity to seek the support of international financiers. In a fragmented, unstable party system still under strong authoritarian sway, no Korean political party saw great benefit in pushing central bank independence in the face of strong state opposition.

In Mexico a relatively sophisticated private financial sector developed in the 1950s and 1960s, earlier than in many other developing countries. Yet the influence of this sector on the actions of political leaders varied with the international financial context. Influence was large when the need to compete for international creditworthiness was high in the 1950s, 1980s, and 1990s and low when the world was awash with petrodollars in the 1970s. Extreme presidentialism and semi-authoritarian one-party domination of national politics allowed the sudden override of different groups' preferred policies. This is evident both in the case of the 1954 devaluation and the related rise in central bank authority and in the case of the 1972 embrace of expansionary policy and the related decline in central bank authority.

Unlike Mexican political elites, Thai leaders had no reason to make sudden populist appeals. Nonetheless Thai proponents of central bank independence, whether private financiers, military men, or technocrats, have found that their fortunes wax and wane, albeit less suddenly and dramatically than in Mexico, with the leverage to be gained from connections to international financiers when the need to compete for international creditworthiness is high.

In all four countries there has been a long-term trend toward increased industrial share of GNP and more sophisticated financial markets. Over the long run financial sector development, including internationalization, will lead inevitably to greater central bank independence for a variety of reasons. In addition to the need to compete for international capital, increasingly sophisticated financial markets both require and reinforce central bank independence. Financial markets require effective regulation and macroeconomic predictability. Financial market actors recognize the importance of the international card in the fight for central bank independence. They also dislike arbitrary power and are likely to reward emerging markets where political systems with a large number of institutionalized veto points protect central bank independence.

Robust financial markets also eliminate the seignorage rationale for central bank subordination. Both the Brazilian and the South Korean country histories illustrate the role that subordinate central banks play in financial repression, which helps to keep both demand for money and government opportunity for seignorage income high.[3] Both of these countries also sustained relatively great restriction on international financial transactions. This partially limited the potential for capital flight and mitigated concern over international creditworthiness in comparison with countries with more open financial markets, such as Mexico and Thailand.[4] As Brazil and South Korea follow the global trend toward financial market deregulation, we should see growing pressure for central bank independence in those countries.

Regression Analysis of Central Bank Independence and Private Investment

The investor-signaling argument developed here requires that politicians *believe* that central bank independence is an effective signal, not that it actually *is* one. Nonetheless the argument should be more convincing if central bank independence and private investment are correlated. While it is difficult to reliably separate domestic from foreign investment in developing countries, it is possible to test the impact of central bank independence on private investment *in general*. Controlling for a series of economic and political variables that also affect private investment in developing countries, we find some association of de jure central bank independence with private investment.[5] These econometric results are consistent with an argument that politicians are more likely to delegate authority to central banks the more they make growth of private investment a priority. Although the data do not allow us to distinguish between domestic and international finance of investment, the signaling effect should apply to both domestic and foreign investors.

The regression tested is a reduced-form specification of private investment:

ECONOMIC VARIABLES
PRIVGDP = *f*[EXPGRO(+), PUBIGDP(+), DEBTEXP(–), INFL(+), INFLSQ(–),

POLITICAL VARIABLES
CBI(+), DEMOC(+), SCOPE (–)]

where *PRIVGDP* is private investment as a share of GDP, and the first five variables are "economic": *EXPGRO* is the expected growth rate; *PUBIGDP* is the (lagged) rate of public sector investment as a share of GDP; *DEBTEXP* is a measure of the expected debt burden, or "overhang," as deflated by exports; *INFL* is the (lagged) inflation rate; *INFLSQ* is the square of *INFL*; *DEMO* is democracy; and *SCOPE* is the level of public intervention in the economy. Table 9.2 provides detailed explanations of the variables' sources, actual construction, and lag structure.

The rationales for the signs on the economic variables are straightforward extensions of traditional theory.[6] Expectations of faster growth, for example, should increase investment. We expect public investment to have a positive effect on private investment; that is, we postulate that the "crowding in" effect dominates in the developing world.[7] We also expect that higher ratios of external debt will lower private investment, primarily because a large debt burden acts as a sort of expected "tax" on future output.[8] The inflation variable is a proxy for macroeconomic stability, a factor clearly important in determining the degree of confidence investors attach to their expectations of future growth and hence their need for additional capital stock. Moderate rates of inflation, however, may actually enhance investment by raising short-term profit expectations (since nominal wages often lag, particularly in developing economies); only when rates are high does the instability effect dominate and produce lessened investment. This suggests that the

TABLE 9.2
Economic and Political Variables in the Investment Equation: Definitions and Sources

PRIVGDP	Private investment as a percentage of GDP. Taken from Guy P. Pfefferman and Andrea Madarassy, "Trends in Private Investment in Thirty Developing Countries 1993: Statistics for 1970–91," International Financial Corporation Discussion Paper 16 (Washington, D.C.: World Bank, 1992).
EXPGRO	Expected growth rate. Calculated as the growth rate for the previous year, following Joshua Greene and Delano Villanueva, "Private Investment in Developing Countries: An Empirical Analysis," *IMF Staff Papers*, 38, 1 (March 1991), and Luis Serven and Andrés Solimano, "Private Investment and Macroeconomic Adjustment: A Survey," *World Bank Research Observer* 7, 1 (1992). Growth rates from World Bank, *World Debt Tables* (Washington, D.C.: World Bank, various years).
PUBIGDP	Public investment as a percentage of GDP. Data from Guy P. Pfefferman and Andrea Madarassy, "Trends in Private Investment in Thirty Developing Countries 1993: Statistics for 1970–91," International Financial Corporation Discussion Paper 16 (Washington, D.C.: World Bank, 1992).
DEBTEXP	A measure of the debt overhang calculated as the ratio of total external debt to exports, with both measures from *World Debt Tables*. Entered as a lag.
INFL	The natural log of the inflation rate. Calculated using the GDP deflator from World Bank Tables, since this price index proxies the producer price index most relevant to the investment decision more closely than the Consumer Price Index–based rate. The variable is entered as a lag because of adaptive expectations assumptions and to reduce any simultaneity problems.
INFLSQ	The square of INFL.
DEMOC	An additive 10-point scale determined by quantitative ratings of competitiveness of political participation, competitiveness of executive recruitment, openness of executive recruitment, and constraint on chief executive. From Ted Robert Gurr, *Polity II: Political Structures and Regime Change, 1800–1896* (Ann Arbor: Inter-University Consortium for Political and Social Research [magnetic tape], 1990).
SCOPE	A measure of the extent of government intervention in the economy ranging from 1 (highest) to 9 (lowest). From Ted Robert Gurr, *Polity II: Political Structures and Regime Change, 1800–1896* (Ann Arbor: Inter-University Consortium for Political and Social Research [magnetic tape], 1990).
CBI	Alex Cukierman, Steven B. Webb, and Bilin Neyapti, "Measuring the Independence of Central Banks," *World Bank Economic Review*, 6, 3 (September 1992), and coding of post-1989 charters.

inflation-investment relationship may be that of an inverted U—moderate price hikes enhance investment while "excessive" inflation deters investment. This is the specification used.[9] We assume that more democratic political institutions are consistent with better economic performance, partly because of the policy stability gained when more citizens have access to the policymaking process.[10] *SCOPE* allows us to control for the level of government intervention in the economy. *CBI* is a measure of aggregate legal central bank independence taken from Cukierman et al. (1992).[11] Although legal central bank independence is an imperfect measure, it is the only one available for a broad sample of developing countries.

The *CBI* variable we take from Cukierman et al. (1992) is a summary measure across several periods for numerous countries in the developing and developed world. Unfortunately, the constraints posed by our other variables (the private investment measure is only available from 1970, our growth measure begins in 1972, and our democracy and scope measures end in 1986) mean that we can only use two of their periods (1972–1979 and 1980–1989). There are twenty-one countries in the developing world for which we could collect all the relevant data: Argentina, Bolivia, Brazil, Chile, Colombia, Costa Rica, India, Indonesia, Kenya, Korea, Malaysia, Mexico, Morocco, Nigeria, Pakistan, Peru, the Philippines, Thailand, Turkey, Uruguay, and Venezuela. For most of these countries there is no variation in central bank independence between the two subperiods. Thus data limitations only allow a strong test for the cross-sectional impact of *CBI*. We use a random effects (RE) regression technique which captures both cross-section and time effects and allows for time-invariant country-specific variables to be tested and have an effect on the dependent variable.[12]

In Table 9.3 we report the regression results for the various random effects runs.[13] The first column includes just the economic variables. Note that the base regression performs well, if not spectacularly so. The second column introduces *CBI* with less than stellar results; the economic variables remain the same (with *INFL* improving slightly) and *CBI* is signed as expected but with a *t*-score of only 0.776. Columns (3), (4), and (5) explore the political/institutional relations in a step-by-step fashion. In column (3), we first add *DEMOC* to the regression; note that the variable itself is significant at the .05 level, that growth, debt, and public investment remain highly significant, and that the inflation variables are more or less the same as before. *CBI* obtains the expected sign and its *t*-score improves, but only to slightly above one. Column (4) then drops the *DEMOC* variable and introduces only *SCOPE*. We should stress that the sign of this variable, *SCOPE*, is not really what is at issue; more important is controlling for the level of government in-

TABLE 9.3
Private Investment and Central Bank Independence

Dependent Variable = PRIVGDP					
EXPGRO	0.240 (6.857)***	0.255 (6.076)***	0.254 (6.032)***	0.248 (5.810)***	0.243 (5.736)***
PUBIGDP	0.192 (1.914)*	0.194 (1.910)*	0.200 (1.999)**	0.134 (1.273)	0.146 (1.396)#
DEBTEXP	−0.668 (−4.121)***	−0.637 (−3.885)***	−0.574 (−3.507)***	−0.552 (−3.354)***	−0.550 (−3.373)***
INFL	0.599 (1.085)	0.730 (1.300)#	0.889 (1.599)#	0.661 (1.088)	0.690 (1.143)
INFLSQ	−0.105 (−1.653)*	−0.118 (−1.828)*	−0.135 (−2.084)**	−0.116 (−1.703)*	−0.125 (−1.847)*
CBI		0.056 (0.776)	0.072 (1.035)	0.150 (1.980)**	0.134 (1.807)*
DEMOC			0.163 (2.043)**		0.169 (2.129)**
SCOPE				0.656 (1.832)*	0.572 (1.506)#
Adjusted R^2	0.297	0.301	0.297	0.306	0.318
Number of observations	246	246	245	216	216
F-value	18.2***	14.2***	12.1***	11.5***	11.0***

*** Significant at the two-tail 1 percent level.
** Significant at the two-tail 5 percent level.
* Significant at the two-tail 10 percent level.
# Significant at the two-tail 20 percent level.

tervention. *CBI* is positive and significant at the .05 level. Finally, we turn to the full model in column (5). Again the economic variables are more or less as before. Note that *SCOPE* falls slightly in significance while *CBI* is positive and significant at the .10 level.[14]

Although not overwhelming, these results provide indirect quantitative support for the investor signaling model of central bank independence. The test is for legal independence, with all the limitations of concept and measurement noted in previous chapters. Even though we are unable to differentiate between domestic and foreign investors' responses to central bank independence, the signaling effect should apply to both. In fact the signaling effect should be stronger for foreign investors to the extent that "complete" local information is costly for them to obtain.

Desirability of Central Bank Independence in Developing Countries

What do the country experiences surveyed here suggest about the desirability of central bank independence in developing countries, as measured by its impact on growth, distribution, and democracy? Empirical research has moved farthest in addressing questions about growth, although almost all the research focuses on industrial countries. The one exception, noted in Chapter 1, is the 1993 study by Cukierman and his colleagues finding a positive effect on growth in developing countries, but no effect in industrial countries.[15] The results reported earlier in this chapter reinforce the Cukierman et al. (1993) findings; for developing countries, the greater the central bank independence, the higher the private investment. Controversy over how best to quantitatively measure central bank independence suggests that these results are probably sensitive to the measures used.

All four of the country histories examined here reveal periods of high growth that do not necessarily coincide with periods of rising central bank authority. Nor does the relationship appear more conclusive if we evaluate the countries in static cross-national comparison. Mexico and Thailand have had relatively more independent central banks, de facto, than Brazil or Korea. Yet Korean growth has been consistently higher than that of the other three countries.

Even if there is some uncertainty over the extent of the contribution of central bank independence to growth in developing countries, unless there is reason to fear that the impact might be growth reducing, the potential benefits may well outweigh the costs. The costs are more likely to stem from the distributional consequences of central bank independence and its impact on employment.

One of the more common criticisms of central bank independence is that it may lead to economic policy that is less employment-promoting than the ideal policy of the median voter and/or that is not social-welfare optimizing. This critique is related to the fact that central bankers are likely to be more conservative than the average voter and are not directly accountable to the electorate.

One of the problems in evaluating the distributional impact of central bank independence stems from the mixed nature of wage bargaining in most nations. The rationale for central bank independence is stronger when pressure for employment-motivated inflationary monetary policy is greater. The models that show strong pressure assume a unionized labor force.[16] But most countries have both union and non-union labor forces. Under these circumstances Cukierman shows that there is also pressure, and therefore a strong rationale for central bank independence, if the supply of nonunion labor does not correspond to real wage rates or if the supply/demand dynamics of the unionized and nonunionized sectors are more different than similar.[17] The extent to which these conditions fit the empirical reality of developing countries remains an open question. The latest monetary game theory does little to resolve the debate over the strength of the rationale for central bank independence.

Franzese finds empirical support in OECD countries for a slightly different argument. He suggests that there is little inflation-fighting rationale for central bank independence in the context of centralized wage bargaining systems such as Austria's.[18] The more decentralized the wage bargaining system, the greater the inflation-fighting rationale for central bank independence. These findings suggest that in countries, such as Japan, with firm-level wage bargaining, inflation will be lower to the extent the central bank is independent. This argument is hard to extend to non-OECD countries. Consider the countries highlighted here. Korea has enjoyed relatively low inflation rates under a dependent central bank. But one could hardly imagine effective centralized wage bargaining in the authoritarian political environment Korea has had for most of the post–World War II era. Brazil and Mexico have suffered high inflation under a dependent central bank with a relatively centralized wage bargaining system, which is supposedly a recipe for good macroeconomic performance. Thailand is the only country of the four that fits Franzese's model: an independent central bank combined with decentralized wage bargaining yields low inflation.

Like Franzese, Notermans and Garret imply that certain kinds of national labor institutions may facilitate high employment, low wages, and little inflationary pressure.[19] If such labor institutions can be found and built, they could reduce the potential tension between full employment and national ability to attract and keep capital in a world of integrated financial markets. Most work on this topic has focused on advanced industrial countries, but its implications for developing countries are great. The restructuring of Mexican corporatism, for example, involving centralized wage bargaining with labor a visibly weak and quiescent party to the negotiations, is part of an effort to retain labor support for the ruling political party, the PRI, while doing everything possible to build the confidence of domestic and international creditors and investors.

The impact of central bank independence on employment in developing countries is an important area for future research. Nonetheless, engaging in debate over the employment costs of central bank independence could well be viewed as a luxury for those operating within the reference frame of an industrializing country. In 1995, the cost of a history of macroeconomic instability in many middle-income industrializing countries still greatly outweighed any possible employment benefits from subordinating the central bank. Furthermore, financial expertise is so thin in many of these countries that independent central banks arguably provide a net social benefit simply as a training ground for policy-oriented economists.[20]

Concern over the threat central bank independence may pose to democratic accountability could also be somewhat misplaced in a developing country context.[21] As the 1987–88 Korean central bank independence movement illustrates, in an authoritarian political context central bank independence is more likely to be democracy-enhancing than democracy-detracting. Many also interpreted the increased legal independence of the Mexican central bank, legislated in 1993, as a positive contribution to the slow process of political liberalization by reducing the authority of the Mexican presidency, one of the most powerful in the world.

The concern more relevant to the developing country context is that central bank independence can hinder policy coordination. This suggests that provisions for, and institutionalization of, central bank involvement in the budget process may be one of the most important building blocks for a strong, effective, and welfare-enhancing central bank in the developing country context.

Those who agree that the internationalization of finance lurks behind central bank independence make a slightly different argument about its implications for distribution and democracy. To the extent that central bank independence is a function of the globalization of financial markets, Freeman contends that it undermines local and national governments' abilities to "control . . . [the] allocation of credit within nation-states." "This bears directly on governments' capacity," Freeman continues, "to promote distributive justice and . . . promote the welfare of particular groups."[22] As noted in Chapter 1, Epstein also argues that independent central banks can thwart Keynesian-type economic policies often favored by labor and some industrial sectors.[23] These arguments suggest that national politicians are increasingly caught between the demands of internationally mobile capital and the exigencies of domestic politics. The pressures are more disparate the stronger the national, expansion-oriented political coalitions.

The extent of the structural power of international capital and the tension between international economic forces and national economic policy has become a clear theme in the literature on comparative and international political economy. But the empirical bias toward OECD countries also limits the value of this debate for students of developing countries. A host of articles have proved that the structural power of international capital to bring about convergence in national economic policies and institutions is limited in an OECD country context.[24] Although data limitations confound researchers' ability to replicate these studies for non-OECD country samples, more research is needed. Students of developing countries tend to be much less sanguine about the ability of national institutions and policies to withstand the onslaught of international capital.[25]

Although the structural power of international capital may have little impact in OECD countries right now, could it not be that the future of OECD countries will look increasingly like the present in non-OECD countries? As independent national monetary policy becomes more difficult to pursue, it is more and more likely that the economic impact of individual central bank actions in OECD countries will pale beside the role of exchange markets, exchange rate regimes, international shocks, and internationally coordinated responses to them. This book suggests several obvious areas for future work, including constructing data allowing for more rigorous empirical testing in developing country samples of OECD-oriented political arguments about economic policy and institutions, and building formal models of the open-economy politics of economic policy choice implied here. But the notion that the future of the OECD may look like the present in the stylized small, open economy directs our attention to the fundamental factors behind growing capital account openness and the liquidity structure of international financial assets. Commenting on these trends, Pauly argues that lack of control over finance is inevitably undermining the legitimacy of the nation-state and that a new basis for nationhood, exclusive of economic control, must emerge.[26]

Feasibility of Central Bank Independence in Developing Countries

If we assume that for the short and medium term, especially in middle-income developing countries, central bank authority is desirable, what do this book's findings suggest about how it is best achieved? Legal change should not be considered a panacea. Central bank authority comes from financial markets and political leaders, not necessarily independently of each other. Because the risk to central bank independence of overt involvement in politics is great, especially if political instability is rising or polarization is high, the political burden must fall disproportionately on proponents of central bank independence outside the institution itself. Yet the political realm is unpredictable. To the extent possible, the most effective strategy for securing central bank independence is to focus first on financial market development.[27]

Conduct of monetary policy becomes very complex, even if central banks are nominally independent, when "authorities are faced with widespread risk and insolvency among financial institutions."[28] In fact, it is difficult for the central bank to effectively conduct any of the functions outlined in Chapter 1 if financial markets are not robust. In the first and last instance central bank authority will respond to how effectively the central bank conducts its primary tasks. Furthermore, the more robust financial markets are, the easier it is for the central bank to be open and transparent about its operations. It is less risky to provide public information when the bank can "blame the markets" in the face of complaints. Over time, public understanding of how and why the central bank acts is also an important source of authority.

This book has focused on national politicians and the increasingly international financial markets in recently industrialized countries. The preceding chapters have evaluated the politics of central bank independence in middle-income developing countries and have emphasized the impact of financial markets on politicians' decisions to share economic policymaking authority with the central bank.

Notes

Chapter One

1. Sidney Tarrow, "Bridging the Quantitative-Qualitative Divide," *American Political Science Review*, 89, 2 (June 1995), 473.

2. Alberto Alesina and Guido Tabellini, "Rules and Discretion with Non-Coordinated Monetary and Fiscal Policies," *Economic Inquiry*, 25 (1987), 619–630.

3. An excellent survey of recent developments is N. Gregory Mankiw, "A Quick Refresher Course in Macroeconomics," *Journal of Economic Literature*, 28, (December 1990), 1645–1660.

4. Debate over the Phillips curve continues today. Those in the classical camp deny the inflation-output trade-off over any time horizon. Rejuvenation of Keynesian theory, in contrast, has involved specifying the parameters of a short-run trade-off. Laurence Ball, N. Gregory Mankiw, and David Romer, "The New Keynesian Economics and the Output-Inflation Trade-off," *Brookings Papers on Economic Activity*, 1 (Spring 1988), 1–83.

5. Another reason for the declining value of monetary policy discretion in a context of persistent high inflation is that those in charge of the policy were vulnerable to blame.

6. Robert Lenzer, "Baring's Best Buys," *Forbes*, July 4, 1994, p. 67.

7. Paul A. Volcker, "The Role of Central Banks," in Federal Reserve Bank of Kansas City, *Central Banking Issues in Emerging Market-Oriented Economies* (Kansas City: Federal Reserve Bank of Kansas, 1990), p. 5.

8. There is considerable debate about the relative priority of central bank independence, currency convertibility, and currency boards as inflation-controlling institutions in transitional economies.

9. For a thorough elaboration of the theory, see Torsten Persson and Guido Tabellini, *Macroeconomic Policy, Credibility, and Politics* (New York: Harwood Academic Publishers, 1990).

10. Keith Blackburn and Michael Christensen, "Monetary Policy and Policy Credibility: Theories and Evidence," *Journal of Economic Literature*, 27 (March 1989), 3. For a critique of this logic, see Charles A. E. Goodhardt, "Game Theory for Central Bankers: A Report to the Governor of the Bank of England," *Journal of Economic Literature*, 32 (March 1994), 103–105.

11. Edward J. Kane, "Politics and Fed Policymaking: The More Things Change, the More They Remain the Same," *Journal of Monetary Economics*, 6, 2 (April 1980), 199–211.

12. William T. Bernhard, "Legislatures, Governments, and Bureaucratic Structure: Explaining Central Bank Independence" (Ph.D. diss., Duke University, 1995).

13. Douglass C. North and Barry R. Weingast, "Constitutions and Commitment: The Evolution of Institutions Governing Public Choice in Seventeenth-Century England," *Journal of Economic History*, 49, 4 (December 1989), 803–832.

14. John B. Goodman, "The Politics of Central Bank Independence," *Comparative Politics*, 23, 3 (April 1991), 329–349.

15. Greenspan testimony to the U.S. House of Representatives Banking Committee, October 13, 1993. Reuters, "Free Central Banks Check Inflation—Greenspan," October 13, 1993.

16. Vittorio Grilli, Donato Masciandaro, and Guido Tabellini, "Political and Monetary Institutions and Public Financial Policies in the Industrial Countries," *Economic Policy: A European Economic Forum*, 13 (October 1991), 342–392; Alberto Alesina, "Macroeconomics and Politics," in Stanley Fischer, ed., *NBER Macroeconomics Annual* (Cambridge: Cambridge University Press, 1988).

17. William Roberts Clark, Sandra Lynn Thomas, and Kevin L. Parker, "Central Rates and Central Banks: International and Domestic Constraints on the Political Control of OECD Economies," mimeo, Georgia Institute of Technology, December 1994.

18. Alberto Alesina and Lawrence H. Summers, "Central Bank Independence and Macroeconomic Performance: Some Comparative Evidence," *Journal of Money and Banking*, 25 (May 1993). For a summary of most of the quantitative research, see Patricia S. Pollard, "Central Bank Independence and Economic Performance," *Federal Reserve Bank of St. Louis Review* (July/August 1994), 21–36.

19. Alberto Alesina, Gerald D. Cohen, and Nouriel Roubini, "Macroeconomic Policy and Elections in OECD Democracies," *Economics and Politics*, 4, 1 (March 1992), 1–30.

20. Stanley Fischer, "Modern Central Banking," prepared for the Tercentenary of the Bank of England Central Banking Symposium, June 9, 1994, p. 50.

21. I am grateful to Robert Franzese for pointing this out.

22. Alex Cukierman, Pantelis Kalaitzidakis, Lawrence Summers, and Steven B. Webb, "Central Bank Independence, Growth, Investment, and Real Rates," *Carnegie-Rochester Conference on Public Policy*, 39 (Autumn 1993).

23. In other words, strenthening legal independence matters little if laws are not respected, as is the case in many developing countries.

24. Cukierman comes to similar conclusions. See Alex Cukierman, "Central Bank Independence and Monetary Control," *Economic Journal*, 104 (November 1994), 1437–1448.

25. William Grieder, *Secrets of the Temple* (New York: Simon and Schuster, 1987).

26. Stackelberg duopoly is a model showing that unless two equally powerful firms agree to cooperate by designating one or the other price leader, they will drive each other out of business. See Robert Gibbons, *Game Theory for Applied Economists* (Princeton: Princeton University Press, 1992), pp. 61–64. For a discussion of game theory applied to central bank politics, see Charles A. E. Goodhart, "Game Theory for Central Bankers: A Report to the Governor of the Bank of England," *Journal of Economic Literature*, 32 (March 1994), 101–114.

27. Krugman describes this as the problem of hysterisis in international

trade. Temporary shock induced foreign firms to invade the U.S. market, and led U.S. firms to abandon foreign markets and/or move production overseas. These decisions were not reversed when the temporary shock of overvaluation was corrected. Paul Krugman, *Exchange-Rate Instability* (Cambridge: MIT Press, 1989), pp. 57–59.

28. Alan S. Blinder, "Issues in the Coordination of Monetary and Fiscal Policy," NBER Working Paper no. 982; Guido Tabellini, "Central Bank Reputation and the Monetization of Deficits: The 1981 Italian Monetary Reform," *Economic Inquiry*, 25, 2 (1987), 185–200.

29. Doug Henwood, "Democratize the Fed?" *The Nation*, June 27, 1994, pp. 897–900.

30. Steven Greenhouse, "Greenspan Warns against Easing Fed's Secrecy," *New York Times*, October 20, 1993, sec. D, p. 1.

31. Paul A. Volcker, "The Triumph of Central Banking?" 1990 Per Jacobssen Lecture (Washington, D.C.: IMF, 1990), p. 22.

32. Fischer, "Modern Central Banking," p. 42.

33. John B. Goodman, *Monetary Sovereignty: The Politics of Central Banking in Western Europe* (Ithaca: Cornell University Press, 1992); Peter A. Hall, "Central Bank Independence and Coordinated Wage Bargaining: Their Interaction in Germany and Europe," *German Politics and Society*, 31 (Spring 1994) 1–23; Thomas Havrilesky and James Granato, "Determinants of Inflationary Performance: Corporatist Structures vs. Central Bank Autonomy," *Public Choice*, 76 (1993), 249–261; Susanne Lohmann, "Federalism and Central Bank Autonomy: The Politics of German Monetary Policy, 1957–1992," Department of Political Science, UCLA, October 1994.

34. Rosa Maria Lastra, "The Independence of the European System of Central Banks," *Harvard International Law Journal*, 33, 2 (1992), 478–479.

35. Alberto Alesina, Gerald D. Cohen, and Nouriel Roubini, "Macroeconomic Policy and Elections in OECD Democracies," *Economics and Politics*, 4, 1 (March 1992), 1–30.

36. Miguel Angel Centeno, "The New Leviathan: The Dynamics and Limits of Technocracy," *Theory and Society*, 22, 3 (June 1993), 307–336.

37. John R. Freeman, "Banking on Democracy: International Finance and the Possibilities for Popular Sovereignty," paper prepared for the annual meeting of the American Political Science Association, San Francisco, August 29–September 2, 1990, p. 14.

38. Gerald Epstein, "Political Economy and Comparative Central Banking," *Review of Radical Political Economics*, 24, 1 (1992), 13.

39. Quoted by Paul A. Volcker, "The Independence of Central Banks: Its Value and Its Limits," presentation at the Centenary of the Banca d'Italia, Rome, December 11, 1993.

40. Some economists believe there may be a short-run trade-off between price stability and financial stability. E. Baltensperger, "Central Bank Policy and Lending of Last Resort," in F. Bruni, ed., *Prudential Regulation, Supervision, and Monetary Policy* (Paolo Baffi Center, Milan: Bocconi University, 1993); Alex Cukierman, *Central Bank Strategy, Credibility, and Independence* (Cambridge: MIT Press, 1992), chap. 7.

Chapter Two

1. George J. Stigler, "The Economic Theory of Regulation," *Bell Journal of Economics*, 2, 1 (Spring 1971), 3–21.

2. Randall L. Calvert, Mathew D. McCubbins, and Barry R. Weingast, "A Theory of Political Control and Agency Discretion," *American Journal of Political Science*, 3, 3 (1989), 588–612.

3. Sylvia Maxfield, "Financial Incentives and Central Bank Authority in Industrializing Nations," *World Politics*, 46, 4 (July 1994), 556–589.

4. William T. Bernhard, "Legislatures, Governments, and Bureaucratic Structure: Explaining Central Bank Independence" (Ph.D. diss., Duke University, 1995), p. 20.

5. David R. Johnson and Piere L. Siklos, "Political Effects on Central Bank Behavior: Some International Evidence," in P. L. Siklos, ed., *Varieties of Monetary Reforms: Lessons and Experiences on the Road to Monetary Union* (Norwell, Mass.: Kluwer Academic Press).

6. Ibid., p. 224.

7. Larry Elliott, "Governor Toasts Autonomy but Rejects the Poisoned Chalice," *The Guardian*, February 2, 1994, p. 14.

8. Alex Cukierman, Pantelis Kalaitzidakis, Lawrence Summers, and Steven B. Webb, "Central Bank Independence, Growth, Investment, and Real Rates," *Carnegie-Rochester Conference on Public Policy*, 39 (Autumn 1993).

9. John B. Goodman, *Monetary Sovereignty: The Politics of Central Banking in Western Europe* (Ithaca: Cornell University Press, 1992); John T. Woolley, *Monetary Politics* (Cambridge: Cambridge University Press, 1985).

10. Adam S. Posen, "Why Central Bank Independence Does Not Cause Low Inflation: There Is No Institutional Fix for Politics," in R. O'Brien, ed., *Finance and the International Economy*, 7 (Oxford: Oxford University Press, 1993). Posen does not correct for auto-correlation, which leads to understatement of his standard error terms.

11. William Roberts Clark, "The Sources of Central Bank Independence in Developing Countries," paper prepared for the annual meeting of the American Political Science Association, Washington, D.C., September 3–6, 1993.

12. William Roberts Clark, "Party Structure, Regime Stability, and the Governmental Supply of Central Bank Independence," mimeo, Georgia Institute of Technology, School of International Affairs, 1994.

13. Robert J. Franzese, "Central Bank Independence, Sectoral Interests, and the Wage Bargain," Center for European Studies Working Paper Series no. 56, 1995.

14. Endogeneity plagues this reasoning. Financial market development strengthens central bank independence, which in turn fosters financial sector development.

15. Peter A. Hall, "Central Bank Independence and Coordinated Wage Bargaining: Their Interaction in Germany and Europe," *German Politics and Society*, 31 (Spring 1994), 1–23. Havrilesky and Granato do not find support for a model that associates corporatist structures and central bank independence. Thomas Havrilesky and James Granato, "Determinants of Inflationary

Performance: Corporatist Structures vs. Central Bank Autonomy," *Public Choice*, 76 (1993), 249–261.

16. Susanne Lohmann, "Federalism and Central Bank Autonomy: The Politics of German Monetary Policy, 1957–1992," Department of Political Science, UCLA, October 1994.

17. King Banaian, Leroy O. Laney, and Thomas D. Willett, "Central Bank Independence: An International Comparison," in E. F. Toma and M. Toma, eds., *Central Bankers, Bureaucratic Incentives, and Monetary Policy* (Boston: Academic Publishers, 1986), pp. 199–219.

18. John B. Goodman, "The Politics of Central Bank Independence," *Comparative Politics*, 23; 3 (April 1991), 334.

19. Bernhard, "Legislatures, Governments, and Bureaucratic Structure," chap. 5.

20. Alberto Alesina, "Macroeconomics and Politics," in S. Fischer, ed., *NBER Macroeconomic Annual* (Cambridge: Cambridge University Press, 1988), pp. 13–51; Clark, "Party Structure, Regime Stability," Alex Cukierman, "Commitment through Delegation, Political Influence, and Central Bank Independence," in J. A. H. de Beaufort Wijnholds, S. C. W. Eiffinger, and L. H. Hoogdin, eds., *A Framework for Monetary Stability* (The Netherlands: Kluwer Academic Publishers, 1993), pp. 55–74.

21. Delia Boylan, "Holding Democracy Hostage: Central Bank Autonomy in the Transition from Authoritarian Rule," Political Science Department, Stanford University, Mimeo, September 1995.

22. Goodman, "The Politics of Central Bank Independence," p. 334. Emphasis added.

23. Clark, "Party Structure, Regime Stability."

24. Jacob Zielinski, "Political Parties and Central Bank Autonomy," paper prepared for the annual meeting of the Midwest Political Science Association, Chicago, April 6–8, 1995.

25. Alex Cukierman and Steven Webb, "Political Influence on the Central Bank–International Evidence," paper prepared for the annual meeting of the American Political Science Association, New York, August 31–September 4, 1994.

26. Stephan Haggard, Robert Kaufman, and Steven B. Webb, "Democracy, Dictatorship, and Inflation Middle-Income Countries," mimeo, World Bank.

27. Cukierman and Webb, "Political Influence on the Central Bank–International Evidence."

28. Clark, "Party Structure, Regime Stability."

29. Cukierman and Webb, "Political Influence on the Central Bank–International Evidence."

30. John Brewer, *The Sinews of Power: War, Money, and the English State, 1688–1783* (New York: Knopf, 1989); Douglass C. North and Barry R. Weingast, "Constitutions and Commitment: The Evolution of Institutions Governing Public Choice in Seventeenth-Century England, *Journal of Economic History*, 49, 4 (December 1989), 803–832.

31. Cukierman, "Commitment through Delegation, Political Influence, and Central Bank Independence," p. 56.

32. Maxfield, "Financial Incentives and Central Bank Authority in Industrializing Nations."

33. J. Lawrence Broz, "Rent-Seeking and the Organization of the Fiscal-Military State: Central Banking in England and the United States, 1694–1834," Working Paper no. 94–1, Center for International Affairs, Harvard University.

34. Ibid., p. 15.

35. Maxfield, "Financial Incentives and Central Bank Authority in Industrializing Nations."

36. Cukierman, "Commitment through Delegation, Political Influence, and Central Bank Independence."

37. Donald F. Kettl, *Leadership at the Fed* (New Haven: Yale University Press, 1986).

38. There have been several women central bank governors, mostly in former Communist countries: China, Russia, and Poland.

39. Peter A. Hall, *The Political Power of Economic Ideas* (New York: Oxford University Press, 1986), p. 380.

40. Barry Eichengreen, "House Calls of the Money Doctor: The Kemmerer Missions to Latin America, 1917–1931," in Paul W. Drake, ed., *Money Doctors, Foreign Debts, and Economic Reforms in Latin America* (Wilmington, Del.: Jaguar Books, 1994), pp. 110–132; Richard Hemmig Meyer, *Bankers' Diplomacy: Monetary Stabilization in the Twenties* (New York: Columbia University Press, 1970); Paul W. Drake, *The Money Doctor in the Andes: The Kemmerer Missions, 1923–1933* (Durham, N.C.: Duke University Press, 1989).

41. Beth A. Simmons, *Who Adjusts? Domestic Sources of Foreign Economic Policy during the Interwar Years* (Princeton: Princeton University Press, 1994), p. 75. Bordo and Reddish use a related argument in explaining the foundation of the Canadian central bank in the 1930s. Michael D. Bordo and Angela Reddish, "Why Did the Bank of Canada Emerge in 1935?" *Journal of Economic History*, 47, 2 (1987), 405–417.

42. Sylvia Maxfield, *Governing Capital: International Finance and Mexican Politics* (Ithaca: Cornell University Press, 1991).

43. Simmons, *Who Adjusts?*, p. 61. Emphasis added.

44. Johnson and Siklos, "Political Effects on Central Bank Behavior," p. 225.

Chapter Three

1. Epigraph sources: John Woolley, review of *Monetary Sovereignty*, by John B. Goodman, and *Business and Banking*, by Paulette Kurzer, in *Comparative Political Studies*, 27, 2 (July 1994), 302; Mart Laar, "The Politics and Economics of Successful Stabilizations," paper prepared for the Conference on Central Banks in Eastern Europe and the Newly Independent States, University of Chicago Law School, April 21–23, 1994, p. 3.

2. Of course, it is possible that the more independent the central bank, the less financial regulation.

3. On the theory of signaling through policy reform, see Dani Rodrik, "Promises, Promises: Credible Policy Reform via Signaling," *Economic Journal*, 99 (September 1989), 756–772; Brian Portnoy, "Credibility, Institutions, and Ex-

change Rate Commitments in Developing Countries," Program on International Politics, Economics, and Security, University of Chicago, Spring 1995 Speaker Series.

4. Others have focused on differentiating the impact of varying forms of international financial intermediation, with emphasis different from mine. Winters suggests we characterize the political influence of international capital over domestic economic policy according to supplier motives and end-use discretion, which he posits are inversely related. Jeffrey A. Winters, "Power and the Control of Capital," *World Politics*, 46, 3 (April 1994), 419–452. See also Benjamin J. Cohen, "Phoenix Risen: The Resurrection of Global Finance," *World Politics* 48, 2 (January 1996), 268–296; Leslie Elliott Armijo, "Foreign Capital Inflows and Democracy in 'Emerging Markets': An Analytical Framework and Observations from Mexico, Brazil, and India," Political Science Department, Northwestern University, mimeo, April 1995.

5. Others have pioneered use of the asset-specificity concept in political economy. Jeffry A. Frieden, *Debt and Democracy* (Princeton: Princeton University Press, 1991); Beth V. Yarbrough and Robert M. Yarbrough, *Cooperation and Governance in International Trade: The Strategic Organizational Approach* (Princeton: Princeton University Press, 1992).

6. Implicit here is a model of international investment as a contract. "Regarding the security of property across borders as a problem in relational contracting directs attention to characteristics of the assets, product markets and the informational environment that affect the ability of parties to monitor and enforce their contract." Jeffry A. Frieden, "International Investment and Colonial Control: A New Interpretation," *International Organization*, 48, 4 (Autumn 1994), 565.

7. On the different risks, see Stijn Claessens, "Alternative Forms of External Finance: A Survey," Policy Research Working Paper WPS 812, International Economics Department, World Bank, December 1991.

8. Jonathan Eaton and Mark Gersovitz, "Debt with Potential Repudiation: Theoretical and Empirical Analysis," *Review of Economic Studies*, 48 (1981), 289–309; Jeremy Bulow and Kenneth Rogoff, "A Constant Recontracting Model of Sovereign Debt," *Journal of Political Economy*, 97 (1989), 155–187; Donald Lessard, "Country Risks," in Courtenay, Stone et al., eds., *Financial Risk: Theory, Evidence, and Implications* (Boston: Kluwer Academic Publishers, 1988); Donald Lessard, "Beyond the Debt Crisis: Alternative Forms of Financing Growth," in Ishrat Husain and Ishac Diwan, *Dealing with Debt Crisis* (Washington, D.C.: World Bank, 1989).

9. Until the late 1990s government bonds dominated international bond investments in emerging markets.

10. William Glasgall, "The Global Investor," *Business Week*, September 19, 1994, p. 96. The first U.S. banks to enter the ADR business, which began in the early 1990s, were Bank of New York, Citibank, J. P. Morgan, and Morgan Stanley.

11. Miles Kahler, "Politics and International Debt: Explaining the Crisis," in M. Kahler, ed., *The Politics of International Debt* (Ithaca: Cornell University Press, 1986), pp. 11–36; Philip A. Wellons, "International Debt: the Behavior of Banks

in a Politicized Environment," in Kahler, *The Politics of International Debt*, pp. 95–126.

12. Theodore Moran, *Multinational Corporations and the Politics of Dependency* (Princeton: Princeton University Press, 1974); Joseph Grieco, *Between Dependency and Autonomy: India's Experience with the International Computer Industry* (Berkeley: University of California Press, 1984); Dennis Encarnation, *Dislodging Multinationals: India's Strategy in Comparative Perspective* (Ithaca: Cornell University Press, 1989). On the history of expropriation in the World War II era, see E. Williams, "The Extent and Significance of the Nationalization of Foreign-Owned Assets in Developing Countries," *Oxford Economic Papers*, 27 (1975), 260–273.

13. Claessens, "Alternative Forms of External Finance"; Raymond Vernon and Louis T. Wells, *The Economic Environment of International Business* (Englewood Cliffs, N.J.: Prentice-Hall, 1986), pp. 111–117.

14. John Mullin, "Emerging Equity Markets in the Global Economy," *FRBNY Quarterly Review* (Summer 1993), 54–83; David D. Hale, "Stock Markets in the New World Order," *Columbia Journal of World Business* (Summer 1994), 14–29.

15. Richard Roll, "Industrial Structure and the Comparative Behavior of International Stock Market Indices," *Journal of Finance*, 47, 1 (March 1992), 3–41; Asli Demirguc-Kunt and Harry Huizinga, "Barriers to Portfolio Investments in Emerging Stock Markets," Policy Research Working Papers WPS 984, Country Economics Department, World Bank, October 1992.

16. In contemporary Latin America there is government-introduced issue linkage, adding to equity investors' normal market-based leverage over investment-receiving countries. The U.S. government is leading these countries to believe that good treatment of equity investors will not only bring in equity capital but also curry favor with the United States for possible accession to a regional free trade arrangement.

17. Frieden, *Debt and Democracy*. Andrews argues that capital mobility is a structural feature of the international system and should become incorporated into realist theory in order to enhance the theory's predictions of state behavior. David M. Andrews, "Capital Mobility and State Autonomy: Toward a Structural Theory of International Monetary Relations," *International Studies Quarterly*, 38, 2 (1994), 193–218.

18. Przemyslaw Gajdeczka and Mark Stone, "The Secondary Market for Developing Country Loans," *Finance and Development*, 27, 4 (December 1990), 22–26; Walter Molano, "From Bad Debts to Healthy Securities?" Union Bank of Switzerland, mineo.

19. Andrew Atkeson, "International Lending with Moral Hazard and Risk of Repudiation," *Econometrica*, 59, 4 (July 1991), 1069–1990.

20. Kahler, "Politics and International Debt"; Jonathan Eaton, "Debt Relief and the International Enforcement of Loan Contracts," *Journal of Economic Perspectives*, 4, 1 (Winter 1990), 43–56.

21. Barbara Stallings, "International Influence on Economic Policy: Debt Stabilization and Structural Reform," in Stephan Haggard and Robert R. Kaufman, eds., *The Politics of Economic Adjustment* (Princeton: Princeton University Press, 1992), pp. 41–88. As we have learned from the experience of

conditional lending in the 1980s, the bargaining strategy will only work under fairly restrictive assumptions. On the lender side, these are unity and the credibility of the promise of renewed market access. Vincent P. Crawford, "International Lending, Long-Term Credit Relationships, and Dynamic Contract Theory," *Princeton Studies in International Finance*, no. 59 (March 1987). While the lesson about credible incentives hit home in the 1980s, it is a general condition also noted in the 1920s. Eichengreen, for example, argues that the Kemmerer missions to developing countries in the 1920s brought about substantial financial reform because they bore the promise of access to international capital markets. Conditionality would have been much less successful in the 1930s, when "the fashion for foreign lending passed." Barry Eichengreen, "House Calls of the Money Doctor: The Kemmerer Missions to Latin America, 1917–1931," in P. W. Drake, ed., *Money Doctors, Foreign Debts, and Economic Reforms in Latin America from the 1890s to the Present* (Wilmington, Del.: Jaguar Books, 1994), p. 129.

22. Anonymous interviews with employees in New York offices of internationally operating commercial banks, March 1995.

23. Punam Chuhan, Stijn Claessens, and Nlandu Mamingi, "Equity and Bond Flows to Latin America and Asia: The Role of Global and Country Factors," World Bank Working Paper 1160.

24. Gajdeczka and Stone, "The Secondary Market for Developing Country Loans."

25. Barry Eichengreen and Alejandro Portes, "After the Deluge: Default, Negotiation, and Readjustment during the Interwar Years," in B. Eichengreen and P. H. Lindert, eds., *The International Debt Crisis in Historical Perspective* (Cambridge: MIT Press, 1989), p. 16. Government help for bondholders, whether in the form of military intervention or linkage to trade and aid, was sporadic in the nineteenth and early twentieth centuries. Military force was exercised only several times prior to the 1930s, when it became inconceivable given the number and geographic spread of defaults. Barry Eichengreen and Richard Portes, "Dealing with Debt: The 1930s and the 1980s," Discussion Paper no. 300, Center for Economic Policy Research, London, p. 19. This point was later developed by Frieden, "International Investment." The few occasions of military action on behalf of bondholders involve cases of overt host government fraud or discrimination and/or strategic foreign policy concerns.

26. Eichengreen and Portes, "After the Deluge."

27. Philip G. Cerny, "The Deregulation and Re-regulation of Financial Markets in a More Open World," in P. Cerny, ed., *Finance and World Politics: Markets, Regimes, and State in the Post-Hegemonic Era* (Brookfield, Vt.: Edward Elgar, 1993), pp. 51–86.

28. Martin Feldstein and Charles Horioka, "Domestic Savings and International Capital Flows," *Economic Journal*, 90 (198), 314–329. For example, Michael Dooley, Jeffrey Frankel, and Donald Mathieson, "International Capital Mobility: What Do Saving-Investment Correlations Tell Us?" *IMF Staff Papers*, 34 (September 1987), 503–530; Maurice Obstfeld, "Capital Mobility in the World Economy: Some New Tests," in G. Calvo, R. Findlay, and J. de Macedo, eds., *Debt, Stabilization, and Development* (Oxford: Blackwell, 1989), pp. 135–155.

29. Jeffrey A. Frankel, "Measuring International Capital Mobility: A Review," *American Economics Review*, 82, 2 (1992), 197–203.

30. Ibid. In addition to confusion stemming from use of different indicators, differences in conclusions about the growth of international capital mobility also stem from differences in the time frame used for comparison. Much of the literature using interest rate differentials compares pre-1973 and post-1973 data. But some argue that, compared with capital mobility under the gold standard, today's level is not high. Ton Notermas, "The Abdication from National Policy Autonomy: Why the Macroeconomic Policy Regime Has Become So Unfavorable to Labor," *Politics and Society*, 21, 2 (1993), 149; Carlo Zacchia, "International Trade and Capital Movements, 1920–1970," in Carlo M. Cipolla, ed., *The Fontana Economic History of Europe* (Sussex: Harvester, 1977), p. 584.

31. William C. Brainard and James Tobin, "On the Internationalization of Portfolios," *Oxford Economic Papers*, 44 (1992), 533–565.

32. Nadeem U. Haque and Peter J. Montiel, "How Mobile Is Capital in Developing Countries?" *Finance and Development* (September 1991), 38.

33. Convergence in securities market regulation across OECD countries and non-OECD countries facilitates this convergence. See Terry M. Chuppe and Michael Atkin, "Regulation of Securities Markets: Some Recent Trends and Their Implications for Emerging Markets," Policy Research Working Papers WPS 829, Economics Department, International Finance Corporation, World Bank, January 1992. See also IMF, "Private Investment in Developing Countries," Occasional Staff Paper no. 33, January 1985.

34. Carmen Reinhart and R. Todd Smith, "Capital Controls: Concepts and Experiences," IMF, mimeo, April 13, 1995; James A. Hanson, "Opening the Capital Account: A Survey of Issues and Results," Policy Research Working Papers WPS 901, World Bank, May 1992; Donald Mathieson and Liliana Rojas-Suarez, "Liberalization of the Capital Account: Experiences and Issues, IMF Occasional Paper no. 103, March 1993.

35. Stephan Haggard and Sylvia Maxfield, "The Political Economy of Internationalization in the Developing World," *International Organization*, 62, 1 (1996), 35–68.

36. Alberto Alesina and Guido Tabellini, "External Debt, Capital Flight, and Political Risk," *Journal of Development Economics* (November 1989); A. Giovannini and M. de Melo, "Government Revenue from Financial Repression," *American Economic Review*, 83 (1993), 953–963; Nouriel Roubini and Xavier Sala-i-Martin, "Financial Repression and Economic Growth," *Journal of Development Economics*, 39, 1 (July 1992), 5–31.

37. On the political obstacles to effective tax policy in developing countries in general, see Richard Goode, *Government Finance in Developing Countries* (Washington, D.C.: Brookings Institution, 1984), Chap. 4.

38. Roubini and Sala-i-Martin, "Financial Repression and Economic Growth."

39. Quoted in Kevin Brown, "Apostle of Low Inflation," *Financial Times*, June 14, 1993.

40. Beth A. Simmons, *Who Adjusts? Domestic Sources of Foreign Economic Policy during the Interwar Years* (Princeton: Princeton University Press, 1994).

41. Alex Cukierman and Steven Webb, "Political Influence on the Central Bank—International Evidence," paper prepared for the annual meeting of the American Political Science Association, New York, August 31–September 4, 1994.

42. Stephan Haggard and Robert R. Kaufman, "The Political Economy of Stabilization in Middle-Income Countries," in S. Haggard and R. Kaufman, eds., *The Politics of Economic Adjustment* (Princeton: Princeton University Press, 1992), p. 279.

43. The irony here is that those leaders most in need of creditworthiness, because of the uncertainty over the future investment environment created by political instability in many developing countries, are least able to get it. Unfortunately, from a methodological standpoint, time horizons may not always be independent of the need for creditworthiness.

44. Charles Lipson, "International Debt and National Security: Comparing Victorian Britain and Postwar America," in Eichengreen and Lindert, *The International Debt Crisis*, p. 216.

Chapter Four

1. Epigraphs: "Narrow Money," *The Economist*, August 28, 1993, p. 16; Paul A. Volcker, "The Triumph of Central Banking?" 1990 Per Jacobssen Lecture (Washington, D.C.: IMF, 1990), p. 3.

2. Alex Cukierman, Steven B. Webb, and Bilim Neyapti, "Measuring the Independence of Central Banks," *World Bank Economic Review*, 6, 3 (September 1992).

3. Because of data limitations, this chapter does not consider cross-regional variation in politicians' tenure security.

4. In addition to the new charter itself, see Economist Intelligence Unit, *Country Report—Portugal*, no. 2, 1992, p. 12; Economist Intelligence Unit, *Country Report—Portugal*, no. 3, 1992, p. 9; Economist Intelligence Unit, *Country Report—Portugal*, no. 1, 1991, p. 9. Discussion of all the charter changes of the 1990s is based on evaluation of the new statutes themselves. Citations to charter summaries and evaluations in the business press are included where possible.

5. Peter Bruce, "Survey of Spain, Banking, and Finance," *Financial Times*, June 23, 1993.

6. "Turkey: Treasury Demands Threaten Central Bank Independence," *Middle East Economic Digest*, April 19, 1991.

7. "Turkey: Central Bank Interview," *Euromoney Treasury Manager*, May 12, 1992.

8. The "divorce" refers to legal changes absolving the Italian central bank of requirements to monetize the government debt. See John B. Goodman, *Monetary Sovereignty: The Politics of Central Banking in Western Europe* (Ithaca: Cornell University Press, 1992); Gerald A. Epstein and Juliet B. Schor, "The Divorce of the Banca d'Italia and the Italian Treasury," in Peter Lange and Marino Regini, eds., *State, Market, and Social Regulation: New Perspectives on Italy* (Cambridge: Cambridge University Press, 1989), pp. 147–167.

9. "The Monetary System," *Business International*, June 1, 1992; Carlo A.

Ciampi, Letters, *Financial Times*, March 13, 1992; Haig Simonian, "Italy's Monetary Parting of the Ways," *Financial Times*, February 19, 1992.

10. Quoted in "French Right Plan Bill on Independent Central Bank," *Reuters*, December 18, 1992.

11. Quoted in "French Centrists to Urge Independent Central Bank," *Reuters*, January 12, 1993.

12. Quoted in "Sapin Wants Independent Bank of France Soon," *Reuters*, January 4, 1993.

13. Samuel Brittan, "Next Stage for the Franc Fort," *Financial Times*, April 5, 1993.

14. Report of an Independent Panel Chaired by Eric Roll, "Independent and Accountable: A New Mandate for the Bank of England" (London: Center for Economic Policy Research, 1993).

15. Larry Elliott, "Governor Toasts Autonomy but Rejects the Poisoned Chalice," *The Guardian*, February 2, 1994, p. 14.

16. Kathleen Hinton-Braaten, "New Central Banks," paper prepared for the Conference on Central Banks in Eastern Europe and the Newly Independent States, University of Chicago Law School, April 21–23, 1994, p. 11.

17. The following discussion is based on Stephen Lewarne, "Central Bank Independence and Inflation Policy in Russia and the Commonwealth of Independent States," paper prepared for the Claremont Institute for Economic Policy Studies and the Lowe Institute of Political Economy workshop on "The Political Economy of Money and Inflation in the Former Soviet Union," April 1–2, 1993; Juliet Ellen Johnson, "The Russian Banking System: Institutional Responses to the Market Transition," mimeo, Princeton University, December 1993; Ardo Hansson and Jeffrey Sachs, "Monetary Institutions and Credible Stabilization: A Comparison of Experience in the Baltics," mimeo, Stockholm Institute of East European Economics and Harvard University, June 1994; Eduard Hochreiter, "Central Banking in Economies in Transition: Institutional and Exchange Rate Issues," mimeo, Austrian National Bank, March 1994; and Hinton-Braaten, "New Central Banks."

18. In November 1994 Yeltsin fired then–central bank governor Geraschenko without consulting parliament. In protest the Duma refused to approve Yeltsin's nomination of Tatiana Paramonova to replace Victor Geraschenko.

19. Gail Buyske, "A Tough Task for Russia's Central Bank," *Wall Street Journal Europe*, December 1–2, 1995.

20. Seemingly arbitrary dismissal *has* occurred, as in the case of Galym Bainazarov.

21. V. A. Yuschenko, "Central Bank Independence: Broader Perspectives and Prospects for the Future," paper prepared for the Conference on Central Banks in Eastern Europe and the Newly Independent States, University of Chicago Law School, April 21–23, 1994, p. 3.

22. For a contemporary discussion of currency boards, see Kent Osband and Delano Villanueva, "Independent Currency Authorities: An Analytical Primer," *IMF Staff Papers*, 40, 1 (March 1993), 202–217.

23. Mart Laar, "The Politics and Economics of Successful Stabilizations," paper prepared for the Conference on Central Banks in Eastern Europe and

the Newly Independent States, University of Chicago Law School, April 21–23, 1994, p. 3.

24. The currency board weathered a severe test eighteen months after it was founded, when three of Estonia's largest banks faced severe liquidity problems. Upholding its commitment to hard money, the currency board, vested with financial supervisory power, closed one of the banks and merged the other two.

25. Estonia enjoys the highest foreign investment of the Baltic countries. Hansson and Sachs, "Monetary Institutions and Credible Stabilization," p. 17.

26. Pierre L. Siklos, "Central Bank Independence in the Transitional Economies: A Preliminary Investigation of Hungary, Poland, The Czech and Slovak Republics," in I. Szekely and J. Bonin, eds., *Development and Reform of the Financial System in Central and Eastern Europe* (London: Elgar, 1994); David M. Kemme, "The Reform of the System of Money, Banking, and Credit in Central Europe," mimeo, Economics Department, Wichita State University, July 1992. On Eastern European development in general, see *Central Banking in Emerging Market-Oriented Economies: A Symposium Sponsored by the Federal Reserve Bank of Kansas City*, Jackson Hole, Wy., August 23–25, 1990.

27. Andrzej Rudka, "Reform of the Banking System in Poland," in D. Kemme and A. Rudka, eds., *Monetary and Banking Reform in Postcommunist Economies* (New York: Institute for East-West Security Studies, 1993), p. 74.

28. "Notices: How a Central Banker Shut Up Her Critics," *Global Finance*, August 1993, p. 9.

29. Kemme, "Reform," pp. 19–23.

30. Siklos, "Central Bank Independence."

31. The wording is crucial: the legislation states that the bank must support government economic policy, but includes an important proviso missing in the Hungarian and Slovenian cases. The bank must support government economic policy *unless* this creates insoluble conflict with monetary stability.

32. Vladimir Jindra, "Problems in Czechoslovak Banking Reform," in Kemme and Rudka, *Monetary and Banking Reform*, pp. 43–71.

33. Harold Jackson and John Glover, "A Long, Slow Haul to Break with the Past," *The Guardian*, January 23, 1993.

34. Kemme, "Reform," pp. 14–15.

35. Siklos, "Central Bank Independence"; Istvan Abel, John P. Bonin, and Pierre L. Siklos, "Crippled Monetary Policy in Transforming Economies: Why Central Bank Independence Does Not Restore Control," in P. L. Siklos, ed., *Varieties of Monetary Reforms: Lessons and Experiences on the Road to Monetary Union* (Norwell, Mass.: Kluwer Academic Publishers).

36. Akos Balassa, "The Transformation of the Hungarian Banking System," in Kemme and Rudka, *Monetary and Banking Reform*, p. 18.

37. Mileti Mladenov, "Money, Banking, and Credit: The Case of Bulgaria," in Kemme and Rudka, *Monetary and Banking Reform*, pp. 99–114.

38. Alejandro Foxley, the opposition *Concertacion*'s designated minister of finance, leaked news of the negotiations in order to tap public support. Foxley's victory in these negotiations, several weeks before the scheduled presidential elections, was seen as a turning point in Chile's transition away from authoritarian rule. Interview, Andres Bianchi, former Chilean central bank president,

Paris, July 6, 1992; Jeffrey Ryser, "Chalk Up Another One for the Monetarists," *Global Finance*, July 1993, pp. 66–68; Osvaldo Larranaga J., "Autonomía y deficit del Banco Central," *Colección Estudios Cieplan*, 32 (June 1991), 121–157.

39. Stephen Fidler, "The IMF in Washington: Argentina Expected to Sign Agreement Soon," *Financial Times*, September 27, 1989.

40. Geoffrey P. Miller, "Constitutional Moments, Precommitment, and Fundamental Reform: The Case of Argentina," *Washington University Law Quarterly*, 71, 4 (1993), 1073–1074.

41. Economist Intelligence Unit, *Country Report—Argentina*, no. 4, 1992, p. 12.

42. Economist Intelligence Unit, *Country Report—Colombia*, no. 1, 1993, p. 9.

43. Stephen Fidler, "Venezuela's Central Bank Keeps Its Head: What Happened When All Around Were Losing Theirs," *Financial Times*, June 23, 1993, p. 8. Ruth de Krivoy resigned from central bank in June 1994.

44. A slightly different interpretation is found in Delia Boylan, "Holding Democracy Hostage: Central Bank Autonomy in the Transition from Authoritarian Rule," Political Science Department, Stanford University, mimeo, September 1995.

45. "Fundamental Fiscal Reforms Are Still Lacking," *Business International*, June 8, 1992.

46. R. Lindsay Knight, "Central Bank Independence in New Zealand," in P. Downes and R. Vaez-Zadeh, eds., *The Evolving Role of Central Banks* (Washington, D.C.: IMF, 1991).

47. Mark Beyer, "New Zealand: Government to Give Independence to Its Central Bank," *Australian Financial Review*, December 14, 1989.

48. Economist Intelligence Unit, *Country Report—New Zealand*, no. 2, 1990, p. 11.

49. "Wise Men from the South," *The Economist*, February 2, 1991.

50. David Clark, "Australia: Case for a More Independent RBA," *Australian Financial Review*, September 8, 1993.

51. Jonathan Friedland, "Pakistan: Stuck in a Rut," *Far Eastern Economic Review*, October 17, 1991.

52. Farhan Bokhari, "Pakistan Central Bank Independence Move," *Far Eastern Economic Review*, September 10, 1993.

53. "Pakistan: Central Bank Independence Reduced," *Middle East Economic Digest*, January 10, 1994; Rashid Ahmed, "Bhutto Backtracks," *Far Eastern Economic Review*, January 13, 1993, p. 79.

54. Murray Hiebert, "From Monopoly to Market Place," *Far Eastern Economic Review*, October 17, 1991.

55. Manik de Silva, "Sri Lanka: Fiscal Phoenix," *Far Eastern Economic Review*, October 17, 1991.

56. "South Korea: Cho to Emphasize Flexibility in Control of Money Supply," *Korea Economic Daily*, March 27, 1992.

57. John Burton, "Korea Central Bank Gets New Governor," *Financial Times*, March 15, 1993; "South Korea: BoK Boss Dismissed," *Korea Economic Daily*, March 17, 1993.

58. "South Korea: Critics Give Financial Reform Program Second Look," *Korea Economic Daily*, June 3, 1993.

59. See, for example, "Japan: Stern Call for Rate Cut Stirs Storm," *Nikkei Weekly*, March 9, 1992.

60. The Bank of Japan also held seminars in central banking for other Asian central banks.

61. "Japan: A Yen for Greater Independence," *Euroweek*, August 3, 1990.

62. Ibid.

63. "The Market Opens," *Middle East Economic Digest*, December 21, 1990.

64. "Iran: The Future of the Iranian Economy," *Middle East Economic Digest*, November 15, 1991.

65. "Iran: Reinforcing the Gains," *Euromoney*, September 1, 1993.

66. Economist Intelligence Unit, *Country Report—Egypt*, no. 3, 1992, p. 16; "Central Bank Role to Be Enhanced, *Middle East Economic Digest*, August 30, 1991, p. 11.

67. "Namibia: Central Bank Chief Stays On," *African Economic Digest*, December 10, 1990.

Chapter Five

1. This research design does not seek to definitively prove the weight of international financial influence in shaping central bank authority. It is intended to show the plausibility of the argument that need for international creditworthiness, as it is defined here, is a necessary, not sufficient, condition for central bank independence. Although I have not selected on the dependent variable, a recent paper proposes that such a practice is not methodologically problematic for evaluation of necessary conditions. See Douglas Dion, "Evidence and Inference in the Comparative Case Study," Political Science Department, University of Michigan, mimeo, July 1994.

2. To guard against selection bias, I conducted the most thorough possible research. For the country histories I interviewed virtually every living former central bank governor and many of their executive branch counterparts.

3. B. R. Shenoy, "The Currency, Banking, and Exchange System of Thailand," *IMF Staff Papers*, 1, 2 (September 1950), 289–314.

4. Richard Doner and Daniel Unger, "The Politics of Finance in Thai Economic Development," in S. Haggard, C. H. Lee and S. Maxfield, eds., *The Politics of Finance in Developing Countries* (Ithaca: Cornell University Press, 1993), pp. 93–123.

5. His family name is commonly shortened to "Phibun."

6. Bank of Thailand, *Annual Report*, 1952.

7. Puey Unphakorn, "Lialong Laenna" (Retrospective), in Rangsam Thanapornpan, *In Honor of Dr. Puey* (Bangkok, n.d.), pp. 163–165; Puey Ungphakorn, "Looking Back, Looking Ahead," in *A Siamese for All Seasons: Collected Articles by and about Puey Ungphakorn* (Bangkok: Komol Keemthong Foundation, 1984), pp. 304–309.

8. See David A. Wilson, *Politics in Thailand* (Ithaca: Cornell University Press, 1962); Suchit Bunbongkarn, "Political Institutions and Processes," in S. Xuto, ed., *Government and Politics of Thailand* (Oxford: Oxford University Press, 1987).

9. Interviews with Ekkamol Siriwat, June 11, 1991, Bangkok; Chavalit Thanachanan, May 23, 1991, Bangkok; Sathaporn Chinajitre, June 5, 1991, Bangkok; Nopporn Ruanngsakul, August 8, 1991, Bangkok.

10. Interviews, Alek Rozental, July 18,1991, Bangkok, and Bunyaraks Ninsanada, July 11, 1991, Bangkok. Because a reputation for honesty and integrity was crucial to his power, Puey declined other lucrative government posts in order to retain his independence as governor of the Bank of Thailand. Many contemporary central bank charters explicitly prohibit high-level central bank personnel from holding any other government position.

11. Laurence D. Stifel, "Technocrats and Modernization in Southeast Asia," *Asian Survey*, 16, 12 (December 1976), 1192–1193.

12. Interview, Prachitr Yossundara, Bangkok, July 19, 1991.

13. Puey, *A Siamese for All Seasons*, p. 315.

14. IMF, *International Financial Statistics* (Washington, D.C.: International Monetary Fund, 1948).

15. Of note for their size and importance in later Thai political history are the United Thai People's Party, the Democrat Party, and the Independent Party.

16. Among the reasons for coup was the threat of a parliamentary vote against the government budget. Members of parliament threatened to veto the budget if they were not granted allocations for development projects they had proposed. Debate over the budget on these terms was preempted by the coup.

17. Richard F. Doner and Anek Laothamatas, "Thailand: Economic and Political Gradualism," in Stephan Haggard and Steven B. Webb, eds., *Voting for Reform: Democracy, Political Liberalization, and Economic Adjustment* (Oxford: Oxford University Press, 1994), pp. 411–452.

18. Doner and Unger, "The Politics of Finance."

19. Interview, Boonchu Rojanastien, July 20, 1991, Bangkok.

20. Personal correspondence with Bank of Thailand official, February 7, 1992.

21. Interview, Chavalit Thanachanan, May 23, 1991, Bangkok.

22. Somchaii Wongspark, "After Chavalit," *Puujatkarn* (The Manager: Monthly Review), 79 (April 1990), 103–104. Even at this point the Bank of Thailand's authority, although weaker than in the 1960s, was stronger than in many other countries at the time. Snoh did meet frequently with military leaders and had some success in convincing them to limit weapons purchases from abroad and to control the debt ceiling. Correspondence, Chavalit Thanachanan.

23. Somchaii Wongsapark, "After Chavalit," pp. 103–104.

24. Interview, Boonchu Rojanastien, July 29, 1992, Bangkok.

25. Clark D. Neher, "Political Succession in Thailand," *Asian Survey*, 32, 7 (July 1992), 593.

26. Chai-Anan Samudavanija, "Thailand: A Stable Semi-Democracy," in Larry Diamond, Juan J. Linz, and Seymour Martin Lipset, eds., *Politics in Developing Countries: Comparing Experiences with Democracy* (Boulder: Lynne Reiner Publishers, 1990), p. 282; Suchit Bunbongkarn, "Political Institutions and Processes," in S. Xuto, ed., *Government and Politics of Thailand* (Oxford: Oxford University Press, 1987), pp. 41–75; Ansil Ramsay, "Thailand 1979: A Govern-

ment in Trouble," *Asian Survey*, 20, 2 (February 1980), 112–119; Ansil Ramsay, "Thailand 1978: Kriangsak—The Thai Who Binds," *Asian Survey*, 19, 2 (February 1979), 104–114.

27. Doner and Laothamatas, "Thailand: Gradualism."

28. According to the *Far Eastern Economic Review*, "Negotiations over Boonchu took place between Kukrit [Social Action Party leader] and Kriangsak for nearly a month.... Boonchu reportedly demanded wide discretionary powers over the major economic portfolios and control over the central bank." Richard Nations, "A Time for Generalship," *Far Eastern Economic Review*, June 1, 1979, p. 13.

29. Doner and Unger, "The Politics of Finance."

30. Doner and Laothamatas, "Thailand: Gradualism"; Paisal Sricharatchanya, "A Sack Full of Questions," *Far Eastern Economic Review*, September 27, 1984, p. 138.

31. Neher, "Political Succession," p. 594; Suchit Bungbongkarn, *The Military in Thai Politics, 1981–86* (Singapore: Institute of Southeast Asian Studies, 1987); Larry A. Niksch, "Thailand in 1981: The Prem Government Feels the Heat," *Asian Survey*, 22, 2 (February 1982), 190–199; Surachai Sirikrai, "General Prem Survives on a Conservative Line," *Asian Survey*, 22, 11 (November 1982), 1093–1104; Suchitra Punyarataban-Bhakdi, "Thailand in 1983: Democracy Thai Style," *Asian Survey*, 23, 2 (February 1984).

32. Somaii succeeded Boonchu as finance minister. Prem, with close ties to rural Thailand, was sympathetic to the Social Action Party's rural development platform, and he brought Boonchu in as deputy prime minister, in control of the Ministry of Finance, although not with the complete economic control that Boonchu had demanded of Kriangsak. Boonchu, representing the Social Action Party, had to share control over economic policy within the cabinet with ministers representing the Chat Thai Party. Boonchu left the government within a year.

33. Doner and Laothamatas, "Thailand: Gradualism."

34. Paisal Sricharatchanya, "A Sack Full of Questions"; "1984: Year of Financial Crisis," *Dorkbia* (Interest Rates), 112 (January 1985).

35. The commercial banks themselves disagreed about the proposed measure.

36. Somachai Wongsapark and Pathiya Jettasane, "Pramual's Economic Advisory Group," *Phujaakarn* (The Manager: Monthly Review) (July 1989), 78; Paul Handley, "The Gentle Squeeze," *Far Eastern Economic Review*, December 21, 1989, pp. 68–69.

37. Interview, Chavalit Thanashanan, May 23, 1991, Bangkok.

38. Songkiat Chartwatananan, "The New Wave, Vijit Supanit," *Dorkbia* (Interest Rates), October 1990, p. 14.

39. This discussion was promoted by the editor of one of Thailand's leading business periodicals, Banyong Suwanpong.

40. Ravi Amatayakul and Shrikrishna A. Pandit, "Financial Institutions in Thailand," *IMF Staff Papers*, p. 469.

41. James Manas Vongphakdi, "Financial Development in Thailand and the Role of the Central Bank" (M.A. thesis, New England University, 1982); Bank of

Thailand, "Its History and Roles in Managing the Financial System," *Commemorating Opening the Head Office of the Bank of Thailand,* June 12, 1982.

42. On the Thai Bankers' Association, see Anek Laothamatas, "No Longer a Bureaucratic Policy" (Ph.D. diss., Columbia University, 1989), p. 88.

43. Interviews, Boonchu Rojansastien, July 20, 1991, Bangkok; Prachitr Yossundara, July 19, 1991, Bangkok; and Chavalit Thanachanan, July 16, 1991, Bangkok.

44. For a comparison of these, see Chai-Ana Samudavanija, "Political Institutionalization in Thailand: Continuity and Change," paper prepared for the project on "Development, Stability and Security in the Pacific-Asian Region," University of California–Berkeley, March 17–21, 1984.

45. Terry M. Moe and Scott A. Wilson, "Presidents and the Politics of Structure," *Law and Contemporary Problems,* 57, 2 (Spring 1994), 42.

46. Although this is not an exercise in hypothesis "testing" in a statistical sense, for more on the use of counterfactual reasoning in small-*N* research, see James D. Fearon, "Counterfactuals and Hypothesis Testing in Political Science," *World Politics,* 43, 2 (January 1991), 169–196.

Chapter Six

1. See Edgar Turlington, *Mexico and Her Foreign Creditors* (New York: Columbia University Press, 1930).

2. Robin King, "Confrontation and Accommodation: A Multiactor Approach to Mexican External Debt Policy and Macroeconomic Management" (Ph.D. diss., University of Texas, Austin, 1991).

3. The candidate, Luis Montes de Oca, had previously (1927–1932) occupied the post of finance minister. This contributed to Cárdenas's concern that Montes de Oca might find it difficult "to subordinate himself." Eduardo Suárez, *Comentarios y recuerdos* (Mexico City: Editorial Porrúa, 1976), p. 163.

4. Although the subcommittee given this assignment included Montes de Oca, Luciano Wiechers, Manual Gómez Morin, Eduardo Suárez, and Miguel Palacios Macedo, it was Palacios Macedo who single-handedly wrote the draft legislation. The completed draft was brought to a meeting of the charter revision subcommittee at which one of the members tried to bolster his opposition with arguments from the newly published General Theory, to no avail. The rhetoric of the new charter was extremely orthodox; there were nineteen allusions to the real bills doctrine, holding that the money supply should only expand in response to productive activity. Eduardo Turrent Díaz, *Historía del Banco de México* (Mexico City: Banco de México, 1982), p. 399.

5. National Archives, Record Group 59, 812.516, 1930–1939, roll 79.

6. The Cárdenas administration had created a variety of new state development institutions, including special-purpose banks, which all began to try to draw on the central bank's financing facilities. In November 1936 the Banco de México refused to rediscount paper sent by these banks, proposing as a compromise the creation of a new government account at the central bank over which bank officials could try to exercise limits.

7. Although it was not effective, this November 1937 report to the government and spending-limitation agreement is remarkable in Mexican central bank history. It is unlikely that the central bank ever again openly submitted written policy demands to the Mexican president or obtained written agreement to those demands.

8. Turrent Díaz, *Historía*, p. 457. There is a report, however, that the National Banking Commission members resigned en masse in March 1938 rather than sign an audit attesting to the financial health of the Banco de México. National Archives, Record Group 59, U.S. Embassy to State Department, March 30, 1938 812.516/3–3038, 1930–1939, roll 79.

9. The PRI faced an electoral challenge from Miguel Henríquez Guzmán and his party in 1952. The PRI managed to defeat the "henriquista" movement, and its organizational dissolution "was the ultimate episode in the long history of divisions within the revolutionary family [PRI]." Olga Pellicer de Brody and Jose Luis Reyna, *Historía de la Revolución Mexicana: El afianzamiento de la estabilidad política* (Mexico City: El Colegio de México, 1978), p. 60.

10. For a partisan summary of the politico-economic context of this devaluation, see Antonio Carrillo Flores, "Causas y efectos de la devaluación monetaria de abril de 1954," *Problemas agricolas e industriales de México*, 6, 3 (September 1954), 197–204.

11. Interview, Antonio Ortiz Mena, July 6, 1993, Mexico City.

12. Interview, Antonio Ortiz Mena, July 7, 1993, Mexico City.

13. Interview, Victor Urquidi, August 27, 1991, Mexico City; interview, Ernesto Fernández Hurtado, July 7, 1993, Mexico City. Both of these men were working at the central bank at the time. Pamela Starr emphasizes different aspects of the 1954 devaluation episode. She notes that initially the IMF opposed the devaluation, although she does not deny that discussions over it helped build important channels of communication. Starr also implies doubt about the claims of these interviewees that Ruiz Cortines was brought into the policy formulation process at a relatively late stage. Pamela Karen Starr, "Political Coalitions and Economic Stabilization: Argentina, Mexico, and Brazil during the Early 1950s" (Ph.D. diss., University of Southern California, 1993), chap. 3.

14. National Archives, Record Group 59, Mexican Embassy to State Department, September 13, 1954, 812.14/9–1354, Box 4482.

15. Antonio Ortiz Mena, "La relación entre el gobierno federal y Banco de México," in Banco de México, *Rodrigo Gómez: Vida y Obra* (Mexico City: Fondo de Cultura Económico, 1991), p. 120. Interview, Antonio Ortiz Mena, July 6, 1993, Mexico City.

16. Interview, Antonio Ortiz Mena, July 6, 1993, Mexico City.

17. One example was the gradual phasing in of the Ley de Trabajo in order to mitigate potential inflationary consequences. Another was the delay in the imposition of the value-added tax. Economic policy agenda setting was facilitated by a joint working group called the Grupo Hacienda–Banco de México, headed by one of the private sector central bank stockholders, Manuel Sanchez Cuen. The group had a professional technical staff and was explicitly created as a way to centralize information and to allow for discussion of economic prob-

lems that would otherwise have been difficult to achieve because of the "great resistance that existed in normal channels." Interview, Antonio Ortiz Mena, July 6, 1993, Mexico City.

18. Interview, Gustavo Romero Kolbeck, July 8, 1993, Mexico City.

19. Interview, Ernesto Fernández Hurtado, July 7, 1993, Mexico City.

20. Interview, Ernesto Fernández Hurtado, July 7, 1993, Mexico City.

21. Romero was ordered to do as instructed. He huddled with his staff and decided to implement half the requested appreciation at the close of business and the other half at the opening of business the next day. López Portillo took this as a refusal to follow presidential orders.

22. Sylvia Maxfield, "The Politics of Mexican Financial Policy," in S. Haggard, C. H. Lee and S. Maxfield, eds., *The Politics of Finance in Developing Countries* (Ithaca: Cornell University Press, 1993), pp. 253–257.

23. Sylvia Maxfield, "Mexican Financial Liberalization," in Kent Calder et al., eds., *Letting Capital Loose* (Ithaca: Cornell University Press, forthcoming).

24. Luis Alberto Rodriguez, "Autonomía del Banco de México," *La Jornada*, May 18, 1993.

25. It passed with the "symbolic modification" of one word in the document submitted by President Salinas's office. Ricardo Aleman and Ricardo Olayo, "Fue aprobado en comisiones el dictamen sobre autonomía del Banco de México," *La Jornada*, May 19, 1993.

26. Ignacio Ovalle Fernández, "Banco de México, la cereza del pastel," *La Jornada*, May 26, 1993.

27. Leon Bendesky, "Banco de México, Inc.," *La Jornada*, May 23, 1993.

Chapter Seven

1. Choi Byŏng-Sŏn, "Financial Policy and Big Business in Korea: The Perils of Financial Regulation," in S. Haggard, C. H. Lee, and S. Maxfield, eds., *The Politics of Finance in Developing Countries* (Ithaca: Cornell University Press, 1993), pp. 23–54.

2. Arthur I. Bloomfield, *Banking Reform in South Korea* (New York: Federal Reserve Bank of New York, 1951); Arthur I. Bloomfield, "Report and Recommendations on Banking in South Korea," *Monthly Statistical Review*, Bank of Korea, Research Department (June 1952).

3. Kim Chŏny-Ryŏn, *Thirty Years' History of Korean Economic Policies* (Seoul: Chungang Ilbo Sa, n.d.).

4. Han Sŏng-Chu, *The Failure of Democracy in Korea* (Berkeley: University of California Press, 1971).

5. Letter from U.S. Embassy in Seoul to Secretary of State, December 12, 1956, National Archives, Record Group 59, 895B.14/1–1157; telegram from U.S. Embassy in Seoul to Secretary of State, March, 19, 1959, National Archives, Record Group 59, 895B.14/3–1159; telegram from U.S. Embassy in Seoul to Secretary of State, March 11, 1959, National Archives, Record Group 59, 895B.14/3–1159.

6. Chŏng Hye-Yŏng, "The Fact of the Matter, 'Declaration of Independence' by BoK," *Wolgan Kyŏnghyang* (Monthly Trends) (September 1987), 148–159;

Shin Sŏk-Ha, "A Study of the Independence of the Bank of Korea" (M.A. thesis, Department of Economics, Seoul National University, 1990); telegram from Cronk, U.S. Embassy in Seoul to the Secretary of State, December 12, 1956, National Archives, Record Group 59, 895B.14/1–2059.

7. Chŏng, "The Fact of the Matter"; Shin, "A Study of the Independence"; Bae Ŭi-Hwan, *Although We Overcame the Spring Famine: Autobiography of Bae Ŭi-Hwan* (Seoul: Korea Herald, 1991).

8. Interview, Bae Ŭi-Hwan, October 25, 1991, Seoul.

9. Interview, Bae Ŭi-Hwan, October 25, 1991, Seoul; Chung, "The Fact of the Matter"; Shin, "A Study of the Independence."

10. According to the original charter the Bank of Korea had rights to supervise the so-called deposit money banks but not the mutual financing companies and insurance and trust companies. As the portion of the national financial system dominated by these nonbank financial institutions began to grow, concern over who would supervise them began to increase. Furthermore, another large category of credit, that granted by "policy finance" institutions, also lay beyond Bank of Korea control. This made monetary control by the central bank virtually impossible.

11. The January 1962 Law of Foreign Exchange Management transferred decision making on foreign exchange from the Bank of Korea to the government.

12. During the 1970s there was relatively little turnover in the Bank of Korea governorship. This continuity is actually an indication of complete submission to political authorities. It is an example of the caution which should be exercised in relying solely on governor turnover as an indicator of central bank authority.

13. Stephan Haggard et al., *Macroeconomic Policy and Adjustment in Korea, 1970–1990* (Cambridge, Mass.: Harvard Institute for International Development and Korean Development Institute, 1994).

14. Chŏng, "The Fact of the Matter"; interview, Kim Yŏng-Hwan, October 25, 1991, Seoul.

15. Interview, Kim Yŏng-Hwan, October 25, 1991, Seoul.

16. Interview, Chŏng Ŭn-Ch'an, October 24, 1991, Seoul.

17. Interview, Chŏng Ŭn-Ch'an, October 24, 1991, Seoul.

18. Shin, "A Study on the Independence," p. 45.

19. There is considerable literature on this. For example, see Choi, "Financial Policy and Big Business in Korea."

20. Nouriel Roubini and Xavier Sala-i-Martin, "Financial Repression and Economic Growth," *Journal of Development Economics*, 39, 1 (July 1992), 5–31.

21. For an elaboration of this viewpoint, see Lee Kŭn-Shik, "Kwanch'i Kŭmyung Chŏngsanŭi Haekshim Kwaje" (Core Tasks in Liquidation of Government-Led Finance), *Chugan Maegyŏng* (Weekly Daily Economics), August 27, 1987; "Kyŏgje Minjuhwawa Hanŭn Chŏngnip" (Economic Democratization and Neutrality of BoK), *Donga Ilbo* (Donga Daily), July 31, 1987; *Hanguk Ilbo* (Hanguk Daily), April 5, 1988; "Hanûn Manûi Moksori" (The Voice of the BoK Men), *Donga Ilbo* (Donga Daily), August 4, 1987. Articles reprinted in Bank of Korea, *Collection of Journalistic Articles about the Issue of Assurance of Central Bank Independence* (Seoul: Bank of Korea, 1990).

22. They used the analogy of opium to make their point that control over monetary policy should reside with the central bank, not the Ministry of Finance or Economic Planning Board. "Opium may be good medicine when it is well prescribed. . . . But as habitual use of opium does the human body great harm, chronic inflation makes the national economy deteriorate . . . control of the money supply should be directed by the central bank, as the use of opium should be by a doctor." "Hanŭn Tongnipsŏng: Kyŏngje Minjuhwa Pŏtimmok" (BoK's Independence: A Proposition of Economic Democratization), *Maeil Kyŏngje* (Daily Economic News), August 5, 1987; see also "Hanŭn Tongnipsŏng Pojang Hŏnbŏbe Myŏngshi Haeya" (Assurance of the Neutrality of BoK Should Be Included in the Constitution), *Chungang Ilbo* (Chungang Daily), August 1, 1987.

23. High-level Bank of Korea officials were wary of pushing for large-scale change because they feared losing their jobs. Bank of Korea officials are not easily able to get other government jobs.

24. Sŏ Won-Sŏk, "Hanguk Ŭnhaengŭn Kwayŏn Chaemubu Namdaemun Ch'uljangsonya" (Is BoK Really the Namdaemun Office of the BoK?), *Chugan Chosun* (Weekly Chosŏn), August 14, 1987.

25. "Hanŭn Tongnipsŏng Sangbandoen Tu Shigak—Kuk'oe Sokkirok Chisang Chŏngae" (Opposing Two Viewpoints about BoK's Independence-Selected Summarization of Assembly's Stenographic Records), *Maeil Kyŏngje* (Daily Economic News), August 15, 1987.

26. See "Hanŭn Wanjŏn Tongnipsŏng Pojang: Yasamdang Tanil Shian Maryŏn, Yŏkwonbandae Chôngch'i Chaengjŏm Yesang" (Full Independence of Bank of Korea Assured: Three Opposition Parties Made a Unified Proposal, Government Party Opposes, Which Will Become a Political Issue), *Maeil Kyŏngje* (Daily Economic News), July 25, 1988, for a thorough comparison of the existing legislation and the opposition parties' proposal.

27. "Hanûnbôp Kaejôngan, Sae Chaengjômhwa" (Renewed Issue of "Amendment Proposal of Bank of Korea Law"), *Chosun Ilbo* (Chosŏn Daily), July 26, 1988.

28. When questioned about how the Ministry of Finance could control monetary policy when the Bank of Korea governor chaired the Monetary Board, the government party suggested that there would be some distribution of authority between the two agencies. For example, it was suggested that the Economic Cabinet (which excluded the Bank of Korea governor) might decide interest rates while the central bank would be permitted to set margins of interest rate increase and decrease. "Hanŭne Insa, Kyŏngyŏng, Yesankwŏn Puyŏ" (BoK Will Be Awarded the Rights of Personnel, Management, and Budget), *Seoul Shinmun* (Seoul Newspaper), August 2, 1988.

29. Lee Kye-Min, "Chungang Ŭnhaengŭi Tongnipsŏng Pojang" (Assurance of Central Bank's Independence), *Hanguk Kyŏngje* (Hanguk Economic News), July 31, 1988.

30. Kim Sŏk-Kyu and Kim Dae-Mo, "Chaejŏng Kŭmyung Chŏngch'aek: Chohwanya, Kyŏnjenya" (Fiscal-Finance Policy: "Harmony" or "Check and Balance"), *Maeil Kyŏngje* (Daily Economic News), August 9, 1988.

31. Lee Kye-Min, "Hanŭn Kinŭng Sashilsang Ch'ukso" (Functions of Bank of Korea Are Reduced in Fact), *Hanguk Kyŏngje* (Hanguk Economic News), August 9, 1988.

32. "Hanŭnhaengwonhyŏp Kŭmt'ongwiwondŭl Ch'ulse Soksem Maeng-gong" (Council of BoK Employees Attacked Monetary Board Severely, Alleging That the Board Members Seek Promotion), *Hanguk Ilbo* (Hanguk Daily), August 10, 1988.

33. "Habŭichŏm Motch'annŭn Hanŭn Tongnipsŏng" (No Points of Agreement on the Independence of the Bank of Korea), *Chungang Kyŏngje* (Chungang Economic News), August 10, 1988.

34. "Hanŭn Tongnip Konggaenonjŏn Yesang" (Open Debate on the Independence of Bank of Korea Is Predicted), *Yŏnhap T'ongshin* (United Press); "T'onghwa Shinyong Chŏngch'aek Kŭmt'ongwisô Ch'onggwal" (Money and Credit Policies to Be Controlled by Monetary Board), *Chŏngang Ilbo* (Chungang Daily), September 5, 1988.

35. "'Hanŭn Tongnipsŏng Pojang' Saegukmyŏn" (New Phase on the Issue of "Assurance of Independence of Bank of Korea"), *Hanguk Kyŏngje* (Hanguk Economic News), August 8, 1988. The proposal called for the chairman of the Monetary Board to be selected by the president and concurrently hold the position of Bank of Korea governor. It also suggested excluding foreign exchange management from the central bank's authority while including financial institution supervision. For more see "Uri Tangŭi Kyŏngje Chŏngch'aek: Konghwa" (Our Party's Economic Policy: NDRP), *Chungang Kyŏngje* (Chungang Economic News), August 17, 1988.

36. "Kŭmt'ongwi Ŭijangi Hanŭn Ch'ongjae Kyŏmim" (Monetary Board Chairman Should Concurrently Hold the Office of the BoK President), *Chungang Kyŏngje* (Chungang Economic News), November 6, 1988. For a complete comparison of the Bank of Korea government and opposition proposals, see "Kŭmt'ongwijangi Hanŭn Ch'ongjae Kyŏmim" (The Chairman of Monetary Board Will Concurrently Hold the Office of BoK President), *Kyŏnghyang Shinmun* (Kyŏnghyang News), November 10, 1988.

37. "Hanŭn Panbale P'yongmin, Minju, 'Yasamdang' Tanilan Ch'ŏlhoe" (Peace Democratic Party and Democratic Party for Unification Withdraw "Unified Proposal between Three Opposition Parties" due to BoK Resistance), *Chungang Kyŏrgje* (Chungang Economic News), November 16, 1988; "Hanŭn Ch'ongjaega Kŭmt'ongwi Ŭijang Kyŏmim" (BoK President Shall Concurrently Hold the Chairmanship of Monetary Board), *Chungang Kyŏngje* (Chungang Economic News), November 18, 1988; "Hanŭnch'ŭk Kŏsen Panbale Paekp'alshipto Hoejŏn" (180-Degree Turn from Opposition on BoK), *Seoul Kyŏngje* (Seoul Economic News), December 8, 1988.

38. "Tongnipsŏng Pojang Paekmanmyŏng Kadusŏmyŏng Undong" (Street Movement for Collecting One Million Signatures for Assurance of Independence of BoK), *Hangyŏre Shinmun* (Hangyŏrye News), November 15, 1988.

39. "Hanŭnbŏp Kaejŏng Tanilan Mandŭnda" (Unitary Proposal on the Amendment of the Bank of Korean Law Is Supposed to Be Made)," *Kukmin Ilbo*

(Kukmin Daily), January 12, 1989; "Hanŭnbôp Kaejŏng Owoljung Tagyŏldoeldût" (Negotiation about the Amendment of BoK Law Is Expected to Be Completed by May), *Yŏnhap T'ongshin* (United Press), March 23, 1989; Lee Yŏng-Ran, "Hanŭnbŏp Kaejŏng Kongdong Chagŏp" (Joint Work on BoK Law Amendment), *Chŏgan Maekyung* (Weekly Economic News), February 9, 1989.

40. By the early 1990s the Bank of Korea employed roughly 4,000 individuals. For graduates of the country's most prestigious economics department, at Seoul National University, Bank of Korea employment was not as attractive as employment with most government ministries. After more than five years at the Bank of Korea the chances of moving into a more prestigious government job become low.

Chapter Eight

1. Leslie Elliott Armijo, "Brazilian Politics and Patterns of Financial Regulation, 1945–1991," in S. Haggard, C. H. Lee, and S. Maxfield, eds., *The Politics of Finance in Developing Countries* (Ithaca: Cornell University Press, 1993), pp. 259–292.

2. Paulo Neuhaus, *Historia monetaria do Brasil, 1900–1945* (Rio de Janeiro: IBMEC, 1975), p. 144.

3. The first programs were temporary: the 1906 Taubate Agreement and others in 1917 and 1921. In 1924 a permanent program was implemented. The programs were paid for by the federal government except during the period from 1924 until 1930, when they were state funded. See Thomas Holloway, *Immigrants on the Land: Coffee and Society in São Paulo* (Chapel Hill: University of North Carolina Press, 1980); Antonio Delfmin Netto, *O problema do cafe* (Rio de Janeiro: Ed. Fundação Getúlio Vargas, 1979).

4. Steven Topik, *The Political Economy of the Brazilian State* (Austin: University of Texas Press, 1987), p. 47, note 41.

5. Winston Fritsch, "The Montagu Financial Mission to Brazil and the Federal Economic Policy Changes of 1924," *Brazilian Economic Studies*, 9 (1985), 263–325.

6. Otto E. Niemeyer, "Report Submitted to the Brazilian Government," July 4, 1931.

7. Leslie Armijo, "Public Policymaking in a Semi-Autonomous State: Brazilian Financial Modernization, 1950–1987," manuscript, 1989, p. 157.

8. Pedro Aranha Corrêa do Lago, "SUMOC as the Embryo of the Central Bank: Its Impact on Economic Policy-Making, 1945–65" (M.A. thesis, Pontifica Universidade Católica de Rio de Janeiro, 1982), p. 34.

9. Ibid., p. 33.

10. Ibid., p. 40.

11. Ibid., p. 30.

12. They complained about lack of coordination with other important institutions such as the Banco do Brasil and about being cut out of important decisions. See, for example, National Archives, Record Group 59, U.S. Embassy to State Department, August 14, 1959, 832.14/8–1459, Box 4321.

13. Corrêa do Lago, "SUMOC," p. 90.

14. Ibid., p. 153.

15. Armijo, "Brazilian Politics and Patterns of Financial Regulation."

16. See, for example, Memorandum of Conversation, U.S. Embassy, Rio de Janeiro, to State Department, July 2, 1959, National Archives, Record Group 59, 832.14/7–759, Box 4321.

17. Ary Cesar Minella, *Banqueiros: Organização e poder político no Brasil* (Rio de Janeiro: Espaco e Tempo/ANPOCS, 1988).

18. The main proposals were those of Correia e Castro (1947), Faraco (1954), Nogueira da Gama (1959), Faraco (1962), Salvador Lossaco and Contec (1962/63), Goulart (1963), Alkmin (1963), and Bulhões (1964).

19. Joint U.S.-Brazilian Economic Development Commission, *The Development of Brazil* (Washington, D.C.: Institute of Inter-American Affairs, Foreign Operations Administration, 1954), p. 42.

20. Corrêa do Lago, "SUMOC," p. 42.

21. Ibid., p. 91.

22. Donald E. Syvrud, *Foundations of Brazilian Economic Growth* (Stanford: Hoover Institution Press, 1974), p. 75.

23. The Getúlio Vargas Foundation's comprehensive historical-biographical encyclopedia, published in 1984, does not include a listing for the Banco Central do Brasil; instead, it points the reader to the entry for SUMOC.

24. Maria Lucia Teixeira and Werneck Vianna, *A Administração do O Conselho Monetário Nacional 1964–1974* (Rio de Janeiro: Editora Vozes, 1987), pp. 107–109.

25. Ibid., p. 110.

26. Statement in *Visão* quoted in ibid., p. 115.

27. Teixeira and Vianna, *A Administração*, p. 115.

28. Teixiera and Vianna, *A Administração*, p. 116.

29. Ibid., p. 121.

30. J. Carlos de Assis, *A Chave do Tesoro* (Rio de Janeiro: Editora Paz e Terra, 1983), p. 26.

31. This tremendous concentration of power over economic policy decision making led, by the mid-1970s, to considerable debate over the role of the National Monetary Council. In a backlash during the late 1970s the number and extent of sectoral representation on the council was expanded. There was even a brief interlude in which the minister of finance ceased to be the chair. The chairmanship passed to the Planning Ministry in April 1979, then back to the Ministry of Finance in August. Jorge Vianna Monteiro, "Mecanismos decisorios da política económica no Brasil: 1965–1982," *Revista IBM*, 4, 16 (January 1983), 21.

32. Upset by this situation, private bankers, who had initially been given an important role on the National Monetary Council, represented by the São Paulo Bankers Association, presented a proposal in 1972 to return the council more nearly to its original make-up and functions. Apparently no change resulted.

33. "Consolidação de contas publicas vai reduzir Juro," *Jornal do Brasil*, August 17, 1993, p. 1.

34. Ernane Galvêas, "Banco Central ou Frankenstein?" *Jornal do Brasil*, July 6, 1993.

Chapter Nine

1. Alex Cukierman and Steven Webb, "Political Influence on the Central Bank—International Evidence," paper prepared for the annual meeting of the American Political Science Association, New York, August 31–September 4, 1994.

2. James E. Alt and Michael Gilligan, "The Political Economy of Trading States: Factor Specificity, Collective Action Problems, and Domestic Political Institutions," *Journal of Political Philosophy*, 2, 2 (1994).

3. Alberto Alesina and Guido Tabellini, "External Debt, Capital Flight, and Political Risk," *Journal of Development Economics* (November 1989); A. Giovannini and M. de Melo, "Government Revenue from Financial Repression," *American Economic Review*, 83 (1993), 953–963; Nouriel Roubini and Xavier Sala-i-Martin, "Financial Repression and Economic Growth," *Journal of Development Economics*, 39, 1 (July 1992), 5–31.

4. Stephan Haggard and Sylvia Maxfield, "The Political Economy of Financial Internationalization in the Developing World," in R. Keohane and H. Milner, eds., *Internationalization and Domestic Politics* (Cambridge: Cambridge University Press, 1996).

5. These results were obtained in joint work with Manual Pastor. See "Central Bank Independence in the Developing World," Economics Department, Occidental College, mimeo, November 1995.

6. We have followed Serven and Solimano in dropping any measure of credit. This is mostly because we have little confidence in applying the usual "price" or "cost" measures based on interest charges to this developing world data set. Luis Serven and Andrés Solimano, "Private Investment and Macroeconomic Adjustment: A Survey," *World Bank Research Observer*, 7, 1 (1992), 95–114.

7. Lance Taylor, *Varieties of Stabilization Experience* (Oxford: Clarendon Press of Oxford University Press, 1989), and Lance Taylor, "Gap Disequilibria: Inflation, Investment, Saving, and Foreign Exchange," WIDER Working Paper 76, 1989.

8. We deflate debt here by exports, primarily because of the argument, developed in Sachs, that there is less vulnerability to debt problems when a country's export ratios are high. Jeffrey Sachs, "External Debt and Macroeconomic Performance in Latin America and East Asia," *Brookings Papers on Economic Activity*, 2 (1985), 523–573. Various debt overhang variables have been used in Luis Serven and Andrés Solimano, "Debt Crisis, Adjustment Policies, and Capital Formation in Developing Countries: Where Do We Stand?" *World Development*, 21, 1 (1993), 127–140; Manual Pastor, Jr., "Inversion privada y el 'effecto arrastre' de la deuda externa en America Latina," *El Trimestre Económico*, 59, 1 (January–March 1992), 107–151; and Joshua Greene and Delano Villanueva, "Private Investment in Developing Countries: An Empirical Analysis," *IMF Staff Papers*, 38, 1 (March 1991), 33–58.

9. In the econometric testing, we use the log of the inflation rate, making the curve not strictly an inverted U since the right-hand side declines slowly. The rationale is that the negative effects of higher inflation decline as rates increase,

primarily because economic agents have already partially adjusted (that is, an increase in fifty percentage points of inflation is more problematic when the base is 100 percent than when the base is 500 percent).

10. Empirical results on the relationship between democracy and economic growth are inconclusive. But as Pastor and Sung note, the empirical research should focus on the effects on private investment, in part because that is the real focus of the debate (the concern usually is that many democratic voices upset owners of capital) and in part because we have clearer models of the determinants of investment than of the determinants of growth. Manuel Pastor, Jr., and Jae-Ho Sung, "Private Investment and Democracy in the Developing World," *Journal of Economic Issues*, 29, 1 (March 1995).

11. Alex Cukierman, Steven B. Webb, and Bilin Neyapti, "Measuring the Independence of Central Banks and Its Effects on Policy Outcomes," *World Bank Economic Review*, 6, 3 (September 1992).

12. The random effects technique estimates one overall intercept, as opposed to one intercept per country as in fixed effects. The error term is nonspherical and composed of two parts: the traditional error term and a second error component which measures the difference between the country-specific intercept and the overall intercept. The random effects estimation is then just a particular type of estimated generalized least squares regression that corrects for the nonspherical nature of this new composite error term.

13. The regressions also include two dummy variables (as appropriate on the overall specification) which are not reported here. The first arises because our external debt measure sometimes includes short-term debt and sometimes only long-term debt; the World Bank generally does not have collected short-term debt measures prior to 1977 (although short-term debt is available for some countries prior to 1977). Thus we constructed a dummy variable which was equal to one for all those country-years in which our external debt measure included both short- and long-term debt and zero otherwise. The other dummy variable was mentioned earlier; it accompanies *CBI* and is set equal to one for the second time period in Korea, the only time span in which there was an actual change in *CBI*. This implies that these regressions are purely testing for the cross-sectional effects of *CBI*.

14. We also ran this fuller model of the economic and political determinants of private investment with various imperfect measures of the quantity of credit available to the private sector. Such credit quantity can be tested as either a stock or a flow. When tested as a stock (domestic credit as a percentage of GDP, lagged), credit is insignificant and the other results are essentially the same. When tested as a flow (the lagged change in credit to the private sector), the variable is appropriately signed but insignificant at any traditional level, and the pattern for the other variables is basically the same; however, *CBI* slips in significance (to the .22 level), presumably because there is some correlation between central bank independence and private sector credit availability. The actual variable for change in credit to the domestic private sector is calculated by summing: (1) the change in domestic banking claims on the private sector, and (2) net flows (disbursements minus repayments) on long-term private sector nonguaranteed external debt, both as a percentage of GDP. The former is

calculated using line 32d from the International Monetary Fund's *International Financial Statistics* and the latter is taken from the World Bank's *World Debt Tables;* local currency GDP and dollar GDP (used in calculating the actual ratios summed) are taken from *World Tables* with dollar GDP derived by first determining dollar GDP (per capita dollar GNP by the population) and then scaling with a GNP/GDP ratio figured from the constant currency series reported. This credit measure is similar to variables in Wai and Wong and in Blejer and Khan and is entered as a lag. The stock variable mentioned above includes only the level of domestic claims on the private sector owing to data problems with collecting the stock of foreign claims. U Tun Wai and Chom-huey Wong, "Determinants of Private Investment in Developing Countries," *Journal of Development Studies*, 19 (1982), 19–36; Mario I. Blejer and Moshin S. Khan, "Government Policy and Private Investment in Developing Countries," *IMF Staff Papers*, 31 (June 1984), 379–403.

15. Alex Cukierman, Pantelis Kalaitzidakis, Lawrence Summers, and Steven B. Webb, "Central Bank Independence, Growth, Investment, and Real Rates," *Carnegie-Rochester Conference on Public Policy*, 39 (Autumn 1993).

16. Charles A. E. Goodhart, "Game Theory for Central Bankers: A Report to the Governor of the Bank of England," *Journal of Economic Literature*, 32 (March 1994), 104.

17. Alex Cukierman, *Central Bank Strategy, Credibility, and Independence* (Cambridge: MIT Press, 1992), p. 41.

18. Robert J. Franzese, "Central Bank Independence, Sectoral Interests, and the Wage Bargain," Center for European Studies Working Paper Series no. 56, 1995.

19. Ton Notermans, "The Abdication from National Policy Autonomy: Why the Macroeconomic Policy Regime Has Become So Unfavorable to Labor," *Politics and Society*, 21, 2 (1993), 133–67; Geoffrey Garret, "Economic Internationalization and Economic Policy in the Advanced Industrial Democracies," paper prepared for the working group on "Internationalization and Domestic Politics," UCLA, June 10–11, 1993.

20. Anand Chandavarkar, "Of Finance and Development: Neglected and Unsettled Questions," *World Development*, 20, 1 (1992), 138.

21. For an extreme statement of this concern, see Richard McIntyre and Joseph Medley, "Democratic Reform of the Fed: The Impact of Class Relations on Policy Formation," *Review of Radical Political Economics*, 20, 2/3 (1988), 156–162.

22. John Freeman, "Whither Democracy? International Finance and the Prospects for Popular Sovereignty," manuscript, pp. 4–5. See also Miguel Centeno, "Redefining Technocracy," *Theory and Society*, 22, 3 (June 1993), 307–336.

23. Gerald Epstein, "Political Economy and Comparative Central Banking," *Review of Radical Political Economics*, 24, 1 (1992), 2.

24. Geoffrey Garret and Peter Lange, "Political Responses to Interdependence: What's 'Left' for the Left?" *International Organization*, 45, 4 (Autumn 1991); Duane Swank, "Politics and the Structural Dependence of the State in Democratic Capitalist Nations," *American Political Science Review*, 86 (March 1992); Robert Geyer, "Globalization and the Crisis of Social Democracy: Ex-

plaining the Development of the British and Norwegian Labor Parties' EU Policies in the 1980s and 1990s," paper prepared for the Annual Midwest Political Science Association Meeting, Chicago, April 1995. Supporting the convergence prediction in a variety of ways are David R. Cameron, "The Expansion of the Public Economy," *American Political Science Review*, 72 (1978), 1243–1261; David M. Andrews, "Capital Mobility and State Autonomy: Toward a Structural Theory of International Monetary Relations," *International Studies Quarterly*, 38, 2 (June 1994), 193–219; John B. Goodman and Louis W. Pauly, "The Obsolescence of Capital Controls? Economic Management in an Age of Global Markets," *World Politics*, 46, 1 (October 1993), 50–83; Michael C. Webb, "International Economic Structures, Government Interests, and International Coordination of Macroeconomic Adjustment Policies," *International Organization*, 45, 3 (Summer 1991), 309–342; Robert H. Bates, Philipp Brock, and Jill Tienfenthaler, "Risk and Trade Regimes: Another Exploration," *International Organization*, 45, 1 (Winter 1991), 1–18.

25. See, for example, Ricardo Grinspun, "NAFTA and Neoconservative Transformation: the Impact on Canada and Mexico," *Review of Radical Political Economy*, 25, 4 (December 1993), 14–30.

26. Louis W. Pauly, "Capital Mobility, State Autonomy, and Political Legitimacy," *Journal of International Affairs*, 48, 2 (Winter 1995), 369–388.

27. Of course an independent central bank will help promote financial market development, but the political analysis conducted here suggests that the relative public policy emphasis should be on financial market development.

28. Richard D. Erb, "The Role of Central Banks," *Finance and Development* (December 1989), 12.

Index

About the author

Sylvia Maxfield is Associate Professor of Political Science and Management at Yale University. Among her works is *Letting Capital Loose: Financial Liberalization in Interventionist States.*